THE GATEKEEPER

THE GATEKEEPER

60 YEARS OF ECONOMICS ACCORDING TO THE NEW YORK TIMES

ROBERT CHERNOMAS

AND

IAN HUDSON

Paradigm Publishers
Boulder • London

Copyright © 2012 Paradigm Publishers

Published in the United States by Paradigm Publishers, 2845 Wilderness Place, Boulder, CO 80301 USA.

Paradigm Publishers is the trade name of Birkenkamp & Company, LLC, Dean Birkenkamp, President and Publisher.

Library of Congress Cataloging-in-Publication Data

Chernomas, Robert.
  The gatekeeper : 60 years of economics according to the New York Times / Robert Chernomas and Ian Hudson.
    p. cm.
  Includes bibliographical references and index.
  ISBN 978-1-59451-683-2 (pbk : alk. paper)
  1. New York Times. 2. Journalism—Objectivity—United States. 3. Journalism, Commercial—United States. 4. Government and the press—United States—History—20th century. 5. United States—Economic conditions—1945–6. United States—Economic policy—1945–7. United States—Foreign economic relations. I. Hudson, Ian, 1967- II. Title.
  PN4899.N42N3744 2010
  070.4'4965—dc22

                                                              2010038122

Printed and bound in the United States of America on acid-free paper that meets the standards of the American National Standard for Permanence of Paper for Printed Library Materials.

Designed by Straight Creek Bookmakers.
Typeset by Jeska Horgan-Kobelski.

16 15 14 13 12   1 2 3 4 5

CONTENTS

For my sons Todd and Greg—RC
To my parents—IH

PREFACE

Growing up in a suburb of New York City, reading the *Sunday Times* was a ritual. Given its book-length size, the process would begin on Sunday morning but not end until much later in the week, just in time to begin again. Given its cosmopolitan character, finishing the *Times* made you feel up to speed on all things political and cultural. However, even at a young age, purchasing the *Times* provided a sense that you were being sold something akin to the high-end products advertised among the densely packed erudite news, business, sports, and cultural articles. While the black newsprint left on your fingertips at the end of each reading washed off, in a "Name of the Rose" sort of way, there was a sense that a residue of elegantly worded ideological perspective had slipped through into your bloodstream.

We read *Newsday* during the week, which had a more plebian tone than the patrician *Times*, but there didn't seem to be much of a difference in perspective, just a more provincial focus. Years later, Edward Herman and Noam Chomsky's *Manufacturing Consent* gave substance to this feeling of unease by articulating a model for the idea that news was not necessarily fact and that the economic structure of the media influenced its content. However, its focus on foreign affairs was not completely satisfactory for a budding economist and it didn't account for the *Times'* regular attacks on some corporations and some seemingly pro-business policies. More recently, this uncertainty has been reflected in an ongoing debate about the landscape of journalism in the United States. On one side, Robert McChesney's analysis of the evolving ownership structure of the U.S. media strengthened many of Chomsky's arguments about the dangers of pro-corporate bias in a concentrated, privately owned industry. On the other, a new group of economists, armed with the econometric tools of content analysis, claim to have found proof that the media, as a whole, and the *Times*, in particular, were liberal and out of step with the economic opinions of most Americans. Could these things be reconciled?

While attending a conference in Washington, D.C., on the relationship between corporate food production, society, and the environment, populated mostly by progressive academics, we were struck by the response of the participants to a *Times'* editor on a panel. The consensus view of those in line to comment on her presentation was that she (and the *Times*) was on the side of the angels. The line was too long for our intervention to be heard, but the trust these scholars placed in the *Times* left us with a growing sense of curiosity about what role this clearly important institution played in American democracy. When we returned to work, this project was launched.

With the staggering collapse of 2008, brought about by the very economic policies that were supposedly creating U.S. economic success, there has been reconsideration of what exactly sound economic policy might look like. While we would argue that this reconsideration has been remarkably limited in its scope, there is no question that there is a new suspicion about allowing the private sector to dictate the economic policy agenda. At this remarkable American historical conjuncture, the *Times'* role in the "return to sanity" movement that encourages some government oversight of corporate behavior will reinforce its identity with liberal democratic interests. This book argues that at no time should we forget the limits to the *Times'* commitment to a real, progressive alternative to an American corporate powered world.

In the lengthy period between the idea for this book and its rolling off the printing press, we received a great deal of help and encouragement from a number of sources. Our editor, Jennifer Knerr, with irresistible wisdom, kept suggesting additions as history-changing events—the financial crisis of 2008 and the election of President Obama—unfolded. The result was that another thousand articles needed to be scanned, read, and analyzed. Self-interest made us wish the world would settle down just long enough to finish the book. Jessica Priest and Mary Kay Kozyra always responded to our queries with what seemed like instantaneous precision, nurturing our sense of Paradigm's professionalism and caring.

We also received a great deal of encouragement and aid from friends and co-workers. Every time that we mentioned this project, people claimed that they couldn't wait to read it. Clearly it was not only the two of us who were curious about just what type of information was making its way from the pages of the *Times* into the bloodstream of society. Anne-Emanuelle Birn's reading of an early version of our chapter prospectus reinforced our intuition that this was a worthwhile research project, and she suggested some changes of emphasis. We also need to thank our colleague in the economics department, Fletcher Baragar, who helped focus our discussion on the economics of the *Times* and acted as sage arbitrator on those rare occasions when we had irreconcilable differences. Chomsky and McChesney provided encouraging words at an early stage of the project, although Chomsky warned that we should expect to be ignored by the mainstream media no matter how well documented and reasoned our book. The anonymous academics who reviewed our manuscript provided valuable feedback on how to improve the book, generally, and on how to make it more interesting to those in media studies, in particular.

Funding from the Global Political Economics Research Fund of the Faculty of Arts at the University of Manitoba permitted us to hire Anupam Das, Syeed Khan, and Taiwo Soetan as research assistants. They did much of the dirty work in collecting, organizing, and referencing the thousands of articles that were read for this book with a commendable attention to detail. We thank them and many others and trust the reader will benefit from their efforts.

CHAPTER 1
THE NEW YORK TIMES

LIBERAL AND CONSERVATIVE

It will be my earnest aim that the *New York Times* give the news, all the news, in concise and attractive form, in language that is permissible in good society, and give it as early if not earlier, than it can be learned through any other reliable medium; to give the news impartially, without fear or favor, regardless of party, sect, or interest involved; to make of the columns of the *New York Times* a forum for the consideration of all questions of public importance, and to that end to invite intelligent discussion from all shades of opinion.
—Adolph Ochs, Aug. 18, 1896

The *New York Times* is arguably the most influential newspaper in America (some might say the world) and has been so for decades. It is the largest metropolitan newspaper in the country and one of only a very few papers, including the *Wall Street Journal, Chicago Tribune,* and *Washington Post,* that can claim a truly national reach. A half century ago a member of the State Department acknowledged the importance of the *Times,* claiming, "The first thing we do is read *the newspaper*—the *New York Times.*"[1] More recently, a 2009 article in *Vanity Fair* described the *Times* as "the flagship of serious newspaper journalism in America."[2] Its columnists have become public personalities, sought-after figures on the punditry circuit, dispensing wisdom on issues of political and economic import. *Times'* staff has won far more Pulitzer Prizes than any other paper. According to media analyst Jack Lule, "more than any other U.S. news medium, the *New York Times* has become crucial reading for those interested in the news, national politics, and international affairs. . . . Though not the biggest, it may well be the most significant newspaper in the world."[3]

Publisher Arthur Sulzberger Jr. claimed that if the *Times* has any ideology, it is "urbane," by which he means big-city and broad-minded. The paper is certainly erudite. It provides an account of the world rich in eloquent prose, sophistication, depth, and, within certain limits, balanced content. The *Times'* writing is in the long tradition of the Enlightenment, where reason is the primary basis of authority as opposed to irrationality, superstition, and tyranny. It fosters modernism, discriminating taste, and a cosmopolitan outlook as a result of educated editors and correspondents catering to a civilized, cultivated, and cultured readership. The *Times* provides its readers with answers from writers who have paid attention to the facts and arguments and who have a professional commitment to providing answers. The *Times'* modernism, with its belief in science and social progress, provides its readers with a bulwark against the superstition and intolerance represented by media outlets like Fox News and their viewers. The *Times* is a place to feel a sense of community with those who are above a media that panders to the lowest common denominator.

During the time period in this study, the *Times* was the pinnacle of U.S. journalism. Predictably for a newspaper of such importance, it was also the subject of close examination and heated debate. Despite the bold claims by the founder of the *Times* to provide a forum for all shades of opinion and impartial reporting, the *Times*, perhaps more than any other news outlet, has faced a barrage of criticism over its perceived bias. Interestingly, the *Times* finds itself in a bit of crossfire as both the left and right claim that the *Times* is biased, although, of course, they claim that the bias runs in opposite directions.

From the right, well-known conservative pundits like Ann Coulter and Bill O'Reilly frequently pillory the *Times* for its left-leaning views, despite editor Arthur Sulzberger's repeated insistence that his paper is not liberal.[4] In an interview with the *New York Observer*, Coulter claimed, "My only regret with (Oklahoma City bomber) Timothy McVeigh is he did not go to the *New York Times* Building."[5] According to O'Reilly, "Somewhere along the line, the *Times* got out of the news business and into the nation-building business. Its primary intent is no longer to provide objective information and fair-minded analysis to its readers, but to convince them to support a brave new world in the United States. The power of the *Times* is being used to promote the formation of a new America, a bright, shining progressive city on a hill of steep government entitlements. . . . In almost every section the reader is confronted with liberal ideology."[6]

A website, TimesWatch.com, is dedicated solely to "documenting and exposing the liberal political agenda of the *New York Times*." In a more literary vein, in *Journalistic Fraud: How the* NYT *Distorts the News and Why it Can No Longer Be Trusted*, Bob Kohn argued that the *Times* furthers a leftist agenda by presenting ideology as fact. The Cato Institute, whose mission "seeks to broaden the parameters of public policy debate to allow consideration of the traditional American principles of limited government, individual liberty, free markets, and peace," has often featured writers critical of the *Times*. Alan Reynolds accused the paper of "escalating . . . rhetoric to authentic class warfare" for pointing out that workers were not doing particularly well in the economic recovery of the early 2000s.[7] It is important to note that much of the criticism of the *Times*' "left-wing" slant is based on the paper's "cultural" perspective on, for example, women's and gay rights or the separation of church and state. The *Times*' writing in these areas might well reveal a consistent liberal perspective—maddening those opposed to social progress as much as it would be supported by the *Times*' urbane readership—but of little concern to corporate America. This book is about that which is central to corporate needs—economic policy.

From the left, numerous writers argue that the *Times* may be more liberal than some other media outlets, but that as a part of the "mainstream" media, it will inevitably contain a conservative bias. As the title of his book *Lapdogs: How the Press Rolled Over for Bush* suggests, Eric Boehlert claims that the mainstream media gave the Bush-Cheney presidential ticket a remarkably easy ride. According to Boehlert, during Bush's first term, the *Times* was guilty of deliberately killing stories that would have embarrassed the Bush administration and presenting other issues so that they placed the administration in a favorable light.[8]

Perhaps the most famous media critic on the left, Noam Chomsky, argues that as a privately owned corporation, dependent on advertising revenue, the *Times* has little choice but to have a pro-business bias. This is true in its stance on foreign policy in areas like Vietnam and Nicaragua and also in domestic economic issues like taxes on business.[9] Chomsky argued that the "so-called liberal" *Times* offered complete support for the North American Free Trade Agreement. The *Times*' articles that were not directly supportive of NAFTA belittled opponents' ideas, including "tremendous labor-bashing."[10] Similarly, in the late 1970s the *Times* took a "mildly supportive" stance on a tax bill that was opposed by New York businesses. Attributing a small decline in advertising and stock values to its position on the tax bill, the *Times* "shifted its entire editorial staff," purging it of liberals including John Oakes.[11]

Authors from one ideological perspective are convinced that the *Times* is pushing a dangerously liberal, left-wing agenda on its readers, while authors of the opposite stripe claim that it is conservative. Is it possible that both claims are correct? What we are attempting to do in this book is to disentangle the myth from the fact that surrounds so much of the debate on the *Times*.

The Media and Political Economy

Capitalism runs on profits. Maximizing profits is not a matter of morals or ethics for firms, but a condition of survival. The "circuit of capital" demands that businesses first must be concerned with acquiring the least expensive inputs. Second, they must make use of these inputs in a production process that ensures a competitive price in the marketplace. Next they must be able to market these products in order to be able to sell them. Lower-cost capitalists will drive higher-cost capitalists from the market by reducing prices and having more profits to invest for the next round of production and sales. The firm that is able to introduce techniques that lower unit labor costs has profits available to invest in new techniques, which enables it to successfully compete with rivals. Being pushed from below (workers), while being squeezed from the sides (other capitalists) is what drives the system to ever-greater increases in productivity and lower-cost commodities. Without competitive profits, research and development, investment, and advertising all become impossible and the fate of the firm is sealed.

Samuel Bowles, David Gordon, and Thomas Weisskopf once wrote that profits are the spoils of a three-front war that firms must continuously wage with their workforce, the government, and other companies (especially those from other countries).[12] The conflict with their workers is over containing wages while at the same time convincing them to increase production as much as possible. The struggle with the government is over the extent to which the state will impact a firm's bottom line by altering its costs through such things as regulations, taxes, subsidies, or its revenues, through government purchases, for example. This places the firm in conflict with a wide variety of citizens who expect the government to undertake various profit-constraining activities, from those who pressure the state to implement environmental protection; to those who think that the government has a responsibility to provide for the collective good with respect to health, education, and welfare; to those who want to contain the exploitation and rent-seeking activities on which profits are based. The third and final front is a battle with other firms to reduce any input costs and increase revenues from product sales. On this front, firms may have an important ally in their national governments, which attempt to tilt the rules of the international economy in favor of their own firms. This can be done by changing trade rules, altering exchange rates, or using military force.

Corporate profitability, indeed the very survival of the enterprise, depends to a great extent on factors that lie well outside the internal working of any one firm. Firms' profits depend on government decisions on fiscal and monetary policy, regulations, infrastructure, education, research, foreign policy, and the legal system. In an extreme case, the government could decide that the very structure of private ownership could be done away with, through nationalization, for example. So the amount of profit, in fact the very opportunity to make profit, depends on the good will of the government. In a democratic society, this means the opinions of the voting public become crucial.

The court of public opinion largely reaches its verdict with the expert guidance of the media. After all, it is through the media that people obtain much of their information on what is going on in the economic world. From the standpoint of corporate profitability, it would, therefore, be highly desirable if the media largely contained information that would sway the public toward policies that were generally business friendly.

Yet right-wing critics accuse the media, in general, and the *Times* particularly, of everything from Marxism to liberal bias. If these critics are correct, then the media is not playing a role in assisting corporate profitability. Indeed, the media would be actively harming the ability of companies to make money. While accusing the privately owned media of Marxism is the stuff of undisciplined hysteria, it is possible that news may contain a strong liberal presence for reasons that have nothing to do with the right-wing claim that the media is inundated with liberal, bleeding-heart journalists and owners, eager to foist their anti-business agenda on the American public. First, some liberal policies (defined as a crucial role for the state in correcting for those occasions in which markets fail) may actually increase corporate profitability, as is the case with state spending on research and development or education. Second, liberal policies that may, at first glance, appear to run counter to the short-term interests of corporate America may be necessary to maintain the long-term profitability of the economic system. For example, a liberal policy to provide government oversight of the accounting industry might constrain the short-term profitability of companies like Enron, but it might also be necessary to protect the profits of the broader corporate sector. Finally, liberal policy can also support the long-term interest of business when the results of conservative economic policy are sufficiently disastrous that they compromise the public's willingness to support the economic system on which business depends. For instance, if conservative policy resulted in environmental damage, as it did with the BP oil spill in the Gulf of Mexico, that was so devastating to the population that they began to question the economic system that produced these results, liberal policy, even if it were to dampen business profits through pollution taxes or environmental regulations, would be in the long-run interests of the corporate world, since it maintains the legitimacy of the entire system.

This is not to say that all liberal policy at all times is profit enhancing. Some conservative policies, at some times, will be more advantageous for profitability than liberal alternatives. The hallmark of conservative economic theory is that firms should not be constrained by the state in their pursuit of profit. While many take this to mean that the state should not intervene in the market, this is not quite accurate. Conservative economists frequently call on the state to take deliberate action that would increase the profits of corporations, by making it difficult to form unions, for example. Regulation of the accounting industry may be profit enhancing in the long run, but in many other instances the conservative distaste for state regulatory activity is a more profitable path. To take one obvious instance, a large state role that necessitates a high corporate tax rate is unlikely to be profit enhancing. There are numerous other less obvious examples. A strong regulatory role can also increase costs to business in areas such as environmental protection or worker safety. The long-term interests of capital are, therefore, a balancing act. At times, certain regulatory activity may be necessary to both enhance profits and ensure public support for the system. At others, specific conservative prescriptions to reduce the size of government would be beneficial to the long-term interests of business.

From a business standpoint, what would the ideal media institution look like? We have seen that profitability depends crucially on the information provided to the public by the media. We have also seen that both liberal and conservative elements are necessary in order to promote profitability and to maintain the legitimacy of the broader economic system. An ideal media institution, from the corporate standpoint, would promote whichever liberal or conservative policy was best placed to contribute to the long-term profitability of business.

It could do this by calling on a host of "experts" to influence the political and ideological context so that it is favorable for the expansion of corporate interests. Their role would be to convince the majority of the population that profit-enhancing economic policy is common sense. This does not mean that there would be no room for complaints and an acceptance of the need for reform when the system seems to be producing pathological results, but the core values underlying the system would be beyond question. After all, a debate over how the pie gets divided is very different from an open public discussion about who owns the bakery. A media institution that fulfilled this role would be invaluable to corporate America.

Why the *Times*?

The *Times* is ideally situated to speak from the perspective of the long-term interests of business. In addition to being observers of our capitalist democratic system, media outlets like the *Times* are also participants in it, driven, like all private firms, to make a profit. What is it about the *Times* that results in a private, for-profit firm becoming the leading voice of forward-thinking business? The *Times* is especially well placed among media outlets to fulfill this role due to its ownership structure, the individual desires of its owners, and its customer base.

The usual economic assumption about any privately owned firm, including the media, is that its goal is to maximize short-run profits. It is unwilling to take actions that do not maximize revenues and minimize costs. Since revenues in the newspaper world come from readers and advertisers, content should not discourage people from purchasing the paper or firms from marketing in it. This would imply that there is little room for the owners in the media to influence content; rather it would be driven by the tastes of readers and the requirements of advertisers. Interestingly, media analysts from both the left and right side of the spectrum share this view. From the left, Robert McChesney argues that the corporations that own media outlets will limit content to that which shows their own firm and their advertisers in a positive light.[13] From the right, Daniel Sutter argues that it is not advertisers, but consumers, who dictate content, so newspapers must run content that panders to the "tastes" of their readers.[14] In both cases, the actions of the owners of the media are constrained by their need to maximize profits. This short-run profit maximizing is more likely to hold when companies have broad public ownership, since the numerous owners are unlikely to agree on any goal other than immediate profit maximization. What flows from this line of economic reasoning is that any firm whose stock can be bought and sold on the market is unlikely to do anything but profit maximize in the short run since failure to do so would decrease its stock value below its potential and invite an unwanted takeover.

Alternatively, in sectors dominated by a small number of large firms and in places like Japan where there is a different corporate ownership structure, the goals of short-term profit maximizing may be sacrificed for long-term profits based on maintaining and expanding market share. Therefore, there are circumstances in which the desires of owners can play a larger role. According to economist James Hamilton, owners can have more influence on the content of any given media outlet when it is privately, rather than broadly, owned, as is the case with the *Times*.[15] The current publisher, Arthur Sulzberger Jr., has inherited the company from a family dynasty that stretches back four generations to Adolph S. Ochs, who purchased the paper in 1896 for $75,000. Although the *Times* has been listed on the New York Stock Exchange since 1967, stock in the *Times* is divided into Class A, which is publicly traded and nonvoting, and Class B (91 percent of which was in family control in 2008), which is voting and elects 70 percent of the board of directors.[16] Further, in the event that any family members want to sell their shares, the right of first purchase goes to other family members. This tight control of voting shares means that, while the *Times* must pay a competitive rate of return on its Class A shares to maintain its stock price (which, as we shall see, it has had trouble doing in 2008), it does not have to worry about the company falling out of family hands, providing some leeway to ignore short-term profitability for longer-term goals.

If the owners of media outlets gain some utility from advocating a particular ideology or political perspective, then it is possible that they might be willing to forgo short-term profits in favor of promoting their own point of view. Sulzberger comes from a long line of owners who seemed to be willing to place the reputation of the paper before the base needs of short-term profitability. Russell Baker, a reporter who moved from the *Baltimore Sun* to the *Times* in the 1950s, described with amazement the massive, and in his opinion, unnecessary, levels of staffing. He claimed that reporters would often sit around with little to do but play bridge.[17] As long as the paper made money, the driving motivation was to churn out a quality product. Any return on revenues beyond 1 or 2 percent was seen as unnecessary.[18] According to *Business Week*, before 1967 the *Times*, "barely broke even" because of the Sulzbergers' desire to place prestige and quality journalism ahead of profits.[19] In *Vanity Fair*, Bowden claimed, "To their credit, the Sulzbergers have long treated the *Times* less as a business than as a public trust, and Arthur is steeped in that tradition, rooted in it, trained by it, captive to it. . . . The *Times*' reputation and influence drive him. He is not just a newspaper publisher and a chairman of the board. He is Arthur Ochs Sulzberger Jr., and the pride he feels in that name doesn't have anything to do with how much is in his bank account."[20]

The Sulzbergers did genuinely appear to be determined to turn out a quality product. This clearly meant an expansive staff committed to wide coverage of important domestic and foreign events as well as investigative reporting. It might also mean that there was room not just for "quality" but also for the owners' own ideological perspective. If this were true, what type of economic perspective would we expect from a Sulzberger owner of a large media corporation? The *Times* does appear to favor the Democratic Party, offering them 78 percent of its political contributions between 1999 and 2008, perhaps indicating a preference for slightly liberal economic policy.[21] However, it should not be forgotten that the *Times* is a business and, therefore, has a vested interest in many conservative policies. Their longstanding hostility to unions was very revealing in this respect. In one of the many instances in which the Sulzbergers requested that their paper take a hard line on unions, in 1957 Arthur Hay Sulzberger wanted stories that would "hit these striking motormen hard."[22]

The owners' personal opinions about unions were put into practice in labor relations at the *Times*. Between 1988 and 1992 net income at the *Times* fell from $168 million to $45 million. The *Times* responded as did most profit-driven corporations at the time, by aggressively cutting costs. One of the areas targeted was the wages of its unionized employees, who created a cost disadvantage compared to its national competitors operating in less union-friendly jurisdictions of the southwest United States. Perhaps the most bitter dispute came with the delivery drivers, who were particularly well placed to exercise their union powers. While new technology made it possible to produce a paper without as many unionized workers, delivering the papers is very difficult without drivers. Further, the need for drivers to travel the length of the city in the early hours of the morning made it difficult to protect replacement workers from union retribution. Rather than settle with the union, the *Times* provided a loan to Arthur Imperatore that enabled him to purchase two of the four delivery services used by the paper. Since existing contracts do not survive the sale of a company, the new owner was able to unilaterally impose new cost-reducing work rules and hire new replacement workers.[23]

The point of this section is not to claim that the economic imperative of profit maximization is not valid. It is merely that in certain specific contexts, short-term profit maximization may be sacrificed for other goals, especially if a firm is narrowly owned. If this were true of the Sulzbergers—and it does appear that they were not quite as cost conscious as a truly disciplined economic bean-counter might have been—then there might have been room for the owners and editors to inject some of their own personal opinions into the paper. They donate to the Democrats, but have expressed conservative views and made conservative choices on some important issues, so they appear to have personal views that reflect a mixed ideology.

Would our conclusions change if Sutter is correct and the *Times* is driven by the biases of its consumers? The *Times* has been very successful in capturing a very large and affluent readership. The circulation of the *Times* was 1.1 million in 2008, making it the third-highest newspaper circulation in the country, behind only *USA Today* (2.3 million) and the *Wall Street Journal* (2.0 million).[24] In addition, the *Times* has a very strong presence online. According to Neilson NetRatings, its online website attracted 19.5 million "unique visitors" per month in 2008, up from 15 million in 2007.[25]

Not all customers are equal. The *Times'* subscriber is quite affluent and concentrated in New York. Although the *Times'* push to the national market has resulted in a larger percentage of its circulation coming from outside the city, 46 percent of weekday circulation is still purchased in the thirty-one counties that make up greater New York.[26] Further, the *Times* has never been designed to appeal to the "masses." According to Max Frankel, former executive editor, "our identity has not been primarily geographic, it has been demographic."[27] There is certainly the belief among those who work at the paper that it is consumed by the elite. The affluent readers of the *Times* create a very low price elasticity, so price increases have little impact on sales. Between 1998 and 2004 circulation actually increased at the same time the cost of a subscription rose by 25 percent, taking the annual price to around $480.[28]

In its promotional material to advertisers the *Times* proudly boasts of the quality of its readers. The *Times* ranks fourth (behind only *U.S. News and World Report, House & Garden,* and *Smithsonian*) in its audience of "influentials," the "critical 10 percent of the population who drive what the other 90 percent think, do, and buy." They are defined by their active political participation and contain highly desirable demographic statistics. For example, they are 54 percent more likely to own weekend homes or investment real estate, 58 percent more likely to have drunk more than two glasses of table wine in the past week, 60 percent more likely to have spent more than $1,000 on clothing in the past year, and 60 percent more likely to have spent $40,000 on a vehicle.[29]

Times readers are more educated, wealthy, and influential than the American general public. As Table 1 (see p. 11) shows, 71 percent of *Times* readers hold college degrees, nearly three times the U.S. average. They have a median household income of $96,000, 1.8 times higher than the national average. Twenty-nine percent own a home worth more than $500,000, almost three times the average in the rest of the country, and they are much more likely to have professional or managerial posts than the general population. Newspaper readers as a group might score higher than the U.S. national average in these measures, but the *Times* can boast an "elite" readership even compared to other newspapers. Table 1 also shows that compared to *USA Today, Times'* readers are considerably more educated, affluent, and more likely to belong to professional or managerial occupations.

As there was with the owners of the paper, there is reason to believe that the readers are ideologically disposed to a liberal and conservative policy mix. The voters of New York City favored Obama in the 2008 election, as did much of the rest of the country. More tellingly, they bucked the national trend by casting an overwhelming 74 percent of their votes for Democrat John Kerry's losing 2004 presidential bid. This was not a one-off phenomenon; with very few exceptions since 1960, New York City has favored Democratic Party candidates. To the extent that the Democrats can be associated with liberal economic policy it would appear that the voters of New York lean in this direction. However, as the table demonstrates, the *Times* has succeeded in attracting a particularly well-heeled demographic. Their position as college educated, high income, property-owning professionals creates an incentive toward many conservative policies in economic matters, most obviously lower tax rates for high-income earners. These same readers would also be attracted to the *Times'* liberal position on non-economic social policies like abortion, gay rights, and gun control.

However, it is important to remember that a component of the *Times'* readers is the corporate class itself. The *Times* is certainly communicating its message to the educated and affluent "influentials" in the general public, but it is also a forum for ideas within the business class. As readers, business leaders purchase the paper as a means to keep in touch with what the forward-thinking members of the corporate elite are thinking on the issues of the day. As advertisers, firms need to have a presence in the *Times* despite (in fact because of) a perspective that is often critical of corporate activity in order to signal to both other members of the corporate community and an elite readership that the company is a responsible corporate citizen. In order to maintain this role for the business elite, the *Times* must behave like a good psychiatrist. It has a fiduciary responsibility to its patient, but that does not mean it avoids telling the patient when its behavior is counterproductive. After all, it is not in the interest of the patient to achieve narrowly defined short-term goals at the expense of its systemic long-term health. The *Times'* long-term profitability depends on its willingness to be critical of corporate activity in prescribed historically specific ways.

The *Times'* affluent customer base and position as the voice of responsible corporate America means that firms will continue to advertise in the paper even when it is critical of certain corporate activity. However, this does not mean that the *Times'* revenue is completely unaffected by its criticisms of the corporate world. Advertising managers at the *Times* have complained in the past that the paper was seen as leftist or anti-business, especially by financial firms on Wall Street angered by coverage that encouraged environmental and regulatory policies.[30] During the years of strong economic growth in the early 2000s, advertising revenue at the *Times* lagged behind that of the industry as a whole. Between 2003 and 2005 the advertising revenue of the Times Media Group (NYT, NYT.com, International Herald Tribune, NYT Radio, and Discovery Times Channel) grew by 5.7 percent, an average of only 2.9 percent a year.[31] To provide some measure of comparison, the newspaper industry reported a 9.7 percent gain in national advertising, and local advertising was up 6.6 percent.[32] Of course, the latter part of this decade has been much harder both for the broader economy in general and newspapers in particular. In the 2006–07 year

Table 1 New York Times and USA Today Consumer Profile

	Weekday *Times* Readers	*USA Today* Readers	New York Times Compared to U.S. Avg. = 100
College graduates	71%	47%	284
Median household income	$96,000	$77,000	180
$500,000 + home	29%	N/A	284
Professional/managerial	52%	35%	224

Source: MRI Demographic Profiles 2006.*

the *Times'* advertising revenue fell by 3.6 percent and it dropped by an even more alarming 12 percent in 2007–08.[33] The fact that the *Times'* ad revenue was growing more slowly than the industry average suggests that, while firms had not abandoned the paper, they were finding other venues more suitable for their advertising message.

At the time of this writing the *Times* was having serious, perhaps even fatal, problems. The value of New York Times Company shares that once sold for $50 slipped below $4 in 2009.[34] In an effort to conserve income for company operations, the *Times* suspended dividend payments on shares in 2009. In order to raise capital, the company had to borrow $250 million from Mexican telecommunications billionaire Carlos Slim. The 14 percent interest rate on the loan no doubt reflected the fact that Moody's had downgraded the *Times'* debt to junk status. Only a few years after building a gleaming office tower, it had to sell the building and lease back the space to raise money. It was even looking for a buyer for its share of the Red Sox.

It is important to stress that these troubles are a very recent phenomenon. For much of our period of study, financial problems were not a real issue given the private control of the paper. After the *Times* started issuing non-voting shares, its rate of return was reasonable. Between 1986 and 2003 the share price of the *Times* fared as well as the Standard & Poors 500 Index. It was only after 2004 that the share price of the *Times* dropped below the S&P.[35] Interestingly, despite the worrying decline in revenue and profits, circulation revenue is actually up for the Times Media Group by 3.4 percent between 2007 and 2008.[36]

Furthermore, the current trouble experienced by the *Times* has been shared by others in the print media, which is suffering from the competition of free online content and the 2008 economic contraction. Its fellow big-city paper, the *Chicago*

---

* MRI Demographic Profiles 2006. Available at http://www.nytimes.whsites.net/mediakit/docs/readership/MRI_adult_consumer_profile.pdf and http://www.usatoday.com/media_kit/usatoday/au_general_demographics.htm, accessed on April 5, 2007.

Tribune has also suffered from declining share value since 2004, and was forced to declare bankruptcy. Gannett Company, publishers of *USA Today* and the *Detroit Free Press*, among many others, faced an even more dramatic free fall in share price than the *Times*, dropping to $2.20 in March 2009. The troubles facing the *Times* are both recent and shared by the rest of the industry. The *Times* has fared as well, or as poorly, as any other paper, and so any content that might conceivably anger advertisers has not resulted in a noticeable decline in revenue and profitability for the paper compared to its industry rivals. One possible explanation for this is that the affluent customers (including the "responsible" business community itself) of the *Times* make it a highly desirable place to be seen. Further, the *Times*' is able to keep this attractive customer base precisely because it is willing to be critical of certain corporate behavior. This is not to say that advertisers' interests have no impact on the content of the *Times*. This is patently not the case. However, it does suggest that the *Times* does not have to run, and indeed would be harmed by, content that unabashedly and consistently toed a conservative line.

This leads to the question of whether what we have hypothesized as the *Times*' perspective is likely to help or hinder it with the current twin challenges of the decline of print media and the economic crisis. The *Times*' educated prose and lengthy articles may be a poor fit for what many perceive to be a generation raised on the shallow brevity of texting and the Internet. It would certainly appear that most texters have not been taking advantage of William Safire's column in the *Times*, "On Language," which is "devoted to grammar and English usage." Whether the *Times* can successfully survive as a broadsheet or convert its strengths into an electronic format is at the moment a very open question. It is possible that in a decade the *Times* will be little more than a genteel anachronism, like brandy and cigars after dinner in the drawing room.

On the other hand, the *Times* is particularly well placed to benefit from the economic crisis precisely because of its owners' and readers' rejection of a specifically conservative position. Although the *Times*' perspective should be to support the broad economic system on which corporate profits rest, this requires criticism of specific corporations or industries. This viewpoint should serve the *Times* well in this period of economic crisis. As we will argue in later chapters, the economic crisis was set off by corporate behavior that caused the collapse of the banking and finance industry. The woes in the financial sector rapidly spread in an economy weakened by three decades of economic policies that enhanced corporate profits at the expense of American wage earners. In this context, a paper that stuck to a conservative line, refusing to criticize corporate activities, would be patently unable to provide a satisfactory explanation for a crisis caused by an overarching conservative policy framework and the overwhelming failings of firms in a particular industry. The *Times* is much better positioned than most private media outlets to provide an accurate analysis that must, at the very least, be highly critical of the activities of a number of firms.

It is possible that the election of Barack Obama as president in 2008 in the midst of an economic crisis reflected a change in American perspective that could benefit the *Times* on two fronts. First, the economic crisis has been so severe and affected such a wide section of the population that it might possibly awaken people's interest in "serious" news. Perhaps the threat of job loss is so grave that people will start reading the *Times* rather than *USA Today* in an effort to understand what caused the collapse. Obama was certainly seen as a more intelligent, issue-savvy president than the man he was replacing. Second, it might reflect a growing dissatisfaction with the universally conservative economic policy that had come to dominate U.S. federal politics, shifting the media market away from Fox and Bill O'Reilly and towards media that is able to be more critical of its corporate colleagues.

The narrow ownership structure of the *Times* through the period of our study made ownership influence in media content much more possible than if the paper were more broadly held. Interestingly, it also appears as though the owners' ideological preferences have not negatively affected profits. To the extent that what liberal content exists angers some advertisers, this content would be more likely to still appear when it is demanded by a large and affluent audience, including other firms that have a longer-run perspective on the interests of U.S. business.

The Rest of the Book: The Liberal and Conservative *Times*

Our analysis of the *Times* is divided into several economic themes. We will study the *Times'* coverage of broad macroeconomic issues, foreign economic policy, regulation, the opinions of their star editorial writers, and the economic crisis of 2008–2009. With the exception of Chapter 6 on the star reporters, these issues will be examined using case studies of controversial issues, carefully chosen as a litmus test, and capable of revealing the *Times'* ideology. Each case study will begin with a concise overview of the issue to provide a contrast to the *Times'* coverage. We will then examine the economics of the *Times* for each case, beginning in 1950. We will test our hypothesis about the *Times'* economic perspective by taking a close, perhaps obsessive, look at what the *Times* has written about what we would consider to be the most ideologically revealing political and economic issues.

Chapter 2 examines the existing literature on media bias. We are specifically interested in a new strand of research that attempts to discover the direction and source of bias in the media. Our interest here is to determine how the explicit themes of this book relate to this literature, which tends to focus on Democratic vs. Republican, and its counterpart, liberal vs. conservative, bias.

Chapter 3 tests the conservative and liberal hypotheses concerning the *Times* when it comes to macroeconomic policy. Economic research on the effects of government policy on competitiveness suggests when the revenues from taxation are spent on research and development, education, an effective social safety net, and a highly motivated, skilled labor force, competitiveness is boosted rather than undermined. An appropriately "mixed economy" is not only liberal, but is essential for a competitive, high-profit economy. However, in other economic contexts liberal policies that interfere with businesses' economic prerogatives can be very damaging to corporate profitability. In these contexts conservative policy is the profit enhancing choice. We will examine the *Times'* reporting on the Swedish model of social democracy and U.S. anti-inflation policy.

Chapter 4 studies the *Times'* reporting on U.S. foreign economic policy. The *Times* has been very consistent in its support of the rights of U.S. capital operating in foreign locations. While it might lament the more obviously horrendous consequences of U.S. companies' quest for foreign profits in a predictably liberal fashion, it consistently took a staunchly conservative stance by opposing threats to U.S. corporate profitability from foreign nations. We will use two case studies of *Times* reporting on foreign regimes that threaten the profitability of U.S. international business—Iran and Venezuela.

Chapter 5 takes a look at the *Times'* perspective on regulation. Government regulation, often pilloried by conservatives as an overprotective state intervening between the firm and the consumer to the detriment of corporate profitability and consumers' interests, can actually protect the profits of firms and the legitimacy of the system. On the other hand, certain regulation must be limited in order to ensure profitability and corporate autonomy. It is important that the *Times'* reporting on regulatory activity and corporate regulatory violations indict individual malfeasance, while capitalism and the corporate system are never indicted on a systemic level. This chapter will analyze the *Times'* reporting of three specific regulatory policies—energy deregulation, the Occupational Safety and Health Administration, and corporate crime.

Chapter 6 examines the work of two of the *Times'* star writers. The *Times* has developed an impressive roster of influential columnists. Among the heady newspaper heights of *Times'* opinion writers, we have opted to analyze the work of Paul Krugman and Thomas Friedman for two reasons. First, even among the famous *Times* columnists, these two stand out. Second, more than their colleagues, they focus particularly on the economic issues in which we are interested.

Chapter 7 examines the economic collapse of 2008. The crisis of 2008–2009 resulted from the deregulation of the financial sector and growing indebtedness of U.S. households. It is worth including as both a current test of our hypothesis about the economic perspective of the *Times* and because it may well be the single most important economic event since the Great Depression of the 1930s.

CHAPTER 2
BIAS IN THE MEDIA

Given its role in providing information to the voting public in a democratic system, it is unsurprising that the media has come under considerable scrutiny from researchers interested in explaining political results. This chapter is not meant to be an exhaustive review of the literature on this subject; rather, it will provide the reader with a sampling of some recent research that has been conducted in an effort to answer three questions. First, what is the nature of media bias? These studies attempt to quantify the strength and direction of media bias. Second, what would cause the media to have a particular bias? These studies move beyond attempts to pinpoint the type of bias to create a theoretical explanation for why media outlets would have a particular bias based on the institutional characteristics of the industry. Three, how does this literature relate to the themes of this book?

The Direction of Media Bias

There is a new, but growing, literature that is attempting to move beyond the anecdotal evidence that, according to the authors of these studies, had previously passed for evidence of media bias. John Lott and Kevin Hassett attempt to determine whether there was any difference in reporting similar economic statistics between Democrat and Republican presidencies during three administrations: those of Bush Sr., Clinton, and Bush Jr. Studying the headlines the day after the release of economic statistics in 389 newspapers and wire services in Nexus, with special attention to the top ten papers, they find that the two Bush Republicans received 20 to 30 percent less positive coverage than Democrat Clinton for similar economic numbers.[1] A closer examination of the print media reveals that three of the top ten papers (the *Los Angeles Times, Washington Post*, and *Chicago Tribune*) and the Associated Press had more negative headlines during Republican administrations than the *New York Times* and could, therefore, be characterized as more left wing. The authors conclude that no papers have a Republican bias and all the large national publications have Democratically slanted headlines.[2]

A possible alternative explanation for the Lott and Hassett results is that, in general, the economy was much stronger under Clinton than it was under both Bush administrations. The Clinton administration presided over an economy with federal government surpluses, the strongest economic growth in three decades, and the late 1990s' boom in the stock market. The record of both Bush presidencies was much more mixed. Given these very different economic contexts, it is hardly surprising that the overall tone of reporting for even similar individual statistics should be more optimistic during the economic boom of the Clinton administration.

Tim Groseclose and Jeffrey Milyo construct a creative measure of bias by comparing the media's use of partisan think tanks to that of members of Congress. The assumption is that if a liberal member of Congress (Ted Kennedy) repeatedly cites a particular think tank (Amnesty International) and a media outlet also frequently cites that same think tank, then it can be concluded that the media outlet has a similar ideology to the member of Congress. They study the news sections (as opposed to the editorial page) of several major television, magazine, and newspaper outlets, including what may be called more serious news institutions, like the *Times* and *Newshour with Jim Lehrer*, alongside slightly lighter fare from *USA Today* to *Good Morning America*. The authors conclude that as a whole the media exhibits a strong liberal bias. With the exception of Fox News' *Special Report* and the *Washington Times*, all of the news outlets studied were to the left of the average member of Congress. The *Times* is tied (with CBS evening news) for the second most liberal media outlet studied. In comparison to the members of Congress, the *Times* has a similar ideological score to Joe Lieberman.[3] Interestingly, the most liberal member of the media by this measure is the *Wall Street Journal*.[4]

Lott and Hassett point out that the reliance on the use of think tanks to measure ideology might create slightly misleading results. If media outlets use think tanks to present the liberal side of a story and present the conservative side of the story by citing non–think tank sources, then Groseclose and Milyo's focus on think tanks will artificially make coverage appear biased towards a liberal viewpoint.[5] More importantly, the definition of bias used by Groseclose and Milyo is very relative. By their definition, the media would be unbiased if it cited think tanks similar to the average member of Congress. But, of course, this is not really unbiased. The U.S. Congress hardly spans the ideological spectrum. Most Europeans would probably find the average member of Congress right of center.[6] If the second-most liberal media outlet has an ideological score comparable to Lieberman, a man who has proven himself comfortable in Republican circles, this would hardly suggest an overwhelmingly liberal bias, even on the terms defined by Groseclose and Milyo. The authors defend this by claiming that the media should be targeting the United States, not the European, population and therefore aiming for the center of the U.S. electoral representatives should indicate a bias-free media. At the very best, however, this would indicate not an unbiased media, but a media biased to the attitudes of the median U.S. voter—a bias that the media itself has helped to form. Finally, the Groseclose and Milyo study is not directly comparable with this work because it was not explicitly restricted to economic issues and so would have captured some of the *Times'* self-declared liberal bias on social issues.

Riccardo Puglisi examined the agenda-setting role of the *New York Times* during presidential campaigns. His inquiry into the direction of bias at the *Times* rests on the idea that Democrat and Republican parties are each seen to be stronger at dealing with certain issues. For example, the Democrats are seen as superior on issues like civil rights and health care while the Republicans are seen as being better able to handle defense and foreign policy issues. The *Times'* bias can be unearthed by discovering if it focuses on those issues in which a particular party is seen as being superior. Puglisi finds that between 1946 and 1997 the *Times* ran 26 percent more stories on Democratic issues during presidential campaigns than regularly.[7] Further, this bias is becoming more pronounced. Between 1961 and 1997 the *Times* ran 33 percent more stories on issues that play to perceived Democratic strengths. Interestingly, this finding only holds when a Republican incumbent is in office. The paper seems to want to replace Republican presidents but has little interest in aiding Democratic presidents.

There may be a slight methodological problem with how this study measures bias. The Democratic issues are generally more pertinent to political campaigns than the Republican issues. While foreign issues like war can be expected to attract coverage at any time, it is possible that domestic policy issues would receive increased coverage during presidential campaigns. After all, these are the issues that dominate campaigns, and that politicians continually make speeches about, but that might not generate much coverage outside of elections. It is, therefore, possible that the increased emphasis on stories in which the Democrats are perceived to be stronger could be less a result of media bias and more an inevitable result of the topics covered during political campaigns.

In an effort to quantify media bias since 1948, Dave D'Alessio and Mike Allen conducted a meta-analysis on fifty-nine previous studies of presidential elections. They examined newspapers, magazines, and television for three different types of bias: gatekeeping bias that reflects selection of stories from one party or another, coverage bias that examines how much time is dedicated to each party, and statement bias that deals with whether the coverage favors one party or another. The authors conclude that these previous studies indicate that there is no measurable liberal or conservative bias in the newspaper industry. This does not imply that individual outlets are not biased, but rather that there is no aggregate bias across all the newspapers, at least during presidential elections.[8]

Given the problems that have been identified with each of these studies, it would be something of an understatement to claim that the jury is still out on the direction of media bias. However, with the important exception of the D'Allessio and Allen study, the research seems to suggest a liberal bias, narrowly defined as similar to a Democrat on the U.S. political spectrum, and sometimes, as in the case of Leiberman, not even a particularly liberal Democrat. Of the media outlets, the *Times* consistently places to the liberal side of center. With respect to the hypothesis of this book, the media's preference for Democrats may be associated with the fact that they are more likely to implement a broader range of economic policy alternatives, including both conservative and liberal positions, which are more consistent with corporate interests. After all, the Clinton administration delivered on conservative welfare reform, deregulated the financial sector, and was a big advocate of free trade agreements. Hedge funds were happy enough with Democratic policies to dedicate 65 percent of their total contributions to them in the 2008 election.[9] In satirist Bill Maher's words, "We have the Democrats, who are what the Republicans used to be when I was a kid. They're a pro-business party, a corporate-friendly, pro-business party. And then we have the Republicans, which are just a club for angry white people and Jesus freaks."

The Source of Media Bias

A second strand of research seeks to analyze the media as a profit-maximizing business in an effort to determine why it would have a bias in one direction or another. Several authors have attempted to theoretically construct both a direction and source of media bias. The following section examines the possible sources of media bias: owners, advertisers, journalists, and customers.

The first possible source of bias is the ownership of the paper. James Hamilton's book *All the News that's Fit to Print* is particularly concerned with explaining the paucity of "hard" news about civic and political issues, but also claims that there is a liberal bias in what limited hard news is actually covered. He argues that these trends can be explained through some fairly conventional economic analysis of the specifics of the media industry.

According to Hamilton, bias might come from the desire of liberal owners to promote their own views. If the owners of media outlets gain some utility from advocating a particular ideology or political perspective, then it is possible that they would be willing to forgo profits in favor of promoting their own point of view. As we saw in Chapter 1, an owner's personal perspective is more likely to appear when there is less competition in a particular market. The media industry, especially that of newspapers, does create barriers to entry because it is characterized by high fixed and low variable costs. The cost of producing the first issue of the paper is very large compared with the cost associated with producing each subsequent paper, which can be done at a remarkably low cost.[10] Industries with high fixed and low variable costs make it difficult for new firms to enter, creating at least a theoretical case for established owners to inject their own biases into the news.

Daniel Sutter argues that owners are very unlikely to be the source of liberal bias. Owners are most likely not liberals. While occasional owners might classify themselves as slightly liberal (Ted Turner has been used as an example), it is certainly not universally true throughout a media world populated by such figures as Rupert Murdoch.[11] Further, a broadly owned firm is much less likely to be willing to settle on any other goal than profit maximization. The rise of the corporate form of ownership in the media industry would make owner-caused bias that reduces short-run profitability increasingly unlikely.

Other authors argue that the for-profit ownership structure of media outlets is likely to produce a right-wing media bias. Critics of a corporate-dominated media, most notably Edward Herman, Noam Chomsky,[12] and Robert McChesney,[13] argue that this inevitably biases the information produced by the mass media. According to these authors, privately owned firms in any industry must attempt to maximize their profits, and media corporations are no exception. Given this truth, their commitment to providing information to the public is a means to an end—higher profitability.

If media firms are profit-maximizing entities, it would seem reasonable to claim that they will be unlikely to provide information or run stories that compromise their own corporate profitability. Most obviously this means that the media are unlikely to run stories that criticize their own corporation. It also means that they are unlikely to be particularly critical of the institution of private ownership in general.[14] This has become a larger problem, given the recent deregulation of the media. Prior to the 1980s, government regulation prevented any one corporation from dominating any individual market and restricted the ability of a corporation to expand into different forms of media.[15] These restrictions have gradually been removed since the 1980s, resulting in a wave of mergers in the media. The result is that media outlets are part of a much larger corporate empire: Fox is part of the News Corporation empire, NBC is part of General Electric, and ABC is owned by Disney.[16] This means that news outlets have a much larger group of companies within their corporate umbrella that individual news outlets will be reluctant to sully.

A for-profit media may also be constrained by its need to generate advertising revenue. While this is particularly true of media content that is provided "free" to viewers, such as radio and television, even newspapers, which earn income from direct sales to their audience, earn most of their revenue from advertising. This influences the type of information that will be provided by media outlets in two ways. First, advertisers prefer content that is complementary to their marketing message and that places potential consumers in a purchasing mood. Style and home sections in newspapers are prime examples of where news can very nicely lead into advertising messages. Second, firms may be reluctant to advertise in outlets that portray a particu-lar corporation, or corporations in general, in a negative light.[17] For example, Exxon might not be overjoyed to find its advertisement across the page from an article on the environmental damage done by burning fossil fuels. These two factors should create an incentive for the media in general to emphasize less hard news, especially news that criticizes advertisers.

While Sutter has difficulty seeing any theoretical justification for ownership to create a liberal media bias, he also finds it difficult to believe that advertising makes the media unwilling to criticize either individual corporations or the business class as a whole. According to the Chomsky and McChesney thesis, the need to generate advertising revenue makes firms reluctant to run content that is critical of firms. This can be true for either individual companies that are specifically criticized or for corporations more generally if media firms run broader "anti-business" stories. Sutter dismisses both of these possibilities. While criticizing any particular business might—in fact probably will—result in that single firm refusing to advertise, this is only one firm among countless others that are still willing, and so the media outlet is unlikely to suffer. This is especially true given the relative market power that exists between newspapers and their advertisers. Sutter claims that most papers operate in markets with at most a couple of competitors, and many markets are dominated by a single company.[18] As evidence to support this contention he claims that companies who do halt advertising due to unfavorable coverage only do so for brief periods and then resume advertising, which he takes as proof that it is the newspaper rather than the advertiser that wields the market power.

This is, perhaps, a slight overstatement of the limited advertising avenues open to firms. After all, newspapers must compete with a wide variety of other media outlets for advertising clients. In fact, it is possible that Sutter has the direction of causa-tion reversed. Conceivably, the reason that negatively covered firms only cease their advertising with the offending media for a brief period of time is not that they have few other advertising outlets and must bow to the newspapers' monopoly power. Rather, they know that newspapers' need for advertising revenue will ensure that their brief foray into corporate criticism is unlikely to be sustained.

There is also the possibility that some corporate criticism by the media may spark increases in advertising by the very companies that have been criticized. Firms may use "defensive" advertising in an attempt to offset negative publicity. In their attempt to reach concerned citizens, corporations are much more likely to choose more critical, liberal media outlets with "serious" readers. To take just one current example, when BP's offshore drilling went horribly wrong and millions of barrels of oil spilled into the Gulf of Mexico, the company took out twenty-four full-page ads in the *New York Times* in the five-week period at the height of the crisis between May 20 and June 28. All of the ads were an attempt to reassure readers that BP was doing its utmost to limit the spill and clean up the damage. One ad optimistically promised: "Our beach clean-up operations will continue until the last of the oil has been skimmed from the sea, the beaches and the estuaries have been cleaned up, and the region has been pronounced oil-free."[19]

Sutter also claims that advertising would not result in suppression of more general anti-business stories if a demand for this kind of media content actually existed. Although it is in the best interest of businesses, in general, to maintain a pro-business bias in the media, this suffers from the public good problem. A public convinced of the benefits of the free enterprise system confers benefits on each individual firm even if it has not contributed to this perception in any way. As a result, each firm will hope to free ride on other firms that are willing to incur the costs of maintaining this public sentiment. If advertising in an anti-business media outlet were to increase profitability, no firm would be willing to accept the cost of withdrawing their advertising, hoping that others would incur the losses.[20] Therefore, the argument that advertising causes a broad pro-corporate bias in the media relies on firms being able to form a cartel to solve the free rider problem. Since Sutter views this as extraordinarily unlikely, he concludes that the only plausible reason for the lack of anti-corporate media is the lack of demand.[21]

It is possible that Sutter is overstating the intractability of the free rider problem. The free rider problem exists for any activity that seeks to influence the broad political and social environment. Changes in regulations or tax laws suffer from the same free rider problems that Sutter ascribes to a general pro-business sentiment. However, there appears to be no shortage of lobby groups spending vast sums of money attempting to sway government policy in a manner that Sutter would argue should be subject to free riding. It would appear that many people and businesses are willing to dedicate substantial resources to public goods despite the free rider problem, despite its supposed irrationality from a purely individual, maximizing perspective.

The third source of bias emanating from inside the media corporations could be from the journalists, who are usually postulated to have liberal leanings.[22] If journalists are liberal and have a considerable degree of autonomy over the stories they file, then their desire to slant stories could be responsible for media bias. Sutter correctly points out that this is an unlikely source of bias because firms should be able to take actions that prevent their employees from creating content that would reduce profitability.[23] Despite the alleged autonomy of journalists, it is important to note that they are not part of a profession that is independent or self-regulating in the same manner as doctors or lawyers. Rather, they are employees of a for-profit firm and subject to the same subservient position in the labor process shared by other workers. Although the claim that many journalists are liberal has never been seriously disputed, many have argued that it is unlikely that journalists will be able to express their own individual ideological preferences if they run counter to those of their employer (whether that is determined by the individual desires of the owner or the dictates of profitability). In his book *Lapdogs*, which is, as the title implies, sharply critical of the mainstream media's kid-glove handling of the Bush presidency, especially during the Iraq war, Eric Boehlert argues that journalists who raised uncomfortable questions about the very shaky justification for the war faced ominous career consequences. His example is the NBC journalist Ashleigh Banfield, who claimed that the cable news coverage of Iraq may have been coverage of the war, but it was not journalism, because it raised no difficult questions about the conflict. According to Boehlert, she was disciplined for this statement and her career effectively ended at NBC.[24]

However, David Baron creates the theoretical possibility that firms could increase their profits by permitting their journalists free reign to express their liberal political bias. If Democrat-leaning journalists get some satisfaction from framing stories in a liberal fashion, then they might be willing to accept lower wages to work for a liberal paper. Even if the liberal bias decreases the demand for the paper from the less liberal general public, if the decrease in wages from being liberal outweighs the decrease in revenue from the dissatisfied customers, then it is economically rational for the media to have a bias that does not reflect that held by the majority of the population.[25]

The advantage of this theory is that it jettisons the dubious assumption that media companies are unable to control their employees. However, Baron has to make some very strong assumptions about the labor market for journalists in order to get this result. Most obviously, journalists have to be interested in projecting their own (very slight) liberal bias in their reporting and willing to sacrifice earnings for creative control in their work. He also assumes a sufficiently large supply of journalists that wages will be forced down far enough to exceed the revenue losses from decreased customers. While this story may actually be true, it cannot be taken as a legitimate cause of the liberal media without additional empirical work to determine whether these assumptions are at all realistic.

The fourth potential source of media bias is the demands of its consumers. Even for media that rely exclusively on advertising for revenue, such as television and radio, viewers and listeners are crucial in order to attract advertisers. Newspaper readers are not only important as targets for advertisers, but contribute more directly to revenues by paying for the product. This creates an opportunity for paper consumers to express their strength of preference for a product by paying for specific types of information. Under the assumption that people are more likely to consume information that fits with their interests and ideological perspectives, media firms' informational bias may, in fact, merely represent the bias of their consumers.

Hamilton's analysis of the lack of "hard" (political or civic matters, as opposed to entertainment) news in the United States argues that it is profit-driven media's attempt to attract customers that largely influences content. In general, he finds that in cities with strong support for one political party or another, the local papers will tend to be similarly partisan.[26] He also argues that the trend toward more liberal news content is an attempt to capture the much coveted younger and female customers, who purchase more than older and male readers, making them highly desirable targets for advertisers. He further finds that young females are more likely to have political views that are more liberal than the general population. Survey data do demonstrate that young women are more likely to feel that the media does a good job of providing the information that they want. Only 11 percent of young women, as opposed to 24 percent of men over 50, report that the media are "out of touch" with their interests.[27] So, according to Hamilton, the media does filter information, and it will often contain a political bias; however, this is not due to any particular motivation of the corporations in the media beyond their quest for customers.

Hamilton also claims that newspapers do not need to be quite so obsessed with the young, female demographic as other forms of media, which are solely dependent on advertising revenue. In a sense, each reader is more equal, since they all pay for the paper. Hamilton still assumes that it is consumer demand that drives content, but with newspapers, the consumers themselves, rather than their value to advertisers, carry more weight compared to other media forms. For example, Hamilton finds that the type of "hard" news covered in the local papers reflects the concerns of the population. For example, cities with older populations, and who read more *Modern Maturity*, will have less coverage of issues such as AIDS and computers in their local papers, especially compared to cities with more computer programmers.[28] This suggests that newspapers might more closely reflect the bias of the population in which they operate rather than the population that advertisers want to reach.

Similarly, Matthew Gentzkow and Jesse Shapiro argue that bias arises from media outlets' desire to create a reputation for accuracy. Media outlets will be perceived as higher quality when they provide information that is closely related to the preexisting beliefs of their consumers. So, it is not that consumers want a particular bias—in fact they demand a "quality" paper. However, when media outlets can generate a reputation for quality by meeting their customers' existing expectations, bias will inevitably result. Industry structure can play an important role in this context. Increased competition will expose customers to more information, reducing media bias.[29]

Timothy Cook offers a slightly different take on the idea of consumer-led bias in his book *Governing the News*. He argued that the media should be seen as a political institution in its own right, every bit as important as government itself.[30] What he meant by an "institution" was that the media should be viewed as a single entity, not through the actions of any particular journalist, since they all follow a common set of practices when it comes to things like the objectivity, importance, and interest of news items. He viewed the government and media as having a symbiotic relationship that is interactive and interdependent. While government certainly uses the media for its own purposes and in fact actually subsidizes the media through its press offices and official news releases, journalists, especially those few in charge of what actually appears in the media, have tremendous influence through their selection of stories, the prominence they are given, and the context in which they are placed. It is this selection and framing that can create a certain perspective, according to Cook, but that perspective has been increasingly framed by the customers of the media as opposed to the journalists themselves. As the profit motive became more important in the privately owned news media, outlets came to regard their readers, listeners, or viewers more as customers than citizens. Customers are drawn to media that provides "production value" in the form of reports that are easy, simple, colorful, concrete, and dramatic. Further, the desire of advertisers to reach affluent customers may create an incentive for media to forgo audience size in favor of carefully targeted stories that appeal to the wealthy.[31] Both of these incentives create a tendency for certain stories to make the news, while others are ignored.

Critics of the media from a more left-wing perspective argue that the effort to meet the concerns of consumers created a very different bias in the media. In the early days of the media in the late 1800s, newspapers were much more unabashedly partisan. Papers made no pretense to objectivity but rather supported a particular ideological perspective. In an era of low barriers to entry, every market was served by a number of publications. So, while each individual paper made no effort at "balanced" coverage, the proliferation of papers in each market from a variety of ideological perspectives created a wide range of information.[32] The problem with this partisan model was that accuracy would frequently take a back seat to ideology. As readers came to question the reliability of the information provided by the papers, newspapers responded by moving to a more professional, nonpartisan code in an effort to restore their credibility and maintain their audiences. Ironically, contemporary non-print media—especially talk radio and cable television—seems to be reverting to the partisan press model of yore as contemporary media consumers express preference for media that accords with their own ideological perspective.

While professionalism and objectivity in print media like the *New York Times* have some important advantages over the blatantly biased reporting that it replaced, this very trend to professionalism has created some important biases of its own. Perhaps most important, it has resulted in a reliance on "official" sources, most often those in high government offices or "experts" in business or academia. This does increase the credibility of the news, but also allows those officials and experts to frame the debate.[33] It also creates a dependence on access to "official" sources. This only creates an illusion of objectivity. The media can claim that it is only reporting the news, using expert or official opinions, rather than inserting its own bias. However, it hides the inevitable bias that will be brought forward by the experts or officials. Paul Krugman is quoted as claiming, "Let's be frank: the Bush administration has made brilliant use of journalistic careerism. Those who wrote puff pieces about Mr. Bush and those around him have been rewarded with career-boosting access."[34]

This literature on the likely sources of media bias reveals some structural causes of media bias that we can apply to the *Times*. It is possible for owners to sometimes impose their own beliefs on the content of their media (as opposed to media outlets pandering to the profitable revenue-generating desires of advertisers and consumers). However, for this to happen, the owners must be willing to sacrifice short-term profits to present that bias, have narrow ownership of the firm, and be in a market with entry restrictions, which we have seen in the previous chapter does applies to the *Times*.

Advertising might also introduce a bias. Since ads are a sizeable portion of media income, even for newspapers, it would seem that this would create a reluctance to run content that angered advertisers. However, this does not mean that media firms will never run content that is either critical of broad sectors of business or criticizes specific advertisers. Advertisers may be forced to run "defensive" ads in critical, quality newspapers like the *Times*. Further, as Sutter correctly points out, if critical media outlets can offer advertisers a large and attractive demographic, they would face the problem of foregoing the profits they could make through advertising for the collective gains of attempting to maintain a pro-business public sentiment. This would favor advertising when the audience is particularly large and affluent while the criticism was not particularly damaging, as is the case with the *Times*.

Journalists themselves appear to be an unlikely source of bias. While survey evidence does show that they have personal sympathies that are slightly liberal or Democratic, it is less clear that they will be free to use their jobs as their own personal soapbox. Journalists follow a professional code of ethics that stresses objective and unbiased reporting (although we have seen that this creates a reliance on official sources that can introduce other biases) and we would expect the *Times* to take this especially seriously. Perhaps more important, journalists are employees and, therefore, are unlikely to have free reign to produce material that runs counter to the desires of their employer (or the customers and advertisers from which the profit-maximizing employer derives revenue).

Finally, this brings us to the customers, who might be responsible for the direction of media bias. There is an annoying "chicken and egg" problem when we deal with consumers' demand for a certain kind of information. If consumers demand a specific type of information, it might be that the media is driven to provide it in order to attract customers. However, it is also possible that the reason consumers demand this specific type of information is because this is the type of information that they have been exposed to through the media. Should the preferences of consumers not conflict with profit-decreasing constraints of advertisers or the corporate ownership of the media itself, as is the case with Hamilton's examples, then media content can certainly be influenced by the demands of consumers. The corollary to this statement is that the demands of consumers are more likely to be recognized when they do not conflict with advertisers or corporate interests.

Our Bias

This book will argue that the usual liberal-conservative dichotomy that has been used as the previous spectrum of media bias, while accurate, overlooks a more profound bias. Casting the debate in such a narrow fashion is, in fact, very misleading because the liberal/conservative or Democrat/Republican spectrum is remarkably limited.

An economic debate that limits itself to options pursued by these two camps would be similarly limited. It is also misleading because it omits the real bias of the *Times*, which is that it supports the long-term interests of U.S. business involving both liberal and conservative policies.

Our claim that the economic debate in the *Times* is narrower than most academic analysts have understood is, in some ways, mirrored by Daniel Hallin's analysis of the Vietnam War.[35] He argued that most of the research surrounding the media's role in the war focused on whether it was "antagonistic" or "supportive." The conventional conclusion was that an uncensored media was in opposition to the U.S. government and its role in Vietnam and contributed significantly to the dissatisfaction with the war in America that caused its eventual withdrawal. Hallin claimed that the actual truth is much more nuanced. "Structurally the American news media are both highly autonomous from direct political control and through the routines of the news gathering process, deeply intertwined in the actual operation of government. Culturally and ideologically, they combine the Progressive suspicion of power with a respect for order, institutions, and authority exercised within those institutions that is equally part of twentieth century liberalism."[36]

Hallin argued that the media was often very supportive of the war, in part because journalistic conventions, like reliance on official sources, set bounds on the range of issues that could be seriously discussed. When the *Times* reported on the Gulf of Tonkin incident it did so by documenting quotable facts from official government sources. The fact that the government was deliberately and systematically lying in order to create a justification for entering the war made "the *New York Times* essentially an instrument of the state."[37] The media in general was largely supportive of the entire Vietnam effort prior to the Tet Offensive.[38]

As the war claimed more U.S. lives and the conflict became increasingly intractable, the media did become more critical, but Hallin claims that there were important boundaries on the criticism. While the media became a battleground between different political factions about the war, "it was a conflict over tactics not principles."[39] According to Hallin, some sections of the American public, like college students, were questioning the assumptions about the role of American foreign policy, not merely the management of the war. These critics challenged the benevolence of American power and saw the "intervention" as an "aggressive war motivated by power, comparable to the Soviet intervention in Czechoslovakia," but issues of this sort were simply not on the news agenda. "Never, for example, did I hear an American utter the word imperialism on television."[40] Even in periods of crisis, when the media distance themselves from incumbent officials and their policies, "they do not make the system—or its core beliefs—an issue."[41]

We are making a very similar tactics-versus-core-beliefs claim about economic policy in this book. The tactics of how best to support U.S. business using liberal or conservative policy is an acceptable ground for debate and the *Times* is a crucial venue in which that can happen. The core belief of the system, whether supporting business has unacceptable costs for the rest of society, is not a common topic of discussion.

The perspective by which we analyze both the actual, real-world economy and how that is reflected in the *Times* is through its effects on different groups in the economic system. Economic conditions and policies have important distributional effects that fall unevenly on different groups. Society can be broadly divided into two groups: those who control businesses, and all those whom Alan Budd, professor of economics at the London Business School and chief economic advisor to Margaret Thatcher, refers to as the "working classes"; that Lester Thurow, professor of economics at MIT and former dean of the MIT Sloan School of Management, identifies as "nonsupervisory workers"; that Alan Greenspan characterizes as "traumatized workers"; and that Thomas Piketty and Emmanuel Saez refer to as the bottom 90 percent of American taxpayers.

These "workers" and their families make up the vast majority of the population of the United States. We use two benchmarks in our analysis. One is how these "workers" have fared in comparison to the business class with respect to wages and productivity, profits, wealth, and income distribution. The second benchmark is to compare the economies of different countries (e.g., Sweden and the United States) with respect to indicators—like wages, hours of work, pensions, health indicators, and work safety—that matter to the vast majority of the population. In other words, what are the class effects of different policy options? There is often an implied assumption that liberal Democratic policies would favor the "workers" and conservative Republican policies would benefit businesses and their owners. However, this is not a particularly accurate assumption. While conservative policies rarely benefit the "workers," liberal policies can improve business profits, especially in the long run, often without improving conditions for workers and the citizenry at large.

In attempting to examine how the *Times* reports on a specific group or class in society, we are more closely following Diana Kendall in her book *Framing Class*. Her primary focus is how the popular media, including entertainment, frames its content about different social classes in the United States. According to Kendall, the media masks the gulf between the income groups by depicting the upper class as being similar to the rest of society, in that their cares and concerns are common to John Q. Public. To the extent that they are shown as different, they are represented as admirable characters that others should seek to emulate, especially in their consumption.[42] By contrast, the poor and homeless are portrayed as being the authors of their miserable lot in life and deserving of sympathy only on holidays and in cases of natural disaster.[43] Kendall argues that these portrayals of different income groups in society hide the real causes of inequalities, downplay the extent of inequality, and justify the existence of inequality. Importantly for this work, Kendall pays particular attention to the *Times* because of her view that it best reflects what is being printed by all newspapers in the country and has unequaled influence over public opinion.[44] She claims that the paper is particularly involved in creating these misleading frames in an effort to simultaneously appeal to their readership while maintaining its status as the most influential newspaper in the world with respect to news, national politics, and international affairs.

Identifying the Bias of the *Times*

The ability of the media to shape stories and issues has long been recognized. The press became known as the Fourth Estate precisely to acknowledge that while the first three estates (nobility; clergy; and commoners, which in those days meant the middle class with property) had a formal voice in democracy, the press was the institution most able to advocate for and frame political issues. Over time, those discontented with what they saw to be the cozy role of the mainstream press in supporting the status quo coined the term the Fifth Estate to describe forms of media that challenged the powers that be. In this context we will demonstrate how the *Times* can be seen as the preeminent example of the Fourth Estate, using its prestige and formidable skills to advocate for the U.S. capitalist class as a whole by helping to frame political issues.

Journalists have a code of ethics, and we would expect those at the *Times* to be among the most committed to the highest standards in the industry. This code stipulates that competing points of view should be balanced and fairly characterized. The subjects of adverse news stories should be allowed a reasonable opportunity to respond before the story is published or broadcast. Reporters must test the accuracy of information from all sources and exercise care to avoid inadvertent error. Stories should never misrepresent the ideas of their subjects, nor should they present information out of context. Further, analysis and commentary should be labeled and not misrepresent fact or context. It is this final stipulation that creates the famous insistence that opinion pieces like editorials and op-eds must be kept completely separate from reporting on news pieces, including keeping distinctly different staffs for the two sections.

While these criteria are designed to create an objective press, editors, writers, and owners still have considerable latitude in their role reporting the news. They must decide which stories to follow and which to ignore. Once a story is selected there are a number of different angles or perspectives in which it could be framed. All this creates an environment where, while still upholding a code of ethics, there is still tremendous discretion in what is reported and how it is covered. So, there is the opportunity for bias in the media, and we have shown above in the discussion of the economics of the *New York Times*, that the motive for bias is also present. Our expectation is that it is not only the more explicit opinion or commentary sections of the *Times* that will contain bias, but that it will also be present in its news stories. In order to explicitly test for this, the opinion pieces will be separated from the news stories in all of the issues to be examined.

We suggest that given the particular economic opportunities and constraints that allow the *Times* to play its crucial liberal and conservative gatekeeper role, a critical reader should look for some specific patterns in the *Times'* reporting. These patterns help the *Times* frame issues to legitimize corporate ownership in the economy while criticizing specific firms or policies that might threaten profitability and legitimacy in the long run. First, does the *Times* have a consistent predisposition in its reporting on issues that constrain corporate profitability, especially those that might call into question the legitimacy of corporate power and the policies necessary to sustain it? We would predict that the *Times* would attempt to frame these policies and their agents in a negative light and brand them so that readers know this is someone or something not to be trusted. Conversely, it is also likely to cast supportive policies, and the people or institutions that champion them, more positively.

Second, does the *Times* tend to assume that firms and the policies that support them are innocent until proven guilty? While this is a commendable practice in the court of law, it stands in the way of the *Times* detecting any consistent problems with corporate behavior or even being sufficiently inquisitive when problems emerge as a result of the corporate system. This "malfeasant amnesia" means that the *Times* will not generally extrapolate from the past on matters that might threaten corporate interests in general.

Third, as we have insisted, amnesia does not mean that the *Times* will side with all firms at all times. On the contrary, when evidence does mount about cases of corporate misbehavior, the *Times* would be highly critical of individual members or sections of the business community, since their misdeeds threaten the profitability and legitimacy of the larger corporate world. However, when reporting on these stories the *Times* should ensure that the problems are a result of "bad apples" that are violating the normal code of good business conduct and not a result of systemic flaws.

Finally, timing is important in the media. The *Times* is most influential when it reports on information from which lessons can be drawn for current policy issues. When incontrovertible evidence makes it impossible for the *Times* to credibly avoid criticizing issues or people that run counter to the long-term interests of corporate America, these concessions to the truth can be made belatedly, when they can have less impact on the current policy debate.

CHAPTER 3
THE *NEW YORK TIMES* AND MACROECONOMICS

A *TALE OF TWO COUNTRIES*

Few people genuinely understand the importance of macroeconomic policy. While most people glaze over when the conversation turns to interest rates, government spending, taxation, or labor markets, the reality is that these things provide the broad policy framework that will go a long way toward determining things like the rate of economic growth, inflation, unemployment, and the amount of innovation, degree of inequality, and level of poverty in society. Will a nation enjoy broadly shared prosperity or will it plunge into recession, destroying livelihoods and forcing families into the misery that is poverty? Further, it is extremely unlikely that macro policy will impact all members of society in a similar fashion, meaning that often there will be winners and losers from any given policy choice. Policies that help firms often harm employees, creating a great deal of conflict over what should be the "correct" policy.[1]

With so much riding on macroeconomic policy, and a veritable buffet of alternative policy options, this chapter attempts to determine what the *Times* considered to be "wise." It will examine the *Times'* coverage of macroeconomic policy using two revealing issues. The first is the *Times'* reporting on the monetary policy of the U.S. Federal Reserve and its effects on inflation and unemployment. The second is the *Times'* treatment of the Swedish economy. Sweden is a particularly interesting test case in how the *Times* treated a frequently cited example of a competing macroeconomic structure. In many ways, Sweden is a foil for the United States in terms of capitalist macroeconomic options. Both Sweden and the United States are subject to the vicissitudes of capitalism's expansions and contractions. Of critical interest is how the citizens of each country share the costs and benefits of these dynamics and how well prepared the two economies are to respond effectively to the need for institutional change in the face of crisis. Before turning to the *Times'* coverage of these issues, we will begin with a brief primer on U.S. monetary policy and Swedish social democracy.

U.S. Macroeconomic Performance and Monetary Policy: Anti Inflation or Pro Profit?

The so-called Golden Age of U.S. capitalism, between the late 1940s and the late 1960s, was characterized by rapid capital accumulation, high rates of profit, high levels of investment, rapid productivity growth, low inflation, low unemployment, and rising real wages. The political and social context for the Golden Age was a set of institutional arrangements between U.S. capital and its workers and citizens that enhanced and legitimated profits after World War II.[2] The failures of the free market during the Great Depression and the economic success of government military spending during World War II created a political climate where growth and full employment became the responsibility of the state. The U.S. government sought to reduce severe economic instability using liberal monetary and fiscal policy, including progressive taxes and unemployment insurance to avoid severe downturns. The emergence of a welfare state to mitigate the inequities and hardship resulting from "the market" was also a means of maintaining the legitimacy of the capitalist system. The period immediately after World War II was also one of intense labor-management strife, which forced corporations to seek some kind of accord with the militant labor unions. The state and the corporate sector found a solution. Labor accepted corporate control over production, technology, plant location, marketing, and the labor process in exchange for job security, rising wages, and union recognition. Unions delivered an orderly and disciplined labor force and corporations rewarded workers with a share of the income gains made possible from productivity growth.[3]

The Golden Age did not last. The 1970s were characterized by a falling rate of profit, a productivity slowdown, accelerating inflation, rising unemployment, eventually stagnating investment, and a stagnation of real wages. Generally, the "Great Stagnation" was a worldwide capitalist phenomenon. In the decade of the 1960s the world economy grew at the rate of 5.0 percent, and in the 1970s the real growth rate dropped to 3.6 percent. By the 1980s the rate had dropped to 2.8 percent, and it continued this decline in the 1990s, when it fell to 2.0 percent. In two decades capitalism lost 60 percent of its macroeconomic momentum.[4] Through the 1990s the overall European unemployment rate remained in double digits, while the Japanese economy stagnated for a decade. Even the most successful post-1970 five-year period in the United States, marked by the boom in the new economy between 1995 and 2000, failed to measure up to the period between 1948 and 1970 in terms of growth, productivity, inflation, unemployment, and profits. The only higher indicator was the stock market, and that bubble was soon to burst.

In the United States, business and governments responded to this economic mal-aise by turning to conservative policy prescriptions designed to cut costs to business in an effort to restore profits. In the macroeconomy, this was most obviously done by a high-interest monetary policy to create unemployment and control wages in the 1980s, but it also took the form of a general reduction in any government regula-tion or spending that would increase costs to business. The result has been that the liberal macroeconomic policy of a larger government has, for the most part, been abandoned in favor of the more conservative policy of reducing the size of the state.

U.S. monetary policy both responded to and influenced these changing economic conditions. The three broad economic policy environments have been accompanied by very different monetary policies. During the Golden Age, the Federal Reserve pursued a generally liberal policy of using low interest rates to promote full employ-ment. The inflationary concerns of the Great Stagnation brought on a conservative, tight monetary policy and high interest rates. Finally, the neoliberal late 1990s and 2000s saw a low-interest-rate policy that met with very few critics in either the lib-eral or conservative camp. Monetary policy may have changed considerably, but its overarching goal has not. Contrary to popular belief, and stated monetary policy, that goal is not to control inflation, but rather to preserve profitability.

> By destiny compell'd, and in despair,
> The Greeks grew weary of the tedious war,
> And by Minerva's aid a fabric rear'd,
> Which like a steed of monstrous height appear'd:
> The sides were plank'd with pine; they feign'd it made
> For their return, and this the vow they paid.
> Thus they pretend, but in the hollow side
> Selected numbers of their soldiers hide:
> With inward arms the dire machine they load,
> And iron bowels stuff the dark abode.

From this mythological episode comes the term "Trojan horse," describing an appar-ent gift that is actually a trick; "Trojan horse tactics" are those considered sneaky, underhand, and deceitful. The term can also refer to a "sneak attack" in general.

Inflation is feared because of the effects of uncertain price increases on investment and the bureaucratic costs of estimating future prices in a high-inflation environment. Since the late 1970s, the U.S. Federal Reserve (the Fed) has dedicated itself primarily to the fight against inflation in spite of the fact that its historic mandate (the result of the experiences of the Great Depression) included maximum employment as well as growth without excessive inflation. However, this obsession with inflation is not empirically justified. In study after study tracking the relationship between inflation and growth for the OECD since 1960, there is no evidence that moderate rates of inflation have a negative impact. According to Sepehri, et al., there is no statistically detectable, long-run relationship between inflation and growth that is evident for the OECD countries.[5] Even studies at the International Monetary Fund (IMF) have acknowledged that inflation rates of up to 8 percent do not seem to have any negative effect on the economy. The same studies also fail to demonstrate that zero inflation maximizes economic growth.[6]

The war on inflation is accomplished by restricting the availability of money and credit and therefore keeping interest rates high. This discourages investment and makes it more difficult for low-profit firms, with their relatively inefficient capital, to access finance and stay in business. In the resulting high-unemployment environment, workers tend to quit less, work harder, and receive lower wages as employers get them to compete with one another for increasingly scarce jobs. For some firms, the higher interest rates will be a double-edged sword. The decreased cost of labor will reduce expenses, but higher interests rates increase the price of borrowing. On a broader level, the general economic slowdown will reduce income from sales. While this strategy helps the business class as a whole by tending to lower labor costs in all sectors of the economy, it does have costs for heavy borrowers and firms that have their sales reduced. High interest rates serve the financial sector more unequivocally by preserving the value of debt and therefore their source of profits.

Prolonged periods of high unemployment in the cause of inflationary discipline can be difficult to justify to the out-of-work citizenry, but right-wing "monetarist" economist Milton Friedman made an effort to do so. Friedman theorized a "natural rate of unemployment," which evolved into the "Non-Accelerating Inflation Rate of Unemployment," or NAIRU. Attempts by governments to lower unemployment below the natural rate will have no long-term beneficial impact on employment and only create inflation. The reason for this is that as unemployment falls, workers will demand and receive higher wages. In an effort to restore profitability, firms will raise prices. So in order to avoid this inflationary trend, the economy should not grow beyond the NAIRU. The NAIRU has been used by central banks to justify prolonged unemployment rates of 10 percent in Europe and 8 percent in the United States.

The focus on the unemployment rate in the NAIRU theory inevitably targets labor and wage gains as one of the main sources of inflation. However, prices are not only driven by costs, but also by the need for firms to make a profit. John Kenneth Galbraith had a more double-sided approach to inflation. While Galbraith certainly identified the potential of labor, especially under conditions of full employment and strong labor unions, to increase costs, he argued that inflation was equally likely to come from the ability of firms to increase prices. Indeed the real danger, according to Galbraith, was that in conditions near full capacity both labor and management will be able to increase both wages and prices in an inflationary spiral.[7]

Although the NAIRU theory was repeatedly used to justify high unemployment rates in the 1980s, conservative economists do not argue that it is "natural" in the sense that it cannot change. Rather, they argued that given the economic structure of the time, any lower unemployment rate would worsen inflation, but restructuring the economy could drop the NAIRU, permitting a lower unemployment rate that would not create accelerating inflation. What is interesting is that the economic restructuring prescribed to improve the NAIRU reveals precisely the hidden conflict that we have been arguing is the underlying reason for this so-called anti-inflation policy. For example, labor unions' ability to demand higher incomes and policies like a minimum wage will push up workers' earnings, making more unemployment necessary to combat inflation. Robert Pollin suggests that the "natural rate" is really a social phenomenon measuring the class strength of working people, as indicated by their ability to organize effective unions and establish a livable minimum wage.[8] In the language of the NAIRU, limiting the strength of working people will create lower inflation and higher levels of employment.

To prove his argument about the hidden conflict behind the NAIRU, Pollin points to a 1997 article by economist Robert Gordon. Gordon argues that the large increase in the NAIRU between the early and late 1960s and the decrease in the 1990s in the United States can be explained by the changes in labor militancy, which was high in the late 1960s but quiescent in the 1990s. "In short, class conflict is the specter haunting the analysis of the natural rate and NAIRU: this is the consistent message stretching from Milton Friedman in the 1960s to Robert Gordon in the 1990s."[9] In the UK, Alan Budd, professor of economics at the London Business School and chief economic advisor to Margaret Thatcher, describes, in astonishingly candid terms, what occurred during the 1980s, stating that conservative monetary and fiscal policy was seen by the Thatcher government as "a very good way to raise unemployment. And raising unemployment was an extremely desirable way of reducing the strength of the working classes. . . . What was engineered—in Marxist terms—was a crisis of capitalism which re-created the reserve army of labor, and has allowed the capitalist to make high profits ever since."[10]

It is possible to argue that the basis for the U.S. boom was increasing exploitation of labor. In the words of the chair of the Fed between 1987 and 2006, Alan Greenspan:

> Increases in hourly compensation . . . have continued to fall far short of what they would have been had historical relationships between compensation gains and the degree of labor market tightness held. . . . As I see it, heightened job insecurity explains a significant part of the restraint on compensation and the consequent muted price inflation. . . . The continued reluctance of workers to leave their jobs to seek other employment as the labor market has tightened provides further evidence of such concern, as does the tendency toward longer labor union contracts. The low level of work stoppages of recent years also attests to concern about job security. . . . The continued decline in the state of the private workforce in labor unions has likely made wages more responsive

to market forces. . . . Owing in part to the subdued behavior of wages, profits and rates of return on capital has risen to high levels.[11]

It was Greenspan's "traumatized worker" that enabled the U.S. economy to function at low unemployment rates without producing inflation. The ability of the U.S. economy to withstand low rates of unemployment without creating excessive inflation even surprised Greenspan. Prior to 1997, Greenspan refused to let the unemployment rate drop below 6 percent because he feared this would create inflationary pressures. It was only in early 1997, under the threat of a potential world-wide financial meltdown, that Greenspan relaxed monetary policy sufficiently to let U.S. unemployment fall below the feared 6 percent rate and accidentally discovered that his growth ceiling was artificially low after all. Even when unemployment fell to 4 percent, while wages increased, it did not lead to "wage inflation."[12]

Inflationary policy is not just about doing what is best for "the nation"; it inevitably favors some and disadvantages others. The conservative macroeconomic policies designed to restore profitability during the Great Stagnation did so at great cost to the average U.S. worker. From 1973 to 1997, labor productivity grew by 29 percent in the United States, but there has been a decline in labor's share of corporate sector income and an increase in profitability.[13] According to Lester Thurow, U.S. real per capita GDP rose 36 percent from 1973 to 1995, yet the real hourly wages of nonsupervisory workers declined by 14 percent. In the decade of the 1980s, all of the earnings gains went to the top 20 percent of income earners, and an amazing 64 percent to the already massively wealthy top 1 percent.[14] Joel Rogers, director of the Center on Wisconsin Strategy, calculated that if wages had tracked productivity growth over the last 30 years, "median family income in the United States would be about $20,000 higher today than it is."[15] Thomas Piketty and Emmanuel Saez provide evidence that between 1973 and 2000 the average income of the bottom 90 percent of American taxpayers fell by 7 percent. Incomes of the top 1 percent rose by 148 percent, the top .1 percent by 343 percent, and the extremely well off in the top .01 percent rose by an amazing 599 percent.[16] During this period, the average product per worker grew significantly faster than wages, providing the profit and motivation to invest. However, it also created growing inequality and wage stagnation for the majority of the U.S. working population.

While U.S. employers have been understandably eager to hire in its more tractable labor market, workers have found themselves working longer hours for their meager wages. According to the authors of the *State of Working America* (SWA), employees in the United States work more hours per year than any of the other industrial countries. In contrast to the United States, all of the other G7 countries have been reducing the workweek, some dramatically. In a dramatic turnaround, Americans now work longer hours than the Japanese, who during the 1980s were notorious for their commitment to their firms, and whose intense work ethic was contrasted with Americans' less dutiful approach to their work lives. Between 1979 and 1995 the Japanese reduced their work year by 228 hours while the Americans increased theirs by 47. By 1995, Americans worked 215 more hours per year than Canadians.[17] Europeans get four or five weeks of leave by law and the Japanese have two legally mandated weeks, while the United States is the only industrialized nation with no minimum paid-leave law.

In an effort to maintain their consumption despite stagnant or declining wages, American workers increasingly resorted to credit. Until 1980, U.S. household debt held fairly constant at about 50 percent of GDP, after which it started to grow, reaching 100 percent of GDP in 2007.[18] This increasing debt-to-income ratio was facilitated by many new credit instruments and was backed by the increasing wealth of U.S. households, mostly due to their housing assets. From 1995 to 2007, home prices rose 70 percent more than the general price level, creating an extra $8 trillion in paper wealth for U.S. homeowners.[19] Borrowing to finance consumption was not only a desperate resort of the poorest. It was undertaken by all income levels. Between 1989 and 2004 the middle 20 percent of households acquired 23.6 percent of all debt growth, while the next highest 20 percent acquired 28.8 percent.[20] In fact, it was consumers' willingness to incur debt to maintain their consumption that helped the United States pull out of a potential slide when the stock market collapsed after the Enron accounting scandals. Firms in the United States had restored profitability by reducing their labor costs, and were still able to maintain sales through households' willingness to use credit. Of course, firms also make money off of credit, so now profits were being bolstered both in production and in the financial sector through increased payments from households to firms in the form of interest on debt. Many traditional manufacturing firms were eager to expand into the new world of finance. General Motors and General Electric still made cars and light bulbs but also ventured into the financial industry with General Motors Acceptance Corporation and GE Capital.

In the context of debt-driven consumption it is important to recognize the signifi-cance of the prolonged period of low interest rates starting in the late 1990s. The low interest rates played a dual role in maintaining consumer spending. Most obviously, it kept payments manageable for increasingly indebted households. Secondly, by keep-ing borrowing costs low, it helped inflate the value of the U.S. housing market that was a cornerstone of the growing wealth on which households were borrowing. It was low interest rates and growing debt that propped up the U.S. economic model based on the "traumatized worker." This was a model that was not sustainable.

Swedish Social Democracy

The Swedish economy provides an interesting foil. Although both the Swedish and American economies were successful in establishing high growth rates and low unemployment in the decades following the Great Depression and World War II, they used different policies to achieve their success. The results until the end of the Golden Age suggest that Sweden managed to be competitive with the United States with respect to growth and was far superior by other standards, such as infant mortality, longevity, poverty, and literacy rates. Sweden began the postwar period with substantially lower living standards than America, but by the mid 1970s, the Swedish standard of living was roughly 30 percent higher than in the United States. With growth rates of 3.3 percent in the 1950s and 4.6 percent in the 1960s, by 1970, Sweden's per capita GDP exceeded the average in 15 EU countries by about 24 percent, after adjusting for differences in price levels.[21] In addition, inequality in Sweden was lower than in any other advanced capitalist economy. The richest 10 percent of the U.S. population earned 5.85 times as much as the poorest 10 percent. In Sweden it was a much more equal 2.61 percent. The poverty rate in the United States in 1994 was 17.8 percent. In Sweden it was only 6.6 percent.[22] Pollution levels in Sweden were roughly half that of the United States. Even during the stagnant years from 1973 to 1979, the average rate of unemployment in Sweden was less than a third of the U.S. level.[23] This remarkable conjuncture of wealth and equity should have made the Swedish model a paragon.

By the 1980s Sweden's economy joined much of the capitalist world in its post–Golden Age decline. By 1997, Sweden's unemployment rate had climbed to 10 percent, considerably higher than that in the United States. Both GDP growth and GDP per capita grew very slowly until the mid 1990s, both in historical terms and compared to many other nations, including the United States. The underperforming economy resulted in government budgetary deficits and, as for all other industrialized nations, the specter of inflation haunted central banks.

By the turn of the millennium the Swedish economy had recovered in many respects. The unemployment gap with the United States had been largely eliminated, and economic growth had improved. It has also received a glowing economic report from the World Economic Forum (WEF), a Geneva-based foundation whose annual meeting of chief executives of the world's richest corporations, political leaders (presidents, prime ministers, and others), and selected intellectuals, about 2000 people in all, is usually held in Davos, Switzerland. The WEF is a think tank funded by 1000 corporations, which must have annual revenues of more than $1 billion. The WEF's annual Global Competitiveness Report, first released in 1979, ranks countries in terms of their potential for sustained economic growth. In 2005, the WEF ranked Sweden third on the list of the most competitive economies in the world, just behind the United States. However, unlike the United States, Sweden's social indicators—infant mortality rates, longevity, and literacy rates—are among the very best in the world as well.

Augusto Lopez-Claros, chief economist at the WEF, suggested that,

Integrity and efficiency in the use of public resources means there is money for investing in education, in public health, in state-of-the-art infrastructure, all of which contributes to boost productivity. Highly trained labor forces, in turn, adopt new technologies with enthusiasm or, as happens often in the Nordics, are themselves in the forefront of technological innovations. In many ways the Nordics have entered virtuous circles where various factors reinforce each other to make them among the most competitive economies in the world, with world class institutions and some of the highest levels of per capita income in the world.[24]

The Swedish success story is a social democratic one (taxes consumed over half of the Swedish GNP compared to only a third in the United States), driven in significant part by and for labor. Since the party in power for virtually the entire 1950 to 2000 period was of the democratic left and had a union base, two economists from the labor movement dominated the policy perspective of Sweden. Gosta Rehn and Rudolph Meidner broke with the more simplified and conservative Keynesian policy in vogue, if not always in place, in the United States by identifying excessive profits as the danger to post-war capitalist macroeconomics. They argued that capping profits through taxation would enhance innovation, expand productivity, and curb inflation. Industrial democracy, worker co-determination, solidaristic wage policies, and state interventions in the labor market to ensure full employment were all characteristic of the Rehn-Meidner model of economic management.[25] Starting in the late 1970s, the Swedish Social Democrats even proposed the Meidner Plan, which aimed to "euthanize the rentier," by paying the Swedish capitalist class the value of its stock to transfer ownership of the productive capacity of the economy into worker-owned funds.

The manner in which the *Times* reported the macroeconomic issues of monetary policy and Sweden is of particular interest because it highlights several issues that provide important clues about the economic perspective of the paper. Monetary policy is important because it was one of the major battlegrounds between liberal and conservative economists. Liberals generally preferred expansionary policy and low interest rates to promote higher employment. Conservatives favored tighter monetary policy and higher interest rates to combat inflation. Our analogy of the Trojan horse suggests a more subtle interpretation. When costs, especially labor costs, are squeezing corporate profits, a conservative regime of tight monetary policy will create unemployment and moderate the wage demands of workers. If workers' demands are sufficiently muted, then low interest rates, and the higher level of employment that they bring, can be very beneficial. They increase sales, make debt more manageable, and increase asset values. If our hypothesis is correct, the *Times* should have been much more conservative in the late 1970s when profits were being squeezed than it was in the 1990s when the chief constraint on profitability was lack of disposable income in the U.S. working class. Further, it will be interesting to examine the *Times'* reporting in the 1990s to see if they link the ability of the economy to avoid inflation under an expansionary low interest rate environment to the weakness of the American worker. After all, it is the limited wage gains that created the debt buildup that left the U.S. economy so vulnerable to the financial crisis in 2008.

The U.S. need to trade off corporate profitability with worker incomes in its monetary policy is not inevitable, but a result of the particular structure of the U.S. version of capitalism. Sweden provided a very credible alternative to existing U.S. welfare, labor, and redistribution policies. It also provided an alternative with respect to actual control of the economy, where labor had significant input into policies, up to and including the potential state or labor takeover of key industries. Crucially, Sweden's macroeconomic policies did not rely on restoring profitability through stagnating wages, opting instead for a more collaborative social democratic approach. Interestingly, the more equal income distribution resulted in an economy more resilient than that in the United States. We think the *Times'* assessment of Sweden is a good test of what counts the most at the *Times*: democracy, equity, and growth, or corporate power.

The *Times* on the Federal Reserve, Unemployment, and Inflation: Articles

Reading all of the articles on monetary policy and inflation spanning the entire fifty years would have been Herculean, so we focused our attention on three periods with three very different inflationary contexts. The period 1950 to 1955 was chosen to look at the *Times'* reporting in good economic conditions when profits were high, unemployment low, workers receiving wage gains, and inflation unproblematic. The 1975 to 1985 period marked a rise in inflationary pressure and a very tight monetary response by the Fed that put millions out of work in the name of combating inflation. Finally, between 1995 and 2000 the Fed was able to maintain low interest rates without creating inflationary pressure.

In the 1950 to 1955 period, the *Times* did not dedicate anything like the same amount of column space to Fed policy that it did in later periods. This is not to say that the *Times* did not have some definite opinions on the tradeoff between unemployment and inflation or the causes of inflationary pressure. The *Times* recognized that there was an important debate between the merits of limiting price increases and the costs of "discouraging investment in new plants" and increased unemployment.[26] This highlighted the genuine debate within the business community about the impact of monetary policy on profitability. On one hand it controls costs, especially labor, but on the other, it lowers demand in the economy.

Another theme that emerged in this era was that the *Times* cited labor costs as the key driver of inflation. "The action of some labor leaders in trying to achieve their objectives through exorbitant and unreasonable demands—by superimposing war-time gains on a peace-time economy—looms in the forefront."[27] Later, a 1952 headline declared, "Steel Strikes Effects Spur Inflation Threat."[28] This theme was repeated over and again by the *Times* for the next fifty years, while the idea that corporations might also play a role in the inflation process was never treated seriously. One article even suggested that the public perception that profits or markups might create price increases has "been sedulously implanted by those who have a stake in discrediting the free enterprise system."[29]

By the late 1970s the *Times'* was still debating the inflation-recession tradeoff under the shadow of growing unemployment and inflation. In 1975 it quoted Fed chief Arthur Burns, who claimed that high unemployment and inflation meant that "something was basically wrong with the American economy."[30] The *Times'* economics' reporter during this period, Leonard Silk, understandably featured very heavily in the paper's writing on this issue. In 1977 he worried that after decades of "Golden Age Growth" the United States was suffering its first significant post-war recession. This event "shattered" the confidence "among businessmen and economists alike—that the business cycle has been brought under effective control."[31] However, reports were split over whether inflation or unemployment was darker and more threatening. A representative article contrasted Arthur Okun's estimate that the cost of reducing the inflation rate by one percentage point was $250 billion worth of production and the loss of five million jobs over five years with William Fellner's view that there is no other "credible" way to sweat inflation out of the system.[32]

This tension was personified in the contest between Fed Chair Arthur Burns, the champion of tight monetary policy to control inflation, and the Carter administration, which favored more expansionary policy to stimulate the economy. On one occasion, the *Times* characterized Burns as a man "whose main constituency is the conservative business and banking community," when he criticized the Carter administration for its policies that sapped business profits by promoting inflation and other cost increases tied to the administration's energy, social security, welfare, tax, and health insurance proposals.[33] Only three days later, the *Times* reported on the dangers of inflation and the wisdom of Burns' tight monetary control, arguing that inflation resulted in overstated profits and, therefore, overpayment of business taxes—a problem that could only be solved by corporate tax cuts.[34] When Burns was dismissed in late 1977, the *Times* quoted post-Keynesian economist Paul Davidson, who argued that "Burns' record in office was terrible," countered by Greenspan's regret at the discharge.[35] Despite its often critical reporting on Burns' record, the *Times* was generous with its personal praise. Burns was described as being neither a conservative nor liberal but rather a flexible economist with "strong analytical abilities, comprehensive economic knowledge, a high level of independence of thought and in action, with great moral authority and devoted to the national interest."[36]

In 1975 the *Times* reported that fighting inflation raised the fear of depression and was preferred by only a minority of economists.[37] Silk also pilloried President Ford for ignoring the warnings of economists and labor leaders about the dangers of pursuing an aggressive anti-inflationary policy in 1974.[38] After admitting that the concerns about inflation voiced by Greenspan, the chairman of President Ford's council of economic advisers at the time, were very real, Silk asked: "The question is whether such fears of a coming inflationary boom are premature, and represent a wrongheaded diversion from the immediate task facing policy makers dealing with the worst economic drop since the Great Depression of the nineteen-thirties." While big business and unions are both likely to resist, it is labor that is the intended target of the Fed's anti-inflation "cold-turkey cure." What Greenspan and other Federal Reserve officials want is a "long spell of underemployment that would both sweat inflation down and make the financial system more robust again."[39] Silk also questioned the very core of monetarist economics, that "huge losses in real output and prolonged high unemployment" are the burdens that must be born, "because there is no other way to restore the economy to price stability or economic stability." Rather, it was "time for the business community—as well as national monetary and economic policy makers—to re-examine the high cost of monetarism."[40]

However, the *Times* was also concerned that political pressure to ease unemployment would compromise the Fed's conservative monetary policy, making 1976 a "danger year" for inflation.[41] The inflationary warning was sounded repeatedly in the late 1970s, whether it was concern about a "higher hard-core inflation rate than in the past,"[42] or headlines like "Outlook for 1977: the Dangers of Inflation"[43] or "Another Jolt From Inflation."[44] In mid-1976 the *Times* reported on "a new theory" of inflation, which was "almost the exact opposite of the old." Instead of a little more inflation being a reasonable price to pay for expanded demand and reduced unemployment, inflation became the cause of recession and unemployment.[45] In the most frightening of the *Times'* warnings on inflation, the headline "Inflation at 13.3%: What Is This Rapacious Thing?" connected a host of social disasters to inflation, including declining investment, falling stock prices, black teenage unemployment, and Hitler's rise in Germany.[46]

While the *Times'* news articles were certainly mixed on whether the benefits of low inflation were worth the cost of reduced output and unemployment, it was more unequivocal about what caused inflation. In addition to the obvious explanation of expansionary monetary policy, the *Times* concentrated on a select few structural sources of inflation. The two most common culprits were government policy and cost pressure. Fiscal deficits were often criticized. According to Burns, "the increase in the federal budget was stirring up new fears and expectations of inflation."[47] According to the *Times*, burdensome taxes also ratchet up inflationary pressure.[48] These state-imposed pressures were exacerbated by rising input costs. Interestingly, while oil price increases dominated any economic discussion during the late 1970s, the *Times* was just as concerned with the increasing cost of labor. "A pattern of outsized gains in rubber, electrical and other industries could doom any hopes of further sizable gains on the inflation front."[49] While labor and other inputs were blamed for driving up the costs to firms, the markups by firms themselves were never cited as a potential cause. As the vice president of the American Paper Institute, Norma Pace, insisted in the *Times*, "it's not greed that is pushing up steel prices, it's costs."[50]

The *Times* also searched for a non-monetary solution that might avoid the seemingly no-win choice between increased unemployment and increased inflation. A 1975 article reported that the only way that inflation could be quelled without resorting to even higher levels of unemployment was stringent wage controls that "reduced the upward pressure on prices and thus reduced inflation."[51] In a 1977 article Silk argued that the cure for stagflation was welfare reform that would encourage job search and labor market flexibility, decreased fiscal deficits, and tax reform to stimulate investment.[52] Many of these recommendations for structural change were shared in later articles by Treasury Secretary Miller[53] and the Business Roundtable.[54] All of these policies would help business, and many of them, like corporate tax breaks and welfare reform, do so at the expense of labor.

When Ronald Reagan was ushered into the White House the Fed pursued a much more aggressive role in crushing inflation under the leadership of Paul Volcker, with U.S. Federal Fund rates pushing 20 percent in the early 1980s. During this period the *Times* repeatedly condemned the pain inflicted by this policy. Even worse, it reported that the painful medicine may not even cure the inflationary disease. "The cost of more than nine million workers unemployed, a shattered housing and auto industry, bankruptcies and social suffering" will not win the war over inflation.[55] Under headlines that declared "Interest Rates Must be Cut" the *Times* urged an end to monetary contraction in order to prevent "depression" and restore stable economic growth."[56] These articles reveal the continued debate at the *Times*, and within the economic community, about whether the recessionary cost is worth the anti-inflationary gain.

By 1984 the economy was slowly recovering, with inflation halved and a sharp drop in the unemployment numbers. In this improving context, a *Times'* article identified three "heroes of the economic recovery." Reagan received credit for his Keynesian deficit spending to stimulate the economy. Volcker and the Fed were recognized for throwing the economy into recession to strangle inflation, which permitted the Fed to create the subsequent expansion with lower interest rates. Finally, Congress was applauded for convincing the Fed to ease up on its battle with inflation.[57] Although there was the usual partisan wrangling over who received credit for the revival, the *Times* clearly approved of the return to an expansionary monetary policy and lower interest rates that, it argued, helped move the economy out of recession.

This is not to say that the *Times* ceased to view inflation as problematic. Even at the height of the Fed's battle against inflation, when the *Times* was most vocal about what it saw as the recessionary consequences of high interest rates, it remained insistent that inflation was a real danger. In a 1983 post mortem for the Fed's policy of monetary contraction, Silk wrote that it exacted too high a price on the economy to be a useful antidote for inflation. However, continued high employment was also unsustainable because it would inevitably lead to inflation.[58] When Volcker was reappointed for a second term in 1983, the *Times* reported that Wall Street saw him as "a symbol of the difficult but necessary fight to cool off inflation."[59]

What the *Times* was more consistent on, however, was that controlling labor costs was necessary to tame inflation. Reagan's tough stand on labor resulted in the kind of labor market flexibility that Silk and the Business Roundtable had been calling for in 1977. Reagan's discharging of the striking air traffic controllers was symbolic of his administration's goal of reducing the power of unions. Silk reported that for the coming years, "it looks like hard cheese for labor . . . with stagnation and higher unemployment the only remedy in sight for inflation."[60] In the improved economic context of 1984, the *Times* argued that wages were unlikely to threaten the economic revival. Unemployment may have fallen from 10.7 percent to 7.8 percent, but "sweeping changes in the environment in which labor operates—and in labor's attitudes resulting from those changes" made wage gains unlikely. The article suggested that labor had been too successful in the 1970s and that corporate America had struggled under its high wage yoke. A more sober American workforce had been chastised into moderating its demands by foreign competition.[61] The insistence on wages, not markups or profits, as the main driver of inflation again revealed the *Times'* true economic ideology. While it was willing to risk inflation from expansionary monetary policy in order to avoid recession, it was only willing to do so if wages were controlled.

The *Times'* reporting on the issue of monetary policy in this period revealed a genuine uncertainty about whether monetary policy should be "tight" or "loose," but the intended beneficiary of either policy was much more clear. This was most succinctly stated in headlines like "Falling Corporate Profits Imperil the Economy,"[62] or analysis along the lines of "corporate profits are threatened by government fueled inflation."[63] The theme reappeared constantly, whether it was a story about the Fed reassuring the business and financial community that they would not tolerate inflation[64] or the concern that "businessmen throughout the country are worrying that the underlying inflationary threat will not be fully recognized."[65]

By 1995, the United States had restructured its economy, creating what Greenspan called the "traumatized worker." In this low-wage context, unemployment and recession were not needed to keep costs under control and would likely hurt corporate earnings through weakness in sales. In addition, high-interest policy had a more direct negative impact by increasing the cost of borrowing and debt payments. When lower-than-expected employment numbers were reported in 1995, the *Times* focused on whether the coming interest rate decline that analysts were predicting would compensate businesses for the drop in sales from stagnating demand.[66] During this period, the *Times'* often challenged the Fed to err on the side of growth instead of targeting higher levels of unemployment than may be necessary to suppress inflation: as one headline put it, "Two Cheers for Inflation, Given the Alternative."[67]

The reason that the *Times* could so blithely downplay inflationary fears was that lower levels of unemployment were not increasing wages. The *Times* was pleased to report that despite tightening labor markets, "wages [were] having little impact on inflation."[68] Even as late as 1999 the *Times* could declare "No Alarms Yet On Cost of Labor."[69] One story explained this pleasing turn of events by citing Greenspan's theory that workers' fear of losing their jobs "has been sufficient to hold down inflation without the added restraint of higher interest rates."[70] Workers appeared to be satisfied with less in this new competitive labor environment, according to the *Times*. Modest wage gains in 1997 may not have raised real wages back to the level enjoyed by workers in the 1970s, but "consumers judge small income gains more favorably than they did in the past."[71]

This is not to say that the concern about the impact of rising wages had disappeared. In fact, at the first tentative sign of wage growth in 1997, the *Times* reported on the Fed's concern about the reemergence of inflationary pressures.[72] According to a particularly telling article, "tightening markets for labor need not cause a wage and price spiral in an era of weak labor unions, productivity-obsessed corporate executives and fierce competition from imports." Unfortunately, this sanguine state of affairs could only be temporary and any unemployment below 6 percent would again start to force wages up, threatening inflationary stability.[73] What becomes clear from the *Times*' reporting was that low interest rates and expansionary policy were a desirable monetary course as long as wages were not growing.

The *Times* on the Federal Reserve, Unemployment, and Inflation: Op-eds

Op-ed pieces on the Fed only start appearing in the 1975 period, but after that they appear with great frequency. The authors of the op-ed pieces fell into four categories: academic economists, representatives of government, private economic consultants, and staff writers like Bob Herbert. The *Times*' choice of contributors is revealing about the opinions that it wants to publicize in the debate surrounding Fed policy. Of the twenty-seven academic economists, only one was a conservative. The *Times*' editorial pages were filled with what economists would consider to be heavy hitting liberals like Franco Modigliani, Alan Krueger, and James Tobin. The *Times* gave special prominence to three writers: Thurow, Robert Reich, and James Galbraith, who each appear on several occasions, and none of whom could be described as conservatives.

Despite the presence of these liberal academics, in the late 1970s period of rising inflation and economic stagnation, the *Times* op-eds took a stronger anti-inflationary stance than its news stories. There was one early exception in which Walter Heller claimed that the Fed acted as though the "hellfires of a new inflation were to engulf us and let the devil take the hindmost, the jobless,"[74] but all of the other editorials cheered on the fight against inflation. William Freund, chief economist for the NYSE, wrote "nothing destroys job opportunities more than inflation."[75] In the early days of the Fed's ruthless high-interest policy, op-eds were still supportive; "raising the discount rate to a then record 13% is therefore to be applauded as a courageous and necessary signal of its determination to combat inflationary psychology."[76]

However, as the harsh recessionary economy that was the inevitable result of record high interest rates began to bite, the op-eds in the *Times* took a very different line. Headlines like "Volcker's Monetarist Policy: Painful Costly" highlighted the unanimous opinion among the op-ed contributors that the Fed was unnecessarily squeezing the economy into recession.[77] Thurow claimed that the Fed "threw an already slipping economy off the economic cliff" and lamented that the burden fell on skilled blue-collar workers.[78] Again, this is not to say that inflation was not a concern. After sharply criticizing the tight money of the early 1980s, Paul Samuelson argued that "the Fed has not abandoned the fight against inflation. It has recognized that the alternative risks of unemployment and inflation have to be soberly balanced."[79] During the early 1980s, *Times'* editorials argued for a return to that balance.

In contrast to news reporting, op-eds did, albeit very occasionally, posit that business as well as labor might bear some of the responsibility for the seemingly intractable unemployment-inflation tradeoff during this period. Democrat Gary Hart agued that inflationary tendencies were exacerbated by the fact that "free enterprise (was) being eaten alive by big enterprise while the government acquiesces."[80] Less polemically, professor Robert Lekachman argued that inflation was caused by company markups since "most sectors of the economy register the force of concentrated market power."[81] Henry Reuss, a Democrat from Wisconsin, argued that inflation was being caused by firms' excessive financial gambling at the expense of productive investment, reducing the supply of goods in the economy and forcing prices up.[82]

As was the case with its economics reporting, *Times* op-ed contributors attempted to think outside the monetary policy box in an effort to find a way out of the seemingly intractable unemployment-inflation dilemma. In a break from his mundane reporter life, Leonard Silk wrote an editorial identifying Keynesian policy as the inflationary culprit because it used monetary and fiscal policy to encourage full employment. The primary source of inflation was labors' willingness and ability to push up wages under full employment. However, the monetarist solution, which would require five to seven years of 8 percent unemployment, would "be politically out of the question." Silk's solution was an income policy that held wage gains to the rate of productivity increases.[83] Interestingly, he does not recommend similar guidelines for prices. Other op-ed pieces also put forward policies that would constrain wages. However, unlike Silk they argued that workers should get something in exchange for their sacrifice, whether it is more "dignity in the workplace and job security"[84] or profit sharing.[85]

Like most other economic commentators during the 1995 to 2000 period, *Times* op-eds became increasingly amazed at the ability of both inflation and unemployment to decline simultaneously. This was in sharp contrast with the economic idea of the NAIRU discussed earlier. In the beginning of this period op-eds were quick to remind their readers that inflation was not beaten.[86] Paul Krugman mocked the claim that the NAIRU was no longer relevant and predicted that unemployment could not fall much below 5 percent without reigniting inflationary pressure.[87] However, as the decade wore on and unemployment remained below 5 percent without any real inflationary pressure, contributors commented with wide-eyed wonder at the destruction of the unemployment-inflation tradeoff that was at the core of the NAIRU theory.[88] In this context, op-eds continuously warned the Fed to cease its fretting over non-existent signs of price increases and keep interest rates low.[89]

In a substantial change of pace from its reporting, the *Times*' op-ed columnists often explicitly recognized the distributional impacts of tight monetary policy. Herbert wrote that the Fed kept unemployment unnecessarily high in the late 1990s, hurting low-wage earners who especially benefit from tight labor markets, lamenting that "the interests of the monied classes will trump the interest of the lower classes every time."[90] A year later he argued that the Fed was too concerned with inflation and was either unaware, or did not care, that low unemployment was needed to increase the income of working families.[91] Galbraith took a similar tack, "He (Greenspan) is not concerned about inflation. He is concerned about the possibility, remote and uncertain though it is, that the American worker might start to demand, and receive, a slightly bigger share of the economic growth."[92] Given this critique of the Fed's irrational inflationary obsession and its damaging impact on workers, it was scarcely surprising that op-ed contributors endorsed low interest rates as a solution to low wages.[93]

The post-1995 boom in profits was even occasionally attributed to the power of firms over their labor force. According to Jeff Madrick, "the willingness of Americans to work long and hard has been one of the foundations of economic growth in the 1990s."[94] Krueger urged analysts to stop treating "bad news for workers as good news for the economy" since the positive indicators of economic growth and inflation came at the expense of stagnant wages. If inflation were really a concern, "profit share could decline to accommodate wage growth and reduce price pressure."[95] Even more strongly, a remarkable article by Stephen Roach, the chief economist at Morgan Stanley Dean Witter, argued that the late 1990s was a "labor-crunch recovery—one that flourishes only because corporate America puts unrelenting pressure on its work force." As a result the recovery was based on the unsustainable trend of more income going to capital and less to labor.[96] Most damningly, staff writer Russell Baker lay the logic of the entire system bare when he wrote that American capitalism was, "a system whose health demands a goodly supply of paupers living on handouts" so that the demands of workers were kept from cutting into the profitability of firms.[97] It was in these few articles (twenty years after the trend began) that the *Times* came the closest to accurately exposing the nasty reality masked by the façade of low inflation and unemployment, acknowledging how power in the labor market had been tilted in favor of corporations. This was at least perceived as profoundly unjust if not often recognized as disastrous in the longer term.

The *Times* on the Federal Reserve, Unemployment, and Inflation: Editorials

As was the case with the op-eds, our sample of editorials yielded few hits between 1950 and 1955. The few editorials on this topic that were written eagerly searched for inflationary signals and sought to prevent inflation from becoming a problem. In 1950 an editorial warned against increases in government spending based on its potential to create inflation.[98] However, the limited attention dedicated to the subject suggests that it was not a particularly pressing concern.

As one would expect, this changed dramatically after 1975. The *Times'* editorials during this period were much more critical of tight monetary policy than were its news reports, revealing a strong liberal streak. One angry editorial railed against the rightward drift of U.S. government economic policy under President Ford. It suggested that the war on inflation was not a good enough reason to keep unemployment at 9 percent, hurting corporate profits, sacrificing tax revenues, and raising the specter of class tensions.[99] This was only one example of a continual theme that expressed dismay and outrage about the debilitating effects of the war on inflation. High interest rates negatively impact growth since they "needlessly restrain business investment,"[100] and are "unduly timorous—and unfair" because the resulting joblessness hits marginal groups more strongly.[101] These attacks continued with even greater fervor as Burns and the 1970s gave way to Volcker in the 1980s.[102] One editorial even made the audacious suggestion that the Fed should commit to the "right to a useful job at fair wages for all adults who are willing and able to work," a true manifesto for full employment, dramatically different from that espoused by the NAIRU theorists.[103]

Editorials were convinced that inflation was caused by "cost-push" factors like increasing wages and energy prices, but they were not fond of the monetary medicine being prescribed by the Fed. Instead, the *Times'* editorial writers favored wage and price controls to break the inflationary spiral. While the *Times* did occasionally mention that the firms in some industries such as steel, autos, and industrial chemicals raised prices even in the face of widespread excess capacity and unemployment[104] and used the term *wage and price controls* on a couple of occasions,[105] its most clearly and frequently articulated policy was income controls to keep wages in line with productivity.[106]

While it may be an example of damning with late praise, one *Times* editorial credited the "Federal Reserve that induced the recession that flattened inflation." However, the same editorial continued to look to more structural reasons for the decline in inflation, arguing that Reagan's hard line on labor and Carter's deregulatory moves in energy and transportation had made the economy more competitive.[107] While this appears to be a conservative exception to the normally liberal editorials on this issue, it is consistent in that the *Times* had argued that it was structural change in the economy, not monetary policy, that was needed to control inflation.

With both inflation and unemployment decreasing in the late 1990s, the *Times* acknowledged that unemployment levels of 5.5 percent showed no signs of creating inflation and urged the Fed to avoid a move to higher interest rates.[108] Despite the seemingly robust economy, editorials pointed out that although average household income grew about 10 percent between 1979 and 1994, 97 percent of those gains went to the richest 20 percent of households.[109] However, an editorial the next year sounded a more triumphant tone, crediting Greenspan for setting monetary policy on a responsible course in "a new world where downturns hardly exist." It also reassured the unfortunate labor force that while some workers have "not enjoyed a wage hike, after accounting for inflation, since the 1970s . . . over the long sweep of American experience, the more workers produce, the more they take home." If on the other hand, wages grew faster than productivity (after 20 years of the reverse), that could lead to price hikes and a Fed crackdown to control inflation, "which would slow the economy and drive up unemployment."[110]

In case there was any doubt about the *Times'* editors' priorities, they defended Greenspan against the "thoughtless barbs" of Senator Harkin who had the audacity to single-handedly block a vote to reappoint him as chairman of the Federal Reserve Board because of the effects of his monetary policies. Celebrating the idea that he would be approved in spite of the senator's efforts, the editors say Greenspan's "errors have been slight and the impact small." "The important fact is that Mr. Greenspan has kept the economy on a steady course through turmoil on Wall Street and a war in the Persian Gulf. Mr. Harkin's carping is not just annoying, it is wrong."[111] While the editorials were unwaveringly liberal in their insistence on low interest rates, they also consistently warned about the dangers of wages causing inflation. Its liberal expansionary policies were very pro-corporate and gave little credence to the idea that the expansionary monetary policy of the late 1990s was made possible by the diminished expectations of traumatized American workers.

The *Times* and Sweden: Articles

The *Times* really did not like the Swedish economy. From 1950 to 1961, and then again from 1977 to 2000, the *Times* was almost always critical. During these periods the *Times* viewed the Swedish political economy as fundamentally flawed, weighed down by high wages, high taxes, high prices, union power, and excessive regulation.[112]

According to the *Times*, the embattled Swedish business class and external factors stood alone as explanations for whatever economic success Sweden could muster. The *Times* portrayed the Swedish economy as stumbling from crisis to crisis, moving from one trough of the business cycle to the next. The successful secular trend and the social and industrial democratic reasons for its existence were barely visible. This was as true in the "Golden" 1950 to 1975 period as it was in the more stagnant period from 1975 to 2000, with the exception of a period between 1962 and 1976 where the *Times* more than occasionally associated Swedish successes with Swedish social democracy. When the *Times* did acknowledged the success of the Swedish system, it was also careful to point out that it was a unique system, unlikely to succeed elsewhere because of the Swedes' cultural and racial homogeneity.[113]

During the 1950s, there were rare articles that would acknowledge Sweden's success.[114] Much more frequently the *Times* was preoccupied with the ever-present threat that social-industrial democracy presented to prosperity. "Perhaps it is ungracious to look under the bed in an economy as neatly kept as Sweden's, but its very external excellence provides an almost irresistible temptation to do so."[115] The *Times* was so preoccupied with looking under the bed for ghosts and goblins that it missed everything that made it solid and comfortable. When analyzing the Swedish model, the *Times* of the 1950s could not seem to identify a pillar or a post unless it was built by a capitalist business.

Those articles that attempted to discover the causes of this success argued that it was due to a combination of fortuitous exogenous factors and the willingness of the labor movement and state to leave the business class free to work its magic. The main source of growth was strong export demand for Sweden's natural resources like timber, pulp, and paper.[116] In 1954, the *Times* actually wrote that Sweden "is a country where indexes seem to go up as if by magic." The country was blessed with two natural resources, iron and timber, "for which there seems to be an insatiable demand."[117] The *Times* stressed that it was Sweden's fortunate possession of highly desirable exports that provided the income necessary to indulge in their social democratic generosity.[118]

Many of the *Times*' articles in this period were a somewhat dry account of strong economic growth in Sweden accompanied by a laundry list of the sectors that had shown the most expansion. So, in 1954 the *Times* reported on the strong growth and low unemployment in Sweden. This was followed by a list of the most rapidly expanding sectors, many of which, including roads, railways, telegraph facilities, and power stations, were the responsibility of the state. However, the reporting failed to connect these crucial infrastructure investments to the long-term growth of the Swedish economy or their importance in creating an atmosphere conducive to private investment. Rather, they were simply reported as a source of jobs, similar to the boom in residential construction.[119]

By 1957, the *Times* could no longer attribute Sweden's growth to exports of natural resources alone. The *Times* reported that its economic growth was driven by sales of office equipment and automobiles, which were high-value-added, manufactured goods. Like so many articles during this period, it merely catalogued the growth in these sectors without attempting to determine why Sweden had succeeded in transforming its economy.[120]

The *Times* did occasionally turn from attributing Sweden's economic success to its bountiful natural resources to its effective policy choices. It credited the socialist government for not preventing industry from earning high profits or taking large depreciation allowances, which the *Times* argued were responsible for Sweden having the highest level of investment in Europe and growing productivity. Similarly, the strong unions fostered by social democracy were complimented for not impinging on profits by moderating their wage demands.[121] Unions and government were not praised for rising wages or excellent public education, but for resisting their natural tendencies to harm business.

Despite the plaudits of the previous article and the unwavering strength of the Swedish economy during this period, the *Times* consistently predicted disaster due to the inevitably negative consequences of the Swedish state's social democratic meddling. "Conservative critics think that the Government and its economists are living in a dream world that will one day crash about the ears of the population, which by that time may have lost its capacity to meet the challenge of adversity."[122] The *Times* was particularly suspicious that strong unions and full employment would lead to inflation. The problem was that these two factors would tend to trigger wage increases, which firms would then pass on to consumers.[123] The *Times* also predicted that low levels of unemployment and accompanying wage growth would undermine Sweden's strength in manufactured exports.[124] Curiously, the *Times* insisted on these conclusions despite reporting evidence to the contrary. In 1954, a *Times* article claimed that high wage settlements did not have the adverse effects on trade feared in business circles, and government borrowing to finance deficits did not create inflationary pressure. However, this was presented as a mysterious stroke of fortune rather than an explainable outcome of the Swedish macroeconomy.[125]

The *Times* also claimed that whatever the current strengths of Sweden, these could not be sustained in an economy threatened by social democracy. In an article titled "Economic Flaws In Sweden Cited" the *Times* wrote that the Swedish system worked astonishingly well in spite of the fact "that the element of stability in the conditions under which investment can be made, usually regarded as essential to the functioning of a private enterprise system, is almost entirely lacking." While the Swedish government had so far shown laudable restraint in limiting its desire to socialize sectors of the economy, there was an "almost unlimited threat hanging over every business that the state will intervene if things do not go to their liking."[126] It was not only the threat of nationalization that hindered social democracy, according to the *Times*. There was ample evidence that current social democratic practices were hurting the Swedish economy. Taxes were so heavy, saving so small, regulation so tight, cradle-to grave security so endemic, that business spokesman believed this would "spread stagnation."[127]

The *Times* also questioned the popularity of a social democratic government that enjoyed remarkably consistent electoral success. In the 1956 election, the Social Democrats lost two seats and the Conservatives gained eight out of a total of 231 seats. Despite the fact that the Social Democrats ended up with 108 seats to the Conservatives' 39, the *Times* reported that Social Democrats and union members alike were privately grumbling about high taxes.[128] An alternative interpretation of the election could have easily been the overall support for Swedish economic policies.

There was no room for even the possibility that the so-called socialist government and its labor economists' industrial democracy may have contributed to Swedish success and insulated their economy from events in the global economy (rising oil prices, for example). Yet, for the next twenty-five years Sweden weathered bad economic events as well as anybody.

Between 1962 and 1976, the *Times*' perspective on Swedish social democracy changed. The reporting on the "Swedish way" in this period ranges from negative[129] to ambivalent, to analysis associating specific policies to positive economic outcomes, to attributing the Swedish miracle to social democracy.

It was in this period that the *Times* began to acknowledge the strength of the Swedish economy. In 1962, a *Times* headline read "Sweden Expects The Year to Be 'Rosy'" due to large increases in productivity that had given its people one of the highest living standards in the world and full employment.[130] Although this article failed to provide an explanation for Sweden's success, several other articles in this period laud different elements of Sweden's model of social democracy. For example, the *Times* praised the Swedish universal public health care model[131] and its labor relocation system for reducing unemployment. However, should readers be tempted to consider such an interventionist model, they were cautioned that it only worked because of Sweden's racial homogeneity.[132]

The *Times* also printed several articles that went beyond mentioning the strength of the Swedish economy or commenting on the benefits of one particular element in their economic model. These articles credited the social democratic system as a whole for the economic success of Sweden. Under the headline "Long-Term Plans A Boon In Sweden," the *Times* argued that "the Swedish economic paragon" rested on government use of "traditional monetary and fiscal policies and the control of its nationalized industries" to smooth out the business cycle and provide a predictable environment in which firms can plan for the future. The article also praised Sweden's comprehensive protection for workers. Companies planning to lay off workers must first notify the government, who then retrain the worker and help sell, or even buy, the worker's house. Job-secure workers and their unions in turn supported productivity-enhancing mechanization, making Swedish industry efficient and competitive in world markets while providing workers with the highest wages in Europe.[133] Interestingly, given the *Times'* continued predictions of inflationary catastrophe for Sweden in its coverage during the 1950s, this article also reported that the degree of inflation in Sweden was no higher than in other European countries.

In a 1968 article, the *Times* continued to compliment Swedish social democracy. It claimed that Sweden's high-wage, privately run economy relied on its government to "direct and stimulate innovation in research and technology."[134] The article went on to suggest that for all the talk of Swedish socialism, the government was less concerned with the ownership of industry than it was with its social and economic usefulness. However, in a return to its 1950s trends, the growth of the economy was traced to the business sector, which had succeeded despite the profit-reducing policies associated with social democracy. "Businessmen have been free to accumulate power and what wealth they could beyond the steeply graduated tax rates so long as they forsook political power, ran internationally competitive industries and financed economic security programs with their taxes."[135]

The *Times* also recognized the contribution of the Swedish model to its populations' job satisfaction. Olof Palme, "the articulate, intellectual" premier of Sweden and head of the Social Democratic party, claimed that the goal of industrial democracy was to "meet people's needs" not just economically but by giving "meaning and dignity to their work."[136] The *Times* even suggested that Sweden might even be meeting this ambitious goal. Under the headline "Sweden Enacts Programs to Make Workers Both Safe And Happy," the *Times* complimented Sweden's increased attention to workplace health and safety as well as increased worker control over the production process.[137] Part of Swedes' job satisfaction was due to the amount of control they had in their workplace. Swedish workers could close a factory if conditions seemed hazardous to their health, and workers sat on the boards of corporations with more than 100 employees. This level of control over their work environment created a relatively content workforce. As a result, Swedish workers rarely went on strike relative to their American or British counterparts.[138] In its most glowing assessment of the Swedish social democratic successes in this period, the *Times* reported that Sweden had the highest per capita income in the world, cradle-to-grave security, and a mixed economy in which private and public sectors peacefully coexist.[139]

This is not to say that the *Times* was unambiguously positive about the Swedish economy in this period. It continued to frequently express doubts about many of the elements of the social democratic system, from its continued obsession with inflation[140] to the power of its unions.[141] In an article that nicely combines many of these elements, under the ominous headline "Inflation Fears Grow In Sweden" the *Times'* pessimistic prediction of economic woes was attributed to excess taxes and public expenditures.[142] Similarly, the *Times* reported that the OECD had advised Europe's most affluent society to restrain its economy, complaining that "government spending had continued rather loose."[143]

In addition to the economic difficulties of the Swedish social democratic model, it was also, according to the *Times*, not universally loved by its own citizens. In a particularly damning article, headlined "White Collar Strike Forces Swedes to Question Welfare State's Future," the *Times* argued that social democracy created an inevitable distributional conflict between the working class, to whom it has promised greater equality, and the middle class, to whom it has promised higher social status. The strike by Sweden's professional classes was due to the highest taxes in the world, "an extravagant cost of living" and working class demands for more economic equality.[144] Not only did this labor unrest threaten Sweden's social democratic system, but the causes of the unrest were directly caused by that system. There can be little question that in the context of widespread strike activity, there must have been considerable dissatisfaction among white-collar workers, but the *Times*' article provided no real evidence in support of its interpretation about the specific causes of the dissatisfaction. The manner in which the reporter discovered that the white-collar workers objected to greater equality with their more blue-collar compatriots, for example, was never divulged.

While several articles did tout the benefits of social democracy to Swedes' on-the-job experience, by the end of this period the *Times* started to become concerned about the degree of control workers had over their firms. In 1976, the *Times* warned that "To Swedish Labor, Equality is Being Boss" because the Social Democrats were planning to pass legislation that would give workers, "at least an equal voice in all aspects of corporate life." They would have input on who got hired and discharged, how work would be organized and managed, and even a company's policies.[145] More ominously for the *Times*, a long-term plan for the whole of Swedish industry to pass into the control of the workers was commissioned by organized labor and authored by Meidner. Companies with more than fifty employees were to set aside stock to be transferred into a "collective employee fund" not allocated to the firm's own workers but held collectively in the fund system. According to the *Times*, the Swedish industrialists "in a state of quiet shock, assailed the plan root and branch" regarding it as "a potential revolution."[146]

The *Times*' ambivalence toward Sweden in this period was well illustrated by its coverage of the proposed Meidner Plan. The *Times* pointed out in no uncertain terms that the business community staunchly opposed the plan and that it would most likely have a negative impact on Swedish economic growth. However, it also assessed the academic controversy surrounding worker control over production, even suggesting the possibility that it might actually increase productivity.[147] A slightly later article neutrally reported the details of the Meidner Plan and documented labor's support and business opposition.[148] However, in 1976, the *Times* attributed the Social Democrat's first election defeat in forty-four years to, among other things, the "demand for change to the growing leverage of trade unions in Government economic policy," especially the "Meidner plan."[149]

Between 1962 and 1976, the *Times* was more positive about the role played by Sweden's social democracy in its economic success than prior to 1962. Indeed, it almost bordered on ambivalent. While Swedish economic success was recognized and occasionally even attributed to social democratic policies, the *Times* remained very quick to either predict disaster or point out failings. When these difficulties, either real or imagined, were reported, it was almost always social democratic policies that were to blame.

By the 1970s, capitalism in general began to lose its macroeconomic momentum. Both Sweden and the United States found their economic indicators in decline. Despite the global nature of the economic malaise, and the fact that during the 1980s Sweden managed to maintain an unemployment rate of less than 3 percent (much lower than that in the United States), the *Times* returned to its 1950s outlook on Swedish social democracy. The welfare state, with its taxes, regulation, and union power sapped the incentives and income from the economy, while embattled business kept the ship afloat. In the words of Jan Carlzon, president of Linjegflyg, Sweden's airline, "We feel ashamed because we said to the Americans and the Germans, 'Look at us.' But we went over the line and couldn't afford all the reforms anymore. It hurts to hear everyone laughing."[150]

While the *Times* was predominantly negative about the future of Sweden's social democratic model, it was not universally so. In an article about the nationalization experience in three European countries, the *Times* was impressed with Sweden's experience, although this was largely down to the business acumen and profitability of a state-run tobacco concern.[151] Two articles also compared the Swedish model of state-funded and -provided day care favorably to the United States both in terms of creating greater gender equality in the working world and delivering happy, well-adjusted toddlers.[152] In the run-up to Sweden's 1980 election, under the dramatic headline "Sweden's Left Is Eager to Spring on a Faltering Foe," the *Times* suggested the Social Democrats were likely to win the next election because of the worst industrial conflict in Sweden since 1909.[153] In a subsequent article the *Times* credited the Social Democrats with giving Sweden a model version of health, education, and welfare, as well as the highest standard of living in the world.[154]

The *Times*' portrait of Sweden during these years was very much of an economy in decline. The most frequent descriptive phrases in this period were "bankrupt"[155] "fatigue,"[156] "cracks,"[157] and, most damningly, "the Swedish disease."[158] In another perfect example of damning with late praise, once the economy was slowing down, the *Times* did, belatedly, comment on the former strength of Sweden but presented it as a faded glory, rapidly deteriorating and unable to compete in the modern global economy. In 1977, for example, the *Times* wrote that while Sweden may have previously enjoyed full employment, rising living standards, and cradle-to-grave security, these luxuries were no longer possible in the new, globally integrated economy.[159] Similarly, an article headlined "Sweden's Economic Success Sours" claimed that the formerly successful Swedish model was rapidly failing. "The backbone of its economy is disintegrating and the country may have entered a long period of decline." Quoting the managing director of Volvo, the *Times* announced that Sweden had "experienced a deterioration of almost unparalleled swiftness in the competitive power of an industrial nation."[160] The language of the *Times* was as remarkable in its animus as its hyperbole, as if they could not wait to spring on a faltering foe.

The overwhelming tone of the *Times* during this period was that Sweden's social welfare system was the cause of an economic malaise. Certainly, high taxes were a major problem. In a 1989 article headlined, "Sweden Social Democrats Veer Toward Free Market and Lower Taxes," the *Times* quoted an investment banker and former conservative deputy minister of finance who claimed that "you'll find that Swedish doctors probably have the lowest average golf score in the world."[161] This was not due to any natural sporting prowess of Swedish physicians, but because high taxes encouraged doctors and other high-income earners to substitute leisure for labor time. This was a specific version of a more general theme that the Swedish welfare state, with its maze of regulatory red tape, high tax levels, and coddled workforce, made its companies uncompetitive.[162] Further, high taxes went into public programs that were not delivering the goods. The public-funded education, medical, and day care systems suffered from lack of attention to quality and efficiency.[163]

While Sweden's social welfare system was creaking during this period, according to the *Times*, its system of industrial democracy was faring little better. The *Times* consistently reported that much of the blame for Sweden's floundering economic performance could be attributed to its increasingly antagonistic workers and their strong unions. Labor unrest hurt the economy directly by stopping production and indirectly as increasingly frustrated employers sought to locate in less union-friendly nations.[164] Further, even the Swedish experiment in worker input on the production line, which the *Times* did cautiously support in the previous period, appeared to be failing. Volvo's experiment to "return dignity to the workplace" by doing away with the alienation of the assembly line and replacing it with creative work teams may have produced satisfied workers, but absenteeism continued and productivity was disappointingly low.[165] The policy prescription, then, became obvious. As early as 1978, the solution, according to the *Times*, was to reduce the power of labor, lower taxes, and encourage entrepreneurial spirit.[166]

Finally, in 1990 the *Times* could claim that its predictions about full employment contributing to inflation had come true. Sweden's inflation rate of 9 percent was about double the Western European average. According to the *Times*, "economists have said that the low unemployment rate, which stands at just over 1 percent, has added to inflationary pressures."[167]

The *Times*' reporting on the popularity of the Swedish system in its own country could not avoid the fact that the Swedes frequently elected the Social Democratic Party. However, when election results indicated support for the Swedish model the *Times* portrayed this as "a nostalgia for the time when Sweden and its so-called 'caring capitalism' were seen as the international model." Further the population's desire to expand social welfare coverage was at "cross purposes with Sweden's need to increase its competitiveness."[168] In contrast, when the voters rejected the Social Democrats, the *Times* reported this as a damning indictment of Sweden's system. According to the *Times*, the 1991 election defeat for the Social Democrats was because voters "punished the party in a rebellion against the world's most extensive welfare state." While the Swedish model gave the Swedes one of the highest standards of living in the world, the state's inefficiency has led to high inflation, anemic growth, fleeing business investment, rampant worker turnover, absenteeism, and a fatally inept health care system.[169] According to the *Times*, the Swedes were "rankled by taxes." Despite this bold headline, the story reported that Swedes accepted all kinds of taxes, and boasted a graphic indicating that Sweden had the most heavily taxed citizens in the OECD. Nowhere did the story provide any support for its assertion that the citizens of Sweden were massively dissatisfied with this state of affairs.[170]

The more ambitious plans of the Social Democrats were also deeply unpopular, according to the *Times*. In 1983, the Social Democrats again mooted the possibility of implementing the Meidner Plan. In an article about Swedish hostility to this proposed economic transformation, the *Times* claimed that in addition to the predictably hostile reception of the business community, "what many see as remarkable is the fact that this opposition is springing from a workforce that is 90 percent unionized." According to the article, workers feared that the nation's traditional welfare state would be jeopardized by union ownership of the corporations, which in turn would undermine the role of the free enterprise system.[171] The article presented these conclusions despite providing no evidence for the "new conservatism" rolling over Sweden or the "new admiration for business" among the 90 percent of the workforce that was unionized.

On those rare occasions that the Swedish economy was being complimented, the *Times* returned to its trend of crediting business for any good news, only approving of the government when it removed impediments to profitability. For example, in a 1987 article the *Times* reported that Sweden's brand of socialism has long been avowedly pro-business. While it had the world's highest personal tax rates, biggest public sector, and most lavish welfare state, "it would be hard to find a country more hospitable to big business." The effective corporate tax rate was only about 25 percent.[172] According to the *Times*, "in an unexpected turnaround, Sweden's economy is now out-performing much of Europe despite maintaining its welfare state." While the government continued to finance health care, education, and many social services, it was the private service sector that was the key to Sweden's success. The new prosperity was due to entrepreneurial deregulation. Although the *Times* referred to an OECD study that reported that "Sweden invested a larger part of its gross domestic product in 'knowledge' (research, training, and education) than any other country in the world" it did not credit the public sector for its undoubted contribution to these kinds of investments.[173]

By 1990 the *Times* was even willing to fete the speculative adventure of "Sweden's New Breed Of Corporate Raider." When Swedish stocks grew tenfold and real estate values tripled, speculators built empires by borrowing against their appreciating real estate, exploiting tax loopholes, and taking advantage of Sweden's favorable treatment of capital gains. Corporate raiders and real estate speculators appear to be a sign of good times in Sweden.[174] This glowing report failed to recognize that these were the very conditions that brought on Sweden's early version of the financial crisis that hit the United States in 2008. In the early 1990s, Sweden's housing bubble burst. Housing prices plummeted, leading to a wave of bank failures. However, Sweden's economic ship was righted with considerably more alacrity than currently appears to be happening in the United States. The reason for the greater Swedish resilience was that its more equal income distribution meant that many of its households were not in as precarious positions as those in the United States, and its much more interventionist government took swift action to nationalize failing banks. The speculation that the *Times* claimed was strength was in fact a weakness, while the social welfare system it viewed as a weakness was actually a strength.

The *Times* and Sweden: Op-eds

The *Times* dedicated little column space to opinion pieces on Sweden, either by its own editorial staff or by guest commentators. However, it is still instructive to determine whether there was a difference in the *Times'* news reporting on Sweden, which is supposed to be balanced and objective, and its admittedly limited editorial commentary, where opinions are given free reign, unfettered by chains of journalistic objectivity.

When the *Times* was toying with the positives offered by the Swedish model in the early 1970s, David Jenkins wrote an op-ed piece that positioned industrial democracy on the forefront of innovative worker relations. He argued that giving workers increasing control of their jobs, including a "no firing" policy, resulted in huge productivity increases for Swedish companies. Even with these admittedly radical changes in employee relations, Jenkins was very clear that these companies were not abandoning basic business principles. "The name of the game is money. Our main job in society is to produce goods and services as efficiently as possible, and that is measured by our return on equity."[175]

Nobel Prize winner Paul Samuelson contributed a textbook version of what we have previously termed damning with late praise. Writing in 1987, he was effusive in his praise for the Swedish miracle, in which welfare-state egalitarianism was improbably wed to impressive productivity growth. However, the fairytale romance of two such incompatible partners was doomed to failure, and "Cinderella's hour seemed to strike around 1973." By "divorcing income from effort" Sweden sacrificed the productivity growth on which it depended. Samuelson even raised the economically terrifying specter of Argentina, a country that tumbled headlong from its prosperous peak in 1945, saying, that it "ought to haunt dreams in the long Nordic winter nights." He was especially scathing of the Meidner Plan, claiming that owner-unionists would not be able to make the hard decisions necessary to run a competitive business.[176]

As with the trend in news stories, by 1992 the "Swedish model" was being skewered on the op-ed pages. William Schmidt commented approvingly on what he saw as the Swedish desire to "abandon socialism and join the free market." He argued that the Swedish welfare state was dragging down the economy due to its high taxes, high public spending, and "vast centralized bureaucracies." In fact, the Swedish welfare state had created a nation of people "unable to take responsibility for their own lives."[177]

The *Times* and Sweden: Editorials

The *Times'* in-house editorial writers struck a similar tone. During the 1950s, Sweden was portrayed as an important bulwark against the Communist Soviet Union, but its socialist tendencies were economically harmful and "when carried to its logical conclusion" created an authoritarian state.[178] When the Social Democrats slipped slightly in the 1952 election, the *Times* saw this as evidence that the "socialist tide is beginning to recede" as Swedish voters finally came to realize the "fallacies of socialism," including the "doctrines of class warfare" and "common ownership of the means of production."[179] As with the news articles, editorials were willing to give Sweden the benefit of the doubt on certain specific policies, like its "experiment" in nationalized health care, but would only do so with the caveat that this is only possible in a "country as small as Sweden and only with a population that is homogenous."[180]

After 1962, the *Times'* editorial page commented consistently on the electoral success of the Social Democrats in Sweden. Under headlines like "The Contented Swedes" editorials praised Sweden's high levels of employment and equal income distribution.[181] At the same time editorials were steadfast in their insistence that the Swedes had distanced themselves from outdated concepts like "common ownership of the means of production"[182] and had "little appetite for doctrinaire socialism."[183]

The 1970s marked a shift in the *Times'* editorial page as well as its reporting. A hint of future opinion pieces came after the 1970 Swedish election, which the Social Democrats won with 46.4 percent of the vote. The fact that this was down slightly from 50 percent in the previous election was labeled a "setback" by the *Times*, which blamed the slide on growing labor unrest and inflation.[184] When the Social Democrats lost the election in 1976, the *Times* attributed the defeat not only to the usual social welfare frailties of high taxes and bureaucracy, but also to "creeping trade union control of industry" and the Meidner Plan.[185]

Despite the conventional wisdom that it is the editorial page in which a paper expresses its opinions, it takes a remarkably similar line to that found in the supposedly unbiased news stories. In fact, if anything it is the news stories that contain the stronger opinions and more memorable quotes criticizing the Swedish model.

Conclusion

In the story of the Trojan horse, the Greeks disguise a cunning attack on Troy as a gift. The *Times'* economic reporting on Fed policy did much the same thing by disguising anti-inflationary policy as a gift for the entire nation, while in reality it was an attack on labor. In the late 1970s the *Times'* reporting was full of the dangers of inflation and was certain that labor costs were the primary culprit. Only in rare op-ed pieces was the corporate class identified as the cause of inflation. It may have lamented the extreme cost of the monetary battle against inflation in the early 1980s, but it never disputed that labor costs had to be brought under control. The only non-monetary solution to inflation that was seriously discussed by the *Times* was wage controls on the labor force.

In the wake of the high unemployment and labor market restructuring of the 1980s, the bottom 80 percent of U.S. citizens suffered from falling wages and longer working hours while their productivity grew. In this context the *Times* largely supported the liberal policy of expansionary monetary policy during the 1990s because wages were less of a threat to profits than the costs associated with high interest rates. With the exception of a few prescient op-ed articles that at least pointed out that the rising economic tide was not lifting all, or even very many, of the boats, the overall tone of reporting during this period was one of economic success.

The weakness in household income and mounting levels of debt left the United States in a vulnerable position when the asset bubble popped. The Swedish economy was structured very differently. Its system of industrial democracy and social welfare had created a more equal income distribution and lower levels of poverty. Only a few times, in a relatively short period, did the *Times* have anything like a balanced article on the Swedish economic model. In all other instances it bounced from one conservative account of Sweden to another. The one constant was equating any strength in the Swedish economy with meeting the interests of its capitalist class. What was good for business was good for Sweden, according to the *Times*. Not once could we find the *Times* even suggesting that any of Sweden's real, exaggerated, or invented economic problems could be placed at the doorstep of Swedish business. For the *Times*, this issue is simply not to be investigated. This line was universally true for both opinion pieces and supposedly more fact-based news stories.

In contrast to the *Times'* unwavering support of the corporate Sweden, it was much more inconsistent in its coverage of the welfare state. Economic difficulties were universally blamed on social democratic policies like high taxes and strong unions. While the *Times* would often acknowledge the popularity of these policies it would, often in the same year, blame them for the unpopularity of the Social Democrats.

One has to wonder how much of the R&D, education, and training were paid for by the entrepreneurs relative to how much came from the parasitic Swedish welfare state. The WEF ranked Sweden the third most competitive economy in the world for 2005, primarily for its social democratic economic policy. It is important for our purposes to identify the fact that in fifty years of reporting on Sweden, the *Times* did not identify the so-called Socialist Swedish State with these policy virtues. The WEF understands that state investment in R&D, education, and training has been a hallmark of Nordic state policy, but not the *Times*. The *Times*' reluctance to credit the Social Democratic government with any of that country's innovation and growth is consistent with its general insistence that Sweden's success has come despite, rather than because of, the role played by its state. Swedish economic successes were the product of a business class at worst under siege, at best left to its own devices, as opposed to a business class provided with an economic and social infrastructure within which they could thrive in exchange for sharing the wealth and some of the power.

For the *Times*, Sweden was largely a cautionary tale, warning of the disastrous economic fate that would befall any economy that foolishly followed its overly interventionist path. The *Times* continuously framed Swedish social democracy's threat to corporate economic control in a negative light despite its laudable record in terms of democracy, equity, and growth.

CHAPTER 4

THE NEW YORK TIMES AND
U.S. FOREIGN ECONOMIC POLICY

Economic policy is not only a matter of domestic initiatives. Since the actions of foreign governments can also alter the profitability of U.S. business, it is important to manage international relationships by economic, political, and military means. The U.S. government has historically been assertive in promoting the international interests of its corporations. When faced with a choice between a supposedly inalienable right such as democracy or the interests of its corporate community, the United States has frequently come down on the side of economic prerogatives, using military might and espionage to topple governments in favor of authoritarian strong men more sympathetic to U.S. economic interests. While this chapter only examines a select few examples, chosen to span the fifty-year time period, a similar tale could be told about countless other interventions on almost every continent.[1] When it is not using the barrel of a gun to ensure its economic interests, the United States actively engages in a range of other, more subtle, techniques to make the economic policies of foreign states more amenable to the profitability of U.S. firms.

The ability of the U.S. government to intervene in one form or another in the affairs of a sovereign foreign nation requires either the ignorance or acceptance of its voting populace. The former is possible if media outlets are not overly zealous in the pursuit of information on U.S. foreign activity that is not spoon fed them by the government. If the public is not aware of negotiations behind closed doors or covert activity, it is in no position to disapprove. Of course, many in the media would argue that their primary objective is to peer into the dark, hidden corners of the world and shed light on exactly this sort of activity.

On those occasions in which the public does become aware of the machinations of its chosen government on behalf of U.S. businesses, it will be much easier to continue these policies if the population feels that the United States has the right to intervene. Interfering in others' affairs is usually justified on the broad conclusion that the government of that country is not behaving in the best interests of its own people. In an undemocratic political system this case is often not tough to make. The Taliban was not kind to the people of Afghanistan and Saddam Hussein's capricious treatment of his own populace was easy to vilify. Arguing that a democratically elected government is not acting in the interests of the very people by whom it was elected is substantially more difficult. Yet it is not impossible. The American public would be much more inclined to support foreign intervention if the government in question were incompetent or unpopular. The public can only make this judgment based on the facts at its disposal, which are for the most part provided through the media. The media's portrayal of foreign countries and the actions of the U.S. foreign policy are, then, of crucial importance. This is far from an insignificant issue, given the extent to which the United States is involved in "setting right" countries around the world.

In choosing our two cases, we have deliberately selected examples in which democratic foreign governments have implemented policies that not only threaten the immediate profitability of U.S. firms operating in foreign lands, but also transfer economic control out of the private sector and into the hands of either the state or groups of citizens, like workers or peasant farmers. We have chosen democratic states because this is the most difficult test for our argument. If the *Times* portrayed democratically elected leaders as irresponsible, incompetent, and unpopular, this would be much more telling about its perspective than were it to make the same claims about a ruthless dictator. We have chosen Iran under Mossadegh in the 1950s and the more current example of Venezuela under Chavez. These examples meet the criteria in terms of economic policy and democratic structures. They also nicely span the time period of our study. As was the case with the macroeconomic policies examined in the last chapter, the *Times* must choose how to report on U.S. foreign policy. In each of the cases, the *Times'* coverage of both the foreign government policies and the U.S. response will be examined. Before delving into the *Times'* coverage we need a quick review of issues surrounding Iran and Venezuela.

Iran

The Anglo-Iranian Oil Company (AIOC) enjoyed a very profitable stay in Iran. Between 1901 and 1951, it earned £115 million on a £22 million investment in its Iranian oil operations. It was not only the company that fared well; the British government, the majority share holder in AIOC, earned £175 million from Anglo-Iranian's operations and tax revenue in this fifty-year period.[2]

In 1951, Mohammed Mossadegh, a democratically chosen member of parliament, was elected prime minister of Iran and promptly nationalized the AIOC. The British responded by successfully convincing other countries to impose a global boycott on Iranian oil and placing a naval blockade in the Persian Gulf to prevent it from being exported, bringing Iran's production to a complete standstill.

While the British argued that they were only imposing the blockade until the company could receive "adequate compensation" for its assets, it is clear that the British were not keen on any negotiated settlement that involved Iranian national control. At first, Britain would not even accept the principle of nationalization and had to be persuaded by the United States, who were fearful about Iran joining the Communist camp over the issue, to come back to the table. Throughout the negotiations the British position was to refuse any settlement that accepted the nationalization, frequently submitting new offers that were backward steps from proposals that had previously been rejected by Iran. Underpinning this hard-line bargaining was the belief that without oil revenues, the Iranian economy would collapse and Mossadegh be overthrown. The British position remained unchanged despite a finding in Iran's favor by the International Court of Justice at The Hague.[3]

Inside Iran, a power struggle was developing between Shah Mohammad Reza Pahlavi and Mossadegh over the issue of nationalizing oil production. In 1952, Mossadegh resigned under pressure from the Shah. Mossadegh's resignation sparked three days of rioting in the country, forcing the Shah to reappoint him. He was reelected as prime minister following an overwhelming vote of confidence by the country's parliament.

The United States became involved because of the lure of Iran's large supply of oil, but Mossadegh had also worried the United States by implementing other economic policies, such as state land ownership and collective farming, which smacked of socialism. The joint U.S. and British plan to overthrow the prime minister involved using agents to destabilize the country by funding opposition parties and paying for anti-Mossadegh content in the media, creating conditions of chaos in which the Shah could reasonably seize power. After a great deal of U.S. and UK pressure, the Shah eventually agreed to plan a military coup.[4] The coup started out disastrously from the Shah's perspective, with his troops refusing to fight and popular support all but invisible. Faced with what appeared to be defeat at the hands of pro-Mossadegh forces, the Shah fled to Rome, where he watched in safety as his supporters in the military eventually succeeded in deposing Mossadegh.[5]

Once ensconced in power with U.S. and British backing, the Shah dismantled the democratic structures in Iran. He abolished the multi-party parliamentary system to rule in a one-party dictatorship. To further quash dissent, he created the secret police force SAVAK, which became famous for its ruthless persecution of dissidents.

While the coup may not have done much for Iranian democracy, the Americans and British gained substantially. After the coup, the Iranian oil company was divided among several American oil companies (40 percent), British Petroleum (40 percent), Shell (14 percent), and a French Company, CFP (6 percent). Further, the Shah implemented "Western" reforms, creating a more market-based economic system and encouraging Western-style consumption. His penchant for military hardware made him one of the largest importers of U.S. military equipment. Between 1970 and 1978 he purchased over $20 billion worth of arms from the United States.[6] The coup had a number of advantages for specific U.S. oil and military companies and fit nicely with the broader U.S. imperative of ensuring that countries remained open to U.S. businesses.

Venezuela

It is difficult to overstate the extent of the economic crisis into which Venezuela had fallen prior to Hugo Chavez taking power. Venezuela is in the envious position of being the world's fifth largest oil producer. Like Iran, the political economy of Venezuela is driven by oil, which is the main source of export earnings and contributes heavily to government revenues. Like all oil-producing nations, the 1970s featured strong economic growth fueled by rising oil prices. In an effort to retain more of the earnings from the oil industry, in 1976 Venezuela nationalized (with compensation) foreign-owned oil companies. When oil prices started to decline from their 1977 peak and the global economy dove into the recession of the 1980s, Venezuela's economy went into a tailspin, increasing the country's foreign debt and landing it in the Latin American debt crisis of the early 1980s.

As was the case with many Latin American countries that implemented International Monetary Fund Structural Adjustment Policies (SAP) after running into debt problems in the 1980s, Venezuela's economic restructuring was not kind to the nation's laboring classes over the next two decades. Venezuela instituted the standard boilerplate SAP that involved privatizing state-run corporations, eliminating regulatory intervention in the market, liberalizing trade, and reducing taxes. Between the late 1970s and the late 1990s there was a transfer of approximately 15 percent of GDP from labor income to capital. Even worse, labor incomes declined in absolute terms as well. An average worker's real income in the late 1990s was only half of what it was in 1970.[7]

Venezuela has a long tradition of democratic government, but it has also been characterized by corruption and ineffectiveness in channeling oil wealth into broad economic success. The two political parties that had dominated the Venezuelan political system "were rightly considered guilty of chronic corruption and mismanagement" according to Michael Shifter, professor of Latin American studies at Georgetown University. He continues, "The exclusionary political system they managed was wholly divorced from the central concerns of most Venezuelans."[8] Worsening economic conditions and dissatisfaction with corrupt government led to two failed coup attempts in 1992. The first was led by Chavez himself, earning him a period of incarceration and a reputation among the poor as someone willing to take on the established government. By 1994 economic disaster had truly set in, with a collapse of the country's banking sector, falling oil prices, inflation, and a crushing foreign debt repayment load. The overall toll on the economy was catastrophic. Between 1980 and the end of the 1990s Venezuela had the dubious distinction of having the worst economic performance in poorly performing Latin America. In the two decades of the 1980s and 1990s Venezuelan GDP declined by 40 percent.[9]

In this context Chavez was elected president in 1998 by promising a "Bolivarian" revolution. His election marked a decisive rejection of the established parties in Venezuela that had produced little but corruption and growing inequality. Chavez's transfer of power out of the hands of wealthy business owners did not pass without instigating a vocal resistance. Between 1998 and 2003, the opposition to Chavez used strikes, protests, and one coup to express its displeasure. In 2001, the Venezuelan Chamber of Commerce organized a business strike. In early 2002 Chavez was briefly thrown out of office in a coup by elements of the military and business community. Later that year, a three-month nationwide strike by what the BBC described as "right-wing business groups and unions," who were attempting to oust Chavez, crippled the economy.[10] The strike was especially economically harmful since it started at the state owned oil company, the PDVSA, strangling oil production. In 2002 and 2003 Venezuelan GDP dropped by 24 percent.

The ultimate failure of the strike marked a turning point in the Chavez regime. Prior to the strike, PDVSA was controlled by the anti-Chavez camp. They were resistant to his regime in general but were especially opposed to Chavez's plans to use oil surpluses to fund social programs and economic development policies. At the end of the strike, Chavez fired much of the opposition management and replaced them with people more willing to go along with his plans to transfer oil revenues to the rest of the population. While this could be interpreted as replacing the previous management with Chavez cronies, it was obvious that Chavez's economic policies could not be implemented while PDVSA was in opposition hands. According to the CIA World Factbook, oil revenues "account for roughly 90% of export earnings, about 50% of the federal budget revenues, and around 30% of GDP."[11]

Government control of the oil industry, a return to some semblance of economic stability, and high oil prices all combined to create strong economic growth. Real GDP grew by 87 percent from the low of 2003, and recent growth has been about 10 percent in 2006 and 8 percent in 2007.[12] Unlike the boom in the 1970s, when oil revenues did little to improve the condition of the nation's poor, the Chavez government attempted to implement sweeping increases in social policy spending. Control of PDVSA allowed the government to transfer $13 billion from the oil company into social spending programs, although $1.1 billion of this spending went to the Ministry of Defense, which is a fairly indirect way of helping the poor.[13] Government social spending has also increased dramatically, from 8 percent of GDP in 1998 to 13 percent in 2006. Most of the increases have been in the areas of health, education, and food subsidization.[14] Chavez has also raised the minimum wage in an effort to increase the incomes of low-wage laborers. There has been a remarkable decline in the poverty rate under Chavez. The percent of the population living on less than one dollar per day fell from 14 percent in 1998 to 3.5 percent in 2006.[15] Unemployment, which stood at 15 percent in 1999, fell to 9 percent in 2007.[16] On the downside, the increase in personal consumption and government spending fueled inflation that topped 30 percent in 2008. In addition to using government spending and legislation to increase the incomes of the poor, who make up much of his electoral base, Chavez implemented an aggressive nationalization strategy. In 2007 he nationalized firms in the petroleum, communications, and electricity sectors and in 2008 he placed firms in the cement and steel sectors under public ownership.[17]

Despite the civic unrest, Chavez successfully passed a startling number of democratic hurdles. In the 2000 elections for the National Assembly two years into the Chavez administration he received 59 percent of the vote and won two-thirds of the seats. In 2004, he faced a recall vote to end his presidency in which he won 59 percent of the vote. For a leader who is frequently described as having dictatorial tendencies, he has also been willing to accept democratic defeat. In a December 2007 referendum on whether he would be allowed to run again by ending presidential term limits, 51 percent of the voters rejected the proposal and Chavez accepted the decision. He tried his luck again in 2008 with another proposition to end term limits, and this time it passed with 54 percent of the vote. While this move has been portrayed as undemocratic, many democracies, like Canada and England, do not have term limits. After all, it is still democratic voting that decides whether politicians are elected and how many terms they serve. Margaret Thatcher won four elections and Tony Blair three without any accusations about the lack of democracy in the UK. The elections in Venezuela since Chavez have been certified time and again as free and honest, and the possibility of midterm recall still exists and will be maintained.

Chavez has remained in power despite antagonistic coverage by the privately owned press. The Venezuelan media is deeply ideologically divided, with the 20 percent under government control espousing unswerving support for Chavez and the privately held 80 percent presenting criticism that would border on treason in many countries. In this deeply divided context there have been a number of concerns about Chavez's commitment to free speech. He has temporarily shut down media outlets, opposition media have had their offices raided, and high-ranking journalists have been the subject of intimidation. While this does have the hallmarks of a dictator eager to suppress opposition views, and a number of media watchdogs have claimed that Venezuela is violating the fundamental democratic right of freedom of the press, things are not quite as straightforward as they first appear. Many of the privately owned media outlets that have been sanctioned by Chavez were reporting in a manner that would have been unacceptable in most democratic contexts. In the aftermath of the 2002 coup, one media outlet ran advertisements encouraging the overthrow of the government.[18] A commentator at another station predicted that (like Mussolini) Chavez would end up "hung with his head down."[19] Lobbying for the violent overthrow of an elected government and predicting a grisly death for the head of state are not usually accepted components of freedom of speech. While Chavez has taken extreme actions against some sections of the media, he has done so in exceptional circumstances.

Analyzing the *Times'* coverage of Iran and Venezuela should help reveal its economic position on three important issues. First, both governments have transferred ownership from foreign, private possession to state national control, allowing us to evaluate the *Times'* opinion of who should own the productive capacity in a country. Second, the chapter deliberately examines cases in which these economic policies are brought about by democratically elected governments to examine the *Times'* coverage of countries in which there might be a conflict between the *Times'* promotion of democracy and its support of the rights of private ownership. Third, in Iran, the U.S. and UK governments intervened to help overthrow a democratically elected leader. The downfall of Mossadegh and rise of the Shah resulted in British and U.S. oil firms gaining control of the formerly nationalized state industry and improved both the price and predictability of British and U.S. oil supplies. The *Times'* coverage of this issue will reveal its opinion of the United States (and in Iran the UK) using covert means to aid the profitability of their own domestic capital.

The *Times* and Iran: Articles

The *Times* had little positive to say about Mossadegh and his economic policies. The nationalization of the AIOC resulted in a British blockade of all Iranian oil sales, completely destroying virtually the only source of foreign exchange and a major source of tax revenue for the Iranian economy. Yet, the *Times'* news stories argued it was Iran who was responsible for the oil crisis. Mossadegh was characterized as intransigent and obstinate. "He has sought first to dispossess the Anglo-Iranian Oil Company in Iran and then force Britain to agree to his expropriation terms."[20] In a particularly memorable passage the *Times* claimed that "The Iranian viewpoint is that of an angry woman who goes to divorce court determined to get hers for all the fur coats that her husband did not give her during her married life."[21] The *Times* stuck to the U.S. and UK line that Britain was the reasonable and aggrieved party in this dispute, reporting that it had "reached the limits of her concessions to Iran," that "Dr. Mossadegh . . . has wrung one concession after another out of the Western powers,"[22] and that the United Kingdom and United States had "many times demonstrated their concern with the stability of Iran and the well being of the Iranian people."[23] Interestingly, the *Times* made these claims without actually revealing what these UK concessions actually entailed or what sticking points remained between the sides, making it difficult to determine just who was being the unreasonable party.

The *Times* did very occasionally portray the Iranian position as reasonable or the UK as intransigent, but these claims were far less frequent and relied on either overly optimistic prognostications by the U.S. mediator in the early days of the negotiations[24] or quotes from Mossadegh, making it appear the opinion of one particularly biased man rather than fact or common knowledge. For example, in 1952 the *Times* quoted Mossadegh as saying "the British Government unlawfully supported the company and prevented agreement."[25]

On the issue of the fairness of the nationalization of AIOC, the *Times* argued that the UK-based company deserved ownership of the oil and the extraction machinery because of its investment in the country. "Mossadegh drove a British company from oil wells it had owned and operated for half a century"[26] and "an investment of hundreds of millions of pounds was lost and an industry that had taken three decades to create came to a dead stop."[27] Further, the *Times* saw little merit in the nationalist claim that AIOC particularly, and other foreign multinationals more generally, might exploit the resources of developing nations. Instead, the *Times* claimed that the argument that foreign companies exploited Iranian resources was a scapegoat, promoted by the Iranian elites to falsely create an external enemy to take the blame for Iran's economic stagnation. "For years the oligarchs rode the nationalist wave and turned popular discontent from themselves to the British."[28] The *Times* was correct in pointing out that the system of property ownership in this semi-feudal economy was grossly unfair to the majority of Iranians and massively beneficial to the elite. It may also have been true that the elites saw the nationalist issue as a way to deflect attention from the domestic policies that impoverished their own populace. Yet, even if this were the case, it would not logically mean that the nationalist argument had no foundation in truth. We have seen that Anglo-Iranian was making massive profits in Iran and that very little of this remained in the country. Even in this context, the *Times* insisted that nationalization was a sop for the masses.

There were exceptions to this general rule. Before AIOC's fields were nationalized, the *Times* reported on growing dissatisfaction among the Middle-Eastern states over the distribution of oil revenues. According to the *Times*, the British government received a larger share of oil income than Iran, making Iranians question why foreign countries should get "such a large tax income from 'their oil.'"[29] The added quotation marks around "their oil" were revealing. In a slightly more balanced claim after the coup, the *Times* argued that while the Anglo-Iranian nationalization was a "positive achievement," Mossadegh's hatred of the British prevented him from negotiating an agreement to end the boycott.[30] The most frequent defense of Iran's point of view was left to either Mossadegh and his officials or other less-than-creditable sources. For example, the *Times* ran a story in which an "Armenian Red," the first secretary of the Armenian Communist Party, claimed that "the United States and Britain . . . had carried out a policy of unreined exploitation and plundering of Iran," which was responsible for the lack of development in that country compared to the rocket-like trajectory of the Armenian economy.[31] It also quoted Iranian minister Ayatollah Kashani as saying "Britain had looted Iran's God-given riches, despoiled the people and imposed corrupt, traitorous rulers upon them."[32]

This is an interesting way of presenting balance. The statement made by the Armenian dignitary is strident and antagonistically phrased. It is also from a less-than-credible source in the eyes of the U.S. public. This allowed the *Times* to present both sides of the issue but ensure that one side is not viewed as a reasonable opinion. The idea that Iran did not particularly benefit from the pre-nationalization relationship with AIOC was expressed in much more reasonable tones by individuals less subject to ridicule than an Armenian Communist Party official, or someone with a vested interest in the negotiations like Mossadegh himself.

According to the *Times*, the nationalization of the oil industry was not only unjust, it was also unwise. "Iran has received no revenues from its oil. . . . It is as though a farmer had decided to let his fields lie fallow for a whole crop season."[33] The *Times* was correct in pointing out that the lack of oil revenue would present massive problems for an economy in which the public sector was dependent on oil tax revenues and oil represented almost the sole source of export earnings. However, they were less accurate about the cause of the decline in oil sales, which it largely pinned on the inability of Iranians to operate the oil refinery after the expulsion of British managers and technicians. "Dr. Mossadegh has been told many times by many persons that Britain is the only country in the world that has enough available oil experts to undertake the operation of the Iranian industry."[34]

While the *Times* was undoubtedly correct in claiming that there were problems due to the outflow of skilled workers, the fact remained that the British boycott would have prevented any oil from being sold even if production were completely unimpeded. The *Times'* continued insistence that it was the nationalization, rather than the boycott, that created Iran's economic difficulties further perpetuated the misconception that nationalization of foreign industry by developing-nation governments was the height of irresponsibility. Further, the very fact that there were so few Iranians qualified to work in their own oil refinery speaks to the lack of local opportunities that were created by AIOC and, perhaps, the lack of control that the company was willing to give up over the technology.

The *Times'* commitment to the beneficial role of multinational investment in the developing world was nicely highlighted in an article about U.S. opposition to a UN proposal "approving the right of any country to seize private property, without mentioning obligations to provide compensation." In covering the objections to this resolution the *Times* pointed out that while governments did have the right to take over private property, as long as there is appropriate compensation to its previous owners, it "would halt improvement of living standards which we all consider desirable and would create an unnecessary obstacle to those friendly and equitable relations among nations which lead to world peace."[35]

The *Times* was less critical of the British blockade. Not once, in all of the articles in our sample, did the *Times* question Britain's right to employ this tactic. The boycott was only questioned, and then merely from a tactical standpoint, when other industrial countries became interested in purchasing Iranian oil. The *Times* correctly pointed out that had anyone succeeded in purchasing Iranian oil, it would be a major problem for the British efforts to seek what they considered to be adequate compensation from Iran, since Britain's main bargaining strength stems from "the fact that Iran now receives no revenue from her vast oil resources."[36] The *Times* provided very similar coverage when Italy[37] and Japan[38] attempted to evade the blockade. These stories were reported as a possible strain on the relationships between the developed countries involved and a threat to Britain's ability to win a favorable settlement from Iraq rather than as the cause of Iran's economic woes.

The *Times*' coverage reflected the dilemma facing the U.S. administration on this issue. On one hand the U.S. government was very eager to not let the Iranian government set a precedent for other nations by nationalizing foreign firms, especially without "appropriate" compensation. On the other, U.S. firms, and surely its own government, recognized the opportunity arising from the Iranian desperation to sell oil. This debate was framed in the *Times* as a conflict between two allies with differing concerns about the crisis. The UK was portrayed as being concerned with taking a hard line to protect the assets of this particular company and also sending a message that the many UK businesses in far-flung remnants of its former colonies should not have to endure the same fate. The United States was portrayed as being rather more conciliatory due to its concern that Iranian economic instability would make it susceptible to the siren song of the Communists, who were well represented in Iran by the Tudeh Party. "Washington seems to feel more keenly than London the possibility that Iran may fall over the brink of bankruptcy into communism."[39]

The blockade was very occasionally linked to Iranian economic woes, but this did not accurately reflect events for a couple of reasons. First, it relied on quotes from Iranian officials and was presented very much as a matter of personal opinion. For example, the *Times* quoted Mossadegh saying, "Britain has been subjecting the Iranian people to terrific economic pressure."[40] These articles present the idea that the boycott is responsible for Iranian economic difficulties as attempts to create a foreign scapegoat by Iranian leaders looking to deflect criticism from their own disastrous policies.

Second, the few articles that did not rely on people who could be dismissed as foreign zealots only started to appear either near the very end of Mossadegh's reign or after he was deposed. In an article describing the state of Iranian political instability only days before Mossadegh was overthrown, the *Times* correctly attributed much of the political turmoil to the economic crisis: "the real crisis . . . is the two-year old economic crisis based on the lack of foreign exchange and government revenue resulting from the nationalization of the huge Anglo-Iranian Oil

Company establishment here and the subsequent British blockade of oil sales."[41] What makes these statements noteworthy is that they were the only articles in our sample that linked the economic crisis not only to the nationalization, but also to the blockade that followed. Perhaps most interestingly, a *Times* article on August 30, 1953, urged Britain to help with Iranian rehabilitation after the Shah had seized power by "removing the legal and political obstacles to the sale of Iranian oil."[42] It is surely not a coincidence that this was the first time that the *Times* had urged a removal of the blockade.

The U.S./UK-assisted coup and subsequent reign of the Shah provides an opportunity to analyze how the *Times* viewed the two contrasting regimes. We have seen earlier that the two leaders not only had very different commitments to democracy, but also very differing economic policies. There is little question which leader was preferred by the *Times*.

The first hint of the *Times'* preferences came immediately after the coup, as the paper was attempting to give its readers some insight into the personality of the new leader. The Shah was described in glowing terms as a modern philanthropist, having given away most of his wealth and instituted social reforms. The sub-headline for an article on August 21, 1953, proclaimed "A Friend of West, He Has Given Much of Wealth, Amassed by Father to Aid People." He was further described in a particularly 1950s style as ". . . popular, as evidenced by his election as captain of the football team. . . . A sportsman, and hunter, he enjoys driving automobiles and flying his own plane."[43] In 1956, three years into his rule, "the Shah is a dark, handsome man with searching eyes and a quiet rhythmical voice. By temperament he is calm and unruffled. By inclination he is a philosopher given to musing over the problems of his ancient land."[44] Mossadegh, on the other hand, was described in less flattering terms. To provide just one example, he "was internationally famous for his bizarre habits—receiving diplomatic visitors in bed, weeping profusely and fainting in public, bounding upstairs like a rabbit at formal meetings."[45] Less comically: "he used nationalism and histrionics to remain in power, despite a rapidly worsening economic crisis."[46]

If the Shah was a rather more likeable character than Mossadegh, he also was a more dab hand at managing the economy, according to the *Times*. Tellingly, after the coup the *Times* dedicated more stories to discussing Mossadegh's supposedly failed policies than the current economic platform of the Shah. First among Mossadegh's follies was the oil nationalization. "When Mohammed Mossadegh sought to bring the British to heel in 1951 by nationalizing the Anglo-Iranian Oil Company, he succeeded only in bringing Iran to its knees."[47] According to the *Times*, the failure of the oil nationalization was only one element of the economic mismanagement perpetuated by Mossadegh. In the period after the coup the *Times'* theme was that the ousted leader left the economy on the brink of catastrophe, claiming, for example, that his regime was "economically and politically bankrupt."[48]

The Shah, on the other hand, was a modern ruler with Western ideas. His first big step forward was to resolve the oil dispute with Britain and the United States by abandoning Mossadegh's attempt at nationalization, a move that the *Times* clearly welcomed: "The prospect of an early infusion of oil revenues sent new vigor coursing through the Iranian body politic this week, enabling the once debilitated patient to move confidently at home and abroad." "These developments sent a ripple of confidence through Teheran's bazaars and government offices. They brought optimistic headlines in the press and revived the spirits of workers in the petrified forest of the huge Abadan refinery and oil fields."[49] It was not only the resumption of oil sales that supposedly improved the Iranian economy, but also the more private-sector oriented, Western, forward approach adopted by the Shah. An October 29, 1958, headline read, "Ruler Voices Hope to Lead People to Economic and Political Advancement."[50]

The *Times* was also complementary about the Shah's aggressive denationalization. Although a January 13, 1959, headline read "Iranian Industry Making Headway: Self-Sufficiency Enhanced by Plan That Spurned Private Investment," the article was about the economic successes brought on by private investment. According to the *Times*, the Iranian economy was booming due to "a Government sponsored shift from public to private ownership chalking up corresponding headway. . . . The time is ripe for private investment, domestic and foreign, in industry." In an exceedingly rare case of sloppy copy editing, it is possible that the headline was supposed to read "spurred," rather than spurned.[51]

In addition to the economic issues surrounding the nationalization of foreign assets, we were also interested in how the *Times* reported on the democratic credentials of Mossadegh and the Shah. Despite the fact that he was actually elected, the *Times* rarely conceded that Mossadegh was a democratic leader or had any genuine support from the people of Iran. To provide just one example of a repeated refrain just after the coup, the *Times* wrote, "he demanded more and more power. In the end he was virtually dictator of Iran. But his only support came from Russia, Tudeh and a handful of Army protégés. This was how he maneuvered himself into his fall."[52] The *Times* further claimed that in some ways Mossadegh's violent overthrow was his own fault, since he had "eliminated all means of an orderly change in government and achieved dictatorial powers."[53]

Despite the fact that the Shah came to power on the back of a military coup (which he viewed from the safety of Rome after fleeing the country) and held no elections with legitimate democratic opposition, the *Times* was prepared to give him the benefit of the doubt. Almost a year after the coup, it wrote that the Shah, "still lacks wide popular support. But in a country where popular support often means descending to the most demagogic form of chauvinism, this deficiency is pardonable."[54] Even after several years in power, during which the *Times* itself reported on the lack of democratic elections and sharp clampdown on civil liberties including the imprisonment of "oppositionists,"[55] it felt confident in proclaiming that, "the Shah is universally esteemed by his own people."[56]

Finally, the *Times'* reporting about whether there was any covert outside involvement in the Iranian coup revealed whether it gave any credence to the rumors of

U.S. and UK involvement. While the *Times* did run numerous stories on British and U.S. intervention well after the fact in the 1970s, during the 1950s there was little suggestion that the coup in Iran was anything other than domestically engineered. Reporting on the coup, the *Times* wrote that "the State Department assumed throughout the day a strictly neutral, hands-off policy."[57] The only two examples during this period that suggested foreign covert activity in the affairs of Iran were from sources that would have lacked credibility to American readers. The first came from a speech by Hussein Makki, secretary general of the National Front party, who claimed that the brief deposition of Mossadegh in July of 1952, which sparked riots and his reinstatement, was aided by the United States State Department.[58] The second source was Pravda (the official press agent of the Soviet state), which claimed, "This time the weapon of subversive activity was directed against Iran, which did not wish to become the submissive slave of American monopolies."[59] Again, these stories did not present the U.S. intervention as a possible truth, but as an example of the outrageous stories being engineered about the United States by its rivals.

While the evidence of U.S. involvement in the coup was not recognized, the *Times* was quite concerned about the direction of the Iranian state under the rule of Mossadegh. In the Cold War context of the 1950s, in which virtually the entire world was being cajoled into lining up into "capitalist" and "communist" camps, the *Times* was not a neutral observer. It remained steadfastly vigilant in identifying the dangers of letting Iran choose the wrong side. The *Times* repeatedly warned of the anti-American sentiment in both the general public and the Iranian Parliament. For example, it reported that "the atmosphere in the chamber during (National Front Deputy) Mr. Damavadi's speech was definitely anti American."[60] It also repeatedly wrote about the outside influence of the Soviets and the domestic influence of the Communist Party, the Tudeh, claiming that "the Soviets are exploiting extremist, fanatical nationalists"[61] or that "the Tudeh party was courted dangerously by Dr. Mossadegh."[62]

In stark contrast to the anti-American leanings of Mossadegh, the Shah was continuously feted as a friend of the West and safeguard against communism. Sampling only a few of the many instances, the *Times* claimed immediately after the coup that, "A political miracle on Aug. 19 jerked Iran out from under the Iron Curtain as it was about to be lowered."[63] On the day Mossadegh was deposed, the *Times* was optimistic that the coup would improve "Iran's chances of staying out of the Soviet orbit."[64] By 1956 it could report that Iran was "subversion free."[65]

The *Times* and Iran: Op-Eds

Despite the *Times*' obvious interest in Iran and its nationalization of AIOC, these issues were largely tackled in its news and, as we will see, editorial pages rather than by columnists. Op-eds may have been few in number, but they were strong in opinion.

Iran was most commonly characterized as irrationally xenophobic, especially when it came to "Westerners." One headline described Mossadegh's "right-hand man" and head of the Parliamentary Oil Nationalization Board, Hussein Makki, as "a blazing nationalist fanatic."[66] Elizabeth Munroe claimed that Iran was prejudiced against all things from "abroad" despite the fact that the efforts of the British Oil industry had helped the city of Abadan climb "farther out of the underdeveloped country's rut of ignorance and apathy than any other point in its region."[67]

Like in the news stories, Mossadegh was compared unfavorably to the Shah. Just after the coup that brought him down, Munroe provided one of the kinder eulogies for the former leader, arguing that he was "full of genuine intentions to raise living standards and feed the hungry" but that these "promises were beyond his range to fulfill" due to the lack of both administrative expertise and revenue in his government.[68] However, this portrait of a well-meaning but ineffectual leader was in stark contrast with a 1952 column in which he was portrayed as having two sides. On one hand, he was praised as incorruptible, taking on the landlord classes, setting up a system of rural democracy, and taking on entrenched corruption. On the other, he was described as "a pathetically frail, hysterical, bedridden old man who, as a symbol of his nation's persecution complex, seemed intent on venting his anger at the West's great powers even if it meant chaos."[69] Even more damning, a 1959 column by Hal Lehrman portrayed Mossadegh as a "weeping and swooning" leader who drove the economy into the ground and flirted with the communists. The Shah, on the other hand, was "his country's smartest politician and complete master" and the handsome "little father" to the common people of the country.

Lehrman's tribute to the Shah hit many of the notes sounded by news stories in the *Times*. His economic policy was modern, compassionate, and pro business. "The Shah's on his throne, and all seems right in Teheran, where foreign currency is plentiful, bright new American and European cars dart and dash through the world's wildest traffic and even the moldy bazaars are being remodeled." While Iran may have had its slight difficulties, "contrasted with the Arab world immediately westward, Iran emerges as a tower of strength." The Shah was also lauded for attempting to bring the economy out of its moribund feudal past and embracing Western ideals and expertise. His proposals to reform the agricultural system by "commencing the sale of Crown lands at long and easy terms to villagers," distributing public lands, and reducing oversized estates were hailed as establishing more equal distribution of wealth and modernizing industry. Further, they were part of a variety of policies that demonstrated a "new concern for the average suffering citizen."[70]

Equally important, while Mossadegh was flirting with the communist party, the Shah could be counted on to side with the United States against the Russian bear. In the early 1950s, Iran was "a tempting plum for Russia" due to its vast oil resources and political instability.[71] After a half decade of the Shah's rule, "the West has a strong ally in Iran, on Russia's border." "There is no communist party here . . . no Arab style tendency to flirt with Moscow." "Under Mossadegh, the Communists just missed grabbing power. The Shah is our strongest bulwark against another attempt."[72] The fact that the crackdown on the communist party in Iran was a fundamental part of a broader suppression of civil liberties under a profoundly undemocratic leader was ignored.

The *Times* and Iran: Editorials

The editorial writers of the *Times* took an even stronger line against the nationalization, and Mossadegh's reign in general, than its news stories. They were especially active in writing about the oil nationalization issues, penning a remarkable 35 articles on the issue between 1951 and 1953. The unremitting opinion of the editorial writers was that the Iranian nationalization was expropriation in defiance of international law and therefore "thoroughly and inexcusably wrong."[73] The paper claimed that, "The British case is unassailable on a legal basis; Iran is outraging accepted standards of international law and practice."[74] It was irrational intransigence by the Iranian government, driven by unreasonable feelings of hatred toward all things foreign, "one phase of the wave of xenophobia that is spreading all over the East . . ." that prevented an agreement.[75] The UK was presented as doing "everything to facilitate an amicable solution of the crisis"[76] and "acting with exemplary patience and coolheadedness,"[77] while "the course that the Iranian Premier has taken has seemed to many persons to be singularly reckless."[78] Not a single editorial in this period suggested that the UK was not the long-suffering, patient, aggrieved party and Iran the childish tormentor.

The Iranians were not just the guilty party in the failure to reach an agreement with Britain over the AIOC nationalization, but from an economic perspective the takeover was "reckless,"[79] "short-sighted,"[80] and "economic national suicide"[81] based on the "false premise that their miseries were due to the exploitation of their oil riches by the British."[82] The reason for the inevitable economic catastrophe was that "Iran possess(ed) neither the capital nor the technical skill to run the oil industry."[83] The *Times* portrayed the nationalization as suicide, implying an injury that was entirely self-inflicted. But, of course, this was not the case. There was no mention of the British blockade, with the exception of two editorials condemning other developed countries for harming the British by offering to purchase Iranian oil.[84] The *Times* editorials may have preferred the comparison to suicide, but a more apt description would be murder.

Although Iran's economic stagnation was largely attributed to the oil nationalization, Mossadegh's handling of the overall economy was also heavily criticized. "Iran is slowly strangling without oil revenues, under a regime that has no constructive ideas of any sort—only the purely destructive nationalist policy of driving the Westerners out."[85] After the coup brought the Shah to power, the *Times* argued that

Mossadegh's pursuit of a nationalist economic policy "wrecked the economy of the country in the process" but this "was apparently of little concern to the fanatical, power-hungry man."[86] He had "brought the country to the brink of economic collapse . . . emptied the state treasury, inflated the currency and squandered much of Iran's remaining foreign reserves."[87]

In contrast, when the Shah reopened the oil negotiations with the British, it was portrayed as a move that was both a great sign for the West and beneficial to the Iranian population. It not only provided the immediate benefits of turning on the oil revenue tap but also marked a general turn away from backward nationalism and toward a more progressive, advanced economy.[88]

Editorials in the *Times* also portrayed Mossadegh as a dictatorial demagogue while sparing the Shah from similar scrutiny. In the period of growing conflict between pro-Shah and pro-Mossadegh factions in Iran that culminated in the coup, the *Times* was very critical of what it considered to be undemocratic moves by Mossadegh. It denounced his "bid for dictatorship."[89] He was "in no sense a real popular leader" and only able to hold his post because of the will of "a tight knot of professional terrorists."[90] While Mossadegh, who did actually submit himself to the democratic process, was painted as a tyrant, only holding power through the threat of violence, the Shah was spared a similar level of close scrutiny. When Mossadegh was overthrown it was with a "deep sense of relief in the West" since the Shah was a moderating influence on wild fanaticism and socially progressive.[91] Indeed, the *Times* approved of the Shah's curtailing of political freedom when he rounded up communists and banned the Tudeh Party.[92] The point here is not that Mossadegh was an ideal leader, unwaveringly committed to democratic ideals, but that compared to the Shah he was a paragon of democratic virtue, a contrast that would have been lost to a reader of the *Times*' editorial page.

At least part of the reason for this asymmetry was surely the *Times*' editors' view of Iran through the prism of the Cold War. Editorial writers were very concerned about the influence of the "Soviet controlled Tudeh party" in the oil nationalization, in particular, and Mossadegh's government more generally.[93] This created a fear at the *Times* that Iran and its vast oil reserves would fall under the sway of Russia.[94] Editorials argued that it was not British colonial aggression or U.S. economic expansion but Stalinist communism that was "the real imperialism." They repeatedly warned Mossadegh's Iran that it was in danger of leaving itself vulnerable to potential overthrow by the communists.[95] This makes for interesting reading given that it was not Russia but rather the United States and United Kingdom that ultimately backed the violent transition. The Shah, on the other hand, was continuously praised for firmly ensconcing Iran in the Western sphere of influence. There were far fewer editorials during the Shah's reign than while Mossadegh was in power, but those that were written concentrated on his ability to stand up to "Soviet pressures on Iran"[96] and "defeat a Soviet design."[97]

The *Times* editorials on Mossadegh and Iran's oil nationalization can perhaps best be summarized by an article a year after the coup in which the *Times* triumphantly proclaimed that "underdeveloped countries with rich resources now have an object lesson in the heavy cost that must be paid by one of their number which goes berserk with fanatical nationalism."[98] The idea that Iran might make use of its control over oil revenues for real democratic economic development, which was patently not taking place when British AIOC was making handsome profits, was not part of the *Times*' perspective.

The *Times* and Venezuela: Articles

The *Times* accurately connected the rise of Chavez to anger at the political parties that had governed during conditions of widespread poverty. On the eve of his election victory the *Times* described Venezuela as a country where corruption and sustained neglect of most of the population had fostered dissatisfaction with democratic government. Four out of five people lived in poverty and 40 percent of the population suffered from malnourishment.[99] It was also a profoundly unequal country, in which "an estimated 5 percent of the population owned 80 percent of the country's private land."[100] Ordinary Venezuelans felt that "the country's political elite have either squandered or pocketed billions of dollars of oil revenues that could have been used to make this country and its people rich."[101] In this context of gross inequality and abject poverty, Chavez was seen as a protector and benefactor by the poor. Two months after the election, the *Times* described the economy inherited by Chavez as a shambles. Oil prices were falling, the government budget deficit was 9 percent of the total economy, and foreign debt payment made up more than 30 percent of government expenditure. With the headline, "Venezuelan Leader Plans to Cut Spending to Pare Deficit," the *Times* supported Chavez's moves to tackle the country's dire economic problems instead of currying favor with the electorate through costly government programs.[102]

The giant state-owned oil company, PDVSA, was the second-largest oil company in the world (at the time) and the largest supplier of oil to the United States. Unlike in Iran, the oil industry was already nationalized, so the issue of private versus public ownership had already been settled. Rather, at issue was the level of independence from the rest of the government enjoyed by the state-owned corporation and to what extent oil revenues would be used to finance other economic priorities. The *Times* was critical of Chavez's plans to use earnings from PDVSA to help fund government programs. It cited opponents of the plan who claimed that any government interference was likely to reduce the efficiency of a company that was running much more smoothly than the rest of the state sector. Oil "experts" were also against the move, describing it as a "huge mistake."[103] When Chavez appointed an ally to head the PDVSA in September 1999, the *Times* raised questions about the competence of the new leadership. The outgoing head of the oil company warned against using the oil company as a "cash cow," an apparent allusion, according to the *Times*, to the "populist economic policies favored by some members of the Chavez administration."[104] In an article titled, "The Oil Company as Social Worker," the *Times* described how oil company profits were being used to fund a "radical and wide-ranging social spending program that includes building homes, running literacy programs and developing agriculture." It warned that this "will soak up capital the company needs to shore up production," causing output declines in the future. The *Times* reported that these programs were designed to solidify Mr. Chavez's support among the growing lower classes as he continued to face a potential recall vote.[105] It was similarly critical of a new law that nearly doubled royalty payments and gave majority control of projects operated by foreign MNCs (which produce about one third of the oil in Venezuela) to the government. The *Times* reported that oil industry analysts predicted that this would destroy future investment from the likes of ExxonMobil, crippling the oil industry on which the economy depended.[106] The *Times* also claimed that using oil money to foster "endogenous development" had failed before in Venezuela, leading to privatization of state companies and the opening of the oil industry to foreign investment.[107]

Chavez's changes to the company created divisions and unrest, according to the *Times*. The conflict was portrayed as a struggle by management and workers at PDVSA to ward off unnecessary government interference and protect the operating efficiency of the company. The series of strikes in 2002 that crippled the Venezuelan economy in general, and its oil production particularly, was sparked by labor unrest at PDVSA among white collar workers angered because Chavez was replacing managers at the company.[108] The strike cost the country $4 billion in lost exports, hobbling the economy, causing a crisis in government revenue, and compromising Venezuela's international reputation as a reliable crude oil supplier.[109] The *Times* reported that due to the cutoff in oil production to PDVSA's main customer, Citgo, "no company in America has as much at stake in the toppling of Venezuela's mercurial president . . . as Citgo Petroleum, one of the biggest gasoline marketers in the United States—a wholly owned unit of the Venezuelan state oil company."[110] Despite the crippling economic effects of the strike, Chavez was criticized for declaring it illegal.[111] Removing the right to strike certainly smacks of the activity of a military junta in the vein of Chile's Augusto Pinochet, but it is interesting that the *Times'* reporting on this incident is so sympathetic to the union leaders and critical of Chavez. We saw in the coverage of inflation in the United States and social democracy in Sweden that the *Times* was much less indulgent of any union activity that caused economic damage.

The economic conflicts at PDVSA were a microcosm of the divisions created by the broader economic changes planned by Chavez, according to the *Times*. His economic programs were designed to improve the lot of his impoverished power base in the barrios while opposition came from labor unions, business owners, and the media.[112] The *Times* was sympathetic to the plight of the poor in Venezuela and frequently reported on how the specific programs initiated by Chavez had improved their lives. As a result, many poor Venezuelans preferred him to the opposition leaders who they saw as part of the privileged classes that benefited from previous governments. For example, the *Times* reported the story of Ermis Montilla, who, after living most of his life in a cardboard shack, was able to construct his own house thanks to building materials and engineering advice from the government.[113] However, the *Times* also reported that Chavez's programs and the individual success stories that they foster have not changed the cold, hard statistical reality for the poor in Venezuela, with the poverty rate increasing from "60 to 70 percent" under Chavez's Bolivarian revolution.[114]

The *Times* also reported that these policies were likely to ruin the economy. Eighteen months after he was elected, the *Times* declared that Chavez had gathered the poor into a powerful force demanding change. However, the well-off had spirited $8 billion out of the country, mostly to the United States.[115] When the economic situation improved, buoyed by high oil prices, the *Times* credited Chavez for steering Venezuela through a period of falling inflation, increasing foreign reserves, and increased government spending. However, this good news was outweighed by the bad news of underemployment, labor protests, and increasing crime. Opponents complained that Chavez built paper castles for Venezuelans and "embarrass(ed) the country while driving away investments." Concerns about Chavez's policies were so strong that tens of thousands of upper-class Venezuelans were abandoning the country.[116] The middle class had been "battered" by decreasing investment, high unemployment, and high inflation.[117] The paper was especially critical of his efforts to increase the nationalization of industry in 2007 and 2008. The *Times* reported that nationalizations led to capital flight and demonstrated that Chavez was more interested in consolidating his power over the entire economy than in the welfare of his people.[118]

The *Times* also claimed that the economic strife caused by Chavez's economic policies was the root cause of his supposed lack of popularity. According to the *Times*, 67 percent of Venezuelans had "little or no confidence" in Mr. Chavez. According to the opposition movement, these low polling numbers were due to the crippling of oil production and the climate of hate emerging in the country.[119]

As was the case in Iran, the *Times* questioned the democratic credentials of an elected leader who threatened sweeping changes to the economic power structure. Of course, Chavez's previous coup attempt made him an easy target. The *Times*' headline on the day Chavez was elected declared "Renegade Officer Favored in Venezuelan Election Today." The article portrayed Chavez as a military strongman who planned to seize power violently and had created a list of journalists deemed "shootable." With the Russians no longer available to provide guilt by association, the *Times* was forced to fall back on Chavez's appreciation of "the Cuban way."[120] This would become the template for many of the *Times*' articles on Venezuelan democracy, which branded Chavez a Cuban-style dictator and constantly reminded readers of his failed coup. Under headlines like "Democrat or a Dictator" the *Times* reported that the Chavez government was planning a new constitution that would expand his powers and endanger his opponents, who worried that he was a military strongman in the mold of Castro.[121]

He was also described in less-than-flattering personal terms. Mostly he was painted as an eccentric bungler who craved power and fostered an incomprehensible cult of personality. According to an "acclaimed" Chavez biographer, he was a charlatan who had "reimagined the country as a type of reality show" in which he was the star.[122] This was only one of many instances in which he was accused of a "tyranny of popularity."[123]

These anti-democratic claims persisted in the *Times* even in the context of Chavez receiving substantial electoral victories. In an election to form a national (constitutional) assembly, three-quarters of the seats were won by a Chavez-led coalition, which campaigned on a promise to rewrite the constitution so that Chavez's reforms would be more easy to implement. While this could have been interpreted as an endorsement of the Chavez government by the Venezuelan people, the *Times* was concerned that this would grant him dictatorial powers.[124] The *Times* later argued that since less than half of the eligible voters took part in the referendum, it did not constitute a mandate for Chavez "to rule by decree on economic matters."[125] When the Chavez government hammered out a compromise solution with the opposition-controlled Congress, the *Times* did not portray this as a conciliatory move by Chavez but as being forced by the external pressure of human rights advocates and those celebrated champions of democracy, Wall Street investors, who would have pestered his government with questions about breaches in the rule of law.[126]

Similarly, in the 2000 elections for the National Assembly, in which Chavez won a fairly sizeable 59 percent of the vote, the *Times'* headline read "Chavez Fails to Get Mandate for Absolute Power in Venezuela" because he was short of the two-thirds majority "that would have turned the new-single-chamber legislature into a rubber stamp."[127] The next day, the *Times* warned that "Chavez says he will crush political foes in Venezuela." Despite the fairly large margin of Chavez's victory and the fact that the voting was declared legitimate by Jimmy Carter and other observers, the *Times* focused its reporting on losing anti-Chavez politicians who claimed they were victims of voting fraud.[128] More recently, even when support for Chavez appeared to be growing, the *Times* dismissed this by claiming that "the modern part of the country wants political change."[129]

The *Times* also repeatedly reported on what it saw as Chavez's plans to remove civil liberties and extend his influence into all aspects of Venezuelan civil society, from unions to the media. When Chavez accused the Workers' Confederation, a labor union coalition that had supported the opposition by organizing numerous strikes and protests, of being an aristocracy of labor, a *Times* headline claimed: "Leader Moves To Dominate Civic Groups In Venezuela." It quoted the union president: "The only war the president ought to win, and hasn't been able to, is the war against unemployment, crime, hunger, and misery."[130] The *Times* portrayed a Chavez-initiated national referendum to replace the union leadership as a power grab intended to replace opponents with Chavez loyalists, "where industrialists will negotiate with the government, not the unions." It quoted the United Nations' high commissioner for human rights, who saw this as "concentration of power without a counterweight that can maintain the state of law."[131]

One story reported that Chavez was setting his sights on turning the educational system into a Stalinist-style indoctrination factory. "After vanquishing Congress, the courts, and political parties Chavez has set his sights on the nation's schools" through the "National Education Project." School enrollment had increased by a million since Chavez forbade schools from requiring parents to pay supplementary fees. But he had also earned the enmity of the Teachers' Federation by changing elements of the curriculum to develop Venezuelan "identity and solidarity."[132]

Freedom of the press was also under assault in Venezuela, according to the *Times*. It reported that Mr. Chavez, "former army paratrooper and failed coup plotter," had threatened to revoke the license of a "respected television network while launching blistering critiques of the press," raising worries among free press advocates and Western diplomats. Chavez was faulted for accusing the network "Globovision" of being similar to Hitler's propaganda minister Josef Goebbels, who claimed that a lie could be repeated "100 times until it is true." However, the issue in the story was slightly more complex than just a dictator looking to silence opposing views. Globovision had falsely reported that nine taxi drivers had been killed in one night, sparking chaos as drivers in Caracas shut down several streets in the aftermath of the reports to protest rising crime. Chavez accused the network of fomenting un-rest, and he certainly had a case that they were engaged in some fairly irresponsible journalism.[133] The *Times* did acknowledge the deeply divided nature of the media in Venezuela. During the wave of strikes that gripped the country in 2002, the *Times* reported that the Venezuelan media gave the strikers "hours on end" to accuse Chavez with everything from repression to terrorism to looting the central bank while "government officials are given very little air time on the private media." Of course the opposite was true on the government-owned station.[134]

The *Times* repeatedly asserted that Chavez was using state resources to subvert the democratic process. It reported that he was using trucks to bring voters to the polling stations, forcing public workers to attend rallies, and breaking up opposition rallies with water cannons.[135] The point here is not that Chavez had an unwavering commitment to civic liberties and the democratic ideal. Nor is it that the *Times* was lying to its readership. Chavez certainly provided the *Times* with ample evidence for its claims with his fiery rhetoric and replacement of trade union leadership. Rather, the point is to contrast the treatment of Chavez (like that of Mossadegh) with leaders who are far less democratically inclined but have economic policies that are less radical.

The coup that temporarily ousted Chavez in April 2002 provided an interesting opportunity to contrast the *Times*' reporting on Venezuelan leaders. In reporting the coup, the *Times* referred to its leader, Mr. Carmona, as the former head of Venezuela's largest business association, not a coup plotter or would-be dictator. Chavez, on the other hand, was again referred to as a "strongman."[136] Although the leaders of the coup dismantled the National Assembly, fired the ministers of the Supreme Court, and arrested high-level members of the government, the *Times* portrayed this as a power play by a coalition of powerful business leaders and generals—not a coup or the overthrow of a democratic government.[137]

After the coup in which Chavez was briefly deposed and then restored to power two days later, the *Times* continued to report that Chavez was ruling a country that was, at best, deeply divided and, at worst, in outright rebellion over his rule. These claims were largely based on the growing move to have a referendum that would shorten his term in office and the increasing severity of protests by the anti-Chavez opposition.[138] The paper insisted that despite his democratic mandate, Chavez was not a popular leader and, therefore, had no real approval for his policies. A year after his return to power, with the opposition in disarray, the *Times* cited a poll suggesting that Chavez would only get 34 percent of the vote in 2003, while his opponents would receive 54 percent even though there was no real opposition leader.[139]

This dissatisfaction coalesced with a petition in favor of a constitutional recall election. In the early stages of the signature gathering, the *Times* argued that Chavez's popularity was increasing and that the opposition was unlikely to unseat him.[140] The effort to collect enough names to force a recall election was not a straightforward project. Despite headlines that read "Venezuelans Flock to Sign Petitions for Chavez's Ouster,"[141] the *Times* reported that it took several months and a couple of failed attempts to collect enough legitimate signatures. The *Times* described this opposition movement as disorganized, but also pointed out that Chavez's popularity was not strong.[142] When sufficient signatures were finally collected, it was interesting that the man repeatedly characterized by the *Times* as a power-mad despot submitted to the referendum.

The *Times* pilloried Chavez's campaign style during the referendum. His speeches were described as "rambling monologues on state-run television, some lasting seven hours, filled with references to baseball, Walt Whitman and Jesus."[143] Despite his idiosyncratic lecturing style, Chavez actually won the referendum with a fairly commanding 59 percent of the popular vote. The *Times* attributed this to his ability to firm up support in the "tumble down barrios" through lavish pre-campaign spending on social programs like free dental clinics for the poor.[144] Any reasonable reading of Chavez's economic initiatives, including a shoe factory, clinics, and a subsidized market, might have suggested that these could be the basis for a diversified, sustainable, and more equitable economy. Instead the *Times* argued that "his leftist policies and sharp attacks on his political opponents have alienated Venezuelans who contend Mr. Chavez is taking Venezuela toward tyranny and ruin."[145]

The *Times'* reporting on Venezuela also provided some insight about its opinion on U.S. intervention in the democratic affairs of other nations. Although the *Times* had by now become more suspicious of the state department's role in the convenient toppling of problematic leaders, it claimed that there was no evidence of U.S. intervention during the coup that briefly unseated Chavez. Just after the coup it reminded its readers that the United States had supported, indeed made possible, authoritarian regimes throughout Central and South America in defense of its economic and political interests. However, "there is no evidence that the United States covertly undermined Mr. Chavez. He did a decent job destabilizing himself." "But the open White House embrace of his overthrow will not be lost on Latin American leaders who dare thumb their noses at the United States, as did Mr. Chavez."[146] The *Times* was concerned that the Bush administration's overly enthusiastic rush to support the new regime might have damaged its credibility as a chief defender of democratically elected governments. It also reported that the U.S. embassy was slightly ambivalent about the coup, with one official claiming they "were not discouraging people" while another insisted on sticking within Venezuelan constitutional processes. This lack of clarity continued when a U.S. official stated that although Chavez was elected democratically, "legitimacy is something that is conferred not just by a majority of the voters, however."[147] A few days later an article that chronicled the admittedly hectic few days of the coup and then Chavez's return to power reported that the leaders of the coup had made entreaties to the U.S. embassy but "they did not meet with encouragement."[148]

After the failed recall referendum in 2004, the *Times* was very critical of U.S. support for anti-Chavez parties, arguing that it provided fodder for Chavez's anti-U.S. rants.[149] The *Times* reported that the United States had spent $2.2 million between 2000 and 2003 on donations to opposition parties, but when this was discovered in Venezuela, "anti-American sentiment mined by Mr. Chavez helped him win support. But it did little to dispel claims outside of Venezuela that his government was undemocratic and radical."[150] What is interesting about these claims is that the *Times* was much more concerned with the fact that these attempts backfired on the Bush administration, actually contributing to the Chavez victory, than it was appalled that the United States was spending money to influence a democratic referendum in a foreign country. Perhaps this was because prior to Chavez, "Venezuela was a staunch ally of the US" but "has taken the most profound leftward turn of any large Latin American nation in decades."[151]

The *Times* and Venezuela: Op-eds

The composition of the *Times'* commentary pieces on Venezuela is different than on Iran. Rather than relying on academics and think tanks to contribute analysis, the *Times* took a much more in-house approach. Of the 35 op-eds during this period, 21 were from *Times*' columnists and only 12 came from authors, think tanks, or university academics. Since op-ed columnists are supposed to have more latitude for invective, the opinions expressed by the writers were more strongly articulated than those in the news section, making for a more fertile ground for harvesting memorable quotations. If balance in this section is described as a relatively even number of articles condemning or supporting Chavez, the *Times* op-eds were not balanced. Only four of the articles could be described as supportive. The overwhelming majority were scathing in their assessments of his economic and political record.

Like the news, the commentary page did concede that the pre-Chavez years created some legitimate grievances for Venezuela's poor. One op-ed argued that Chavez came to power because the previous administration protected the privileged and created inequality.[152] A few other commentators recognized that Chavez had made improvements in some economic areas. For example, *Times* writer Simon Romero credited Chavez for making a shopping district safe and pleasant for pedestrian traffic by cleaning up lawless vendors.[153] The most favorable commentary on the economy argued that the *Times*' coverage of the general strike in Venezuela badly mischaracterized the strikers. While the *Times* often portrayed the strikers as labor and management eager to continue the efficient functioning of the company against the capricious interventions of the Chavez government, Amy Chua claimed that the strike was instigated by the "wealthy business elite." In an economy in which income divisions were paralleled by ethnic division, it was also a struggle by the "white minority" to retain its economic privileges.[154] However, these two opinions on the Chavez economic platform were overshadowed by the number of articles that were much more critical.

The overarching theme of much of the commentary was that Venezuela was squandering its petrodollar riches. To the extent that there was any economic improvement it was a "boom fueled by high oil prices,"[155] but the underlying economy was weak because, as Paul Krugman summarized, Chavez's "policies have been incompetent and erratic."[156] Roger Cohen, who wrote several columns on Venezuela, all very critical of Chavez, was even more scathing. He described Chavez's economic policy as "growth from within, whatever that means" but the only tangible economic results were declining investment due to nationalizations and falling production because of price controls. Chavez's economic policies were only enjoyed by a constituency that he had purchased with oil money consisting of the armed forces, bureaucrats in newly nationalized industries, traders grown rich on gaming a corrupt system, and the poor who he has "helped and manipulated."[157] The former chief of the Venezuelan army under Chavez wrote that the government used oil money to buy off the electorate by dispensing "favors, subsidies and alms." Under the burden of high public spending and high import tariffs, the "economy may well come to a crashing halt."[158] Unemployment and underemployment swelled as capital flight accelerated. Even worse, Chavez's supporters among the poor received few tangible dividends.[159]

These economic policies caused profound divisions and made Chavez deeply un-popular among all but the poor.[160] Former Venezuelan minister of trade and industry (and chairman of the Group of Fifty, an organization of the CEOs of Latin America's largest corporations), Moises Naim, wrote that the great majority of Venezuelans did not believe his economic rhetoric, which would force Chavez to ignore the con-stitution to remain in power.[161] Only rarely did *Times'* columnists portray Chavez as anything but a ranting military strongman who resorted to dictatorial methods to retain power. In one of the exceptions, headlined "What We See in Chavez," author Luisa Velenzuela argued that his popularity in Latin America is because of his attrac-tive vision of a strong, united continent.[162] However, this rare show of support was overshadowed by criticisms of his democratic record and mockery of his personality.

Chavez was repeatedly linked to Castro. For example, Cohen criticized him for his "enduring embrace of Cuba and its revolutionary patriarch." In the same column Cohen likened Chavez to Juan Velasco, a leftist military leader of Peru in the 1970s who, according to Cohen, implemented top-down nationalizations but left only high inflation and stagnant production. Velasco's term was cut short by a bloodless coup.[163]

Chavez was frequently accused of having dictatorial tendencies and wanting to remain in power forever. These comments were especially prominent during his quest to abolish term limits. After the defeat of the first term limit referendum, anti-Chavez student activists were portrayed as the true heirs to liberal democracy and were credited with helping to defeat Chavez's quest for "absolute power."[164] Cohen also delivered a particularly scathing backhanded compliment to Chavez on the occasion of the referendum by congratulating him for accepting a marginal de-feat, despite the fact that he was "a menace" and was "accumulating power through threats, slandering opponents as 'traitors,' buying support with $150 million a day in oil money and bent on socialist revolution."[165]

Chavez was also criticized for his attacks on freedom of the press. Alejandro Toledo, the former president of Peru, accused Chavez of trying to "silence anyone with opposing thoughts" when he refused to renew the license of Radio Caracas TV.[166] Cohen was even more critical: "When opposition TV stations are curtailed, when tens of billions of dollars go missing in the national budget, when the judiciary is subservient and corruption a way of life, democracy is challenged."[167]

His personality was characterized as highly eccentric. Thomas Friedman referred to Chavez as a "piece of work," whose rule was like the "Keystone Kops."[168] Much was made of his seemingly unusual policies. One commentator mocked his proposal to move clocks forward by half an hour because Chavez thought "it will create a metabolic effect where the human brain is conditioned by sunlight."[169] He was also chided for attempting to tone down Venezuela's penchant for drink by restricting the sale of alcohol during Holy Week.[170]

Despite Chavez's many failings, *Times'* columnists were also unanimous in con-demning U.S. behavior toward Venezuela. After the failed coup attempt, the United States was criticized for its unseemly rush to support the plotters and encouraged to support democratically elected governments even if they are not "pro-capitalist."[171] Bernardo Alvarez Herrera, Venezuela's ambassador to the United States, wrote a column claiming that the U.S. "support for the Venezuelan junta undermined its pledge to uphold and promote democracy around the world."[172]

The op-ed page argued that the United States should not intervene, but neither should Chavez continue. William Safire summed up the op-ed consensus view. "His search for greater power led to strikes, riots, capital flight, an abortive coup and, despite high world oil prices, an economy nose-diving by 10 percent per year." "Chavez is an ardent admirer of Fidel Castro. Like the Cuban dictator, he intimidates those who dare to oppose, encouraging violent attacks on his critics by thuggish supporters."[173]

The *Times* and Venezuela: Editorials

Immediately following Chavez's initial election victory, the economic theme of rich against poor in a deeply divided Venezuela was established by describing his policies as "a messianic assault on the establishment which captured the imagination of the poor, frightened Venezuela's elite and made Washington nervous."[174] While the *Times* certainly understood that the poor supported Chavez, it was undecided on whether this support was justified. Some editorials claimed the poor saw him as the first national leader to look after their interests through land reform, free literacy classes, and government loans.[175] In the most supportive article of our sample, one editorial, just after his victory in the recall referendum, read: "unlike most of his predecessors he has made programs directed at the everyday problems of the poor—illiteracy, the hunger for land and inferior health care—the central theme of his administration.[176] However, other editorials argued that he had done little to actually benefit the poor. The most commonly used expression was "using the nation's oil wealth to buy up popular support" without bringing any particularly useful results, even for the poor.[177]

The editorial page was completely convinced of the harm Chavez was doing to the rest of the Venezuelan economy. His divisive policies created staunch opposition from a mix of business, middle-class professional, and labor leaders.[178] Two years into his administration the *Times* argued that "oil revenues, disastrously mismanaged in the past, have been no better used under Mr. Chavez," "while his aggressive anti-business rhetoric has helped inspire the flight of at least $8 billion to overseas banks."[179] After a decade of Chavez's economic policies, the only results were soaring food prices, overflowing sewage, and a surge in gang violence.[180]

The editorial page was especially scathing on the issue of nationalization. After Chavez nationalized companies in the telecommunications, steel, cement, and milk industries, the *Times*' editors predicted that it would cause economic chaos. "Mr.

Chavez's cronies have proved that they don't have the skill—or the honesty—to run these businesses." It repeatedly portrayed the move to state control as yet "another attempt to grab control of all of Venezuela's economic and political life while providing more opportunities for patronage and corruption."[181]

The final verdict on the economy was that under Chavez growth was slowing and inflation, fueled by excessive government spending, was the highest in Latin America. The inevitable result of this morass was that the political support for Chavez's economic transformation was steadily eroding despite the continuing support of the poorest elements of the population.[182]

As was the case in the news stories and the op-eds, editorials suggested that Chavez was no friend of democracy. One editorial warned Venezuelans to be suspicious of how this "former paratrooper colonel who served a jail term after attempting a military coup" planned to use his new powers in spite of Chavez's promise of a "peaceful revolution."[183] The editorial page repeatedly referred to Chavez as a power-mad dictator, frequently comparing him to Castro. "If your taste runs to three-hour speeches, chiseling away at democracy and a world-class personality cult, Mr. Chavez is your man."[184] Perhaps the most strident editorial appeared during the brief coup, which claimed that "Venezuelan democracy is no longer threatened by a would-be dictator." The editorial described Chavez's ouster as a "respected business leader" and claimed that the insurrection was caused by "military commanders unwilling to order their troops to fire on fellow Venezuelans to keep him (Chavez) in power."[185] This type of invective was not reserved for extraordinary circumstances. Chavez was regularly referred to as "a standard issue autocrat—hoarding power, stifling dissent, spending the nation's oil wealth on political support."[186] On the eve of the first vote to extend Chavez's term limits the *Times* urged the citizens of Venezuela to vote no[187] in order to stymie Chavez's "efforts to amass power and cling to it as long as he can."[188] His treatment of the media also did not escape the notice of the editorial page. Under the headline "Latin America's Muzzled Press" Venezuela was lumped in with Haiti and Columbia as a place where independent journalists were physically intimidated because they were a threat to Chavez's brand of left-wing authoritarianism.[189]

The editorial page appeared to have difficulty reconciling Chavez's continued democratic success with their predictions of economic and political chaos. Editorials vacillated between acknowledging that Chavez had the support of the population immediately following a supportive election and insisting that he was massively unpopular most of the rest of the time. After his victory in the 2000 election, the editorial page claimed that his political changes have won "overwhelming approval from the voters."[190] Similarly after the failure of the 2004 recall referendum, one editorial wrote that "it is time for President Chavez's opponents to stop pretending that they speak for most Venezuelans."[191] On the other hand, when the opposition won victories in the two largest cities and "5 of 22" provinces in state and municipal elections, the *Times* concluded that Venezuelans did not want him in power.[192] A later editorial asserted that his own citizens have lost patience with his "failed revolution"[193] and that he became so desperate to hold power he used intimidation and mobs.[194]

Only one editorial in our sample could be possibly construed as supportive of the Chavez administration. The overall attitude of the editorial page was nicely captured just following the overthrow of Chavez in 2002. "His forced departure last week drew applause at home and in Washington. That reaction, which we shared. . . ."[195]

Conclusion

In both Iran and Venezuela, democratic governments enacted policies that threatened the interests of both foreign and domestic business. The *Times'* portrayal of these economic policies was overwhelmingly negative. In Iran, the decline of the oil industry was attributed almost exclusively to Iranian intransigence and incompetence rather than the more obvious problem of the British blockade. There can be little question that the *Times* favored the Shah over Mossadegh. Mossadegh's economic policies, especially the nationalization of AIOC, were ridiculed, his commitment to democracy questioned, and his Cold War allegiance doubted. The Shah, on the other hand, was portrayed as a friend of the West, a wise economic manager, and a capable statesman. Comparing the *Times'* coverage of Iran with the actual course of events shows that the coverage could only generously be described as one very selective interpretation of history. The *Times*, most vehemently in its editorials but also in the rest of the paper, defended foreign, private investment when under threat from those that wanted to improve on the exploitative relationship between AIOC and its host nation. Further, the *Times* demonstrated a certain moral flexibility about its commitment to democracy in the context of Cold War alliances.

A half century later, the *Times'* treatment of Venezuela under Chavez was remarkably similar. Although some op-eds had become much more suspicious of U.S. foreign covert activity and the fog of the Cold War had lifted, the coverage of Venezuela's economic policies and its democratic pedigree mirrored that of Iran in the 1950s. The *Times*, on occasion, acknowledged that before Chavez Venezuelan leaders orchestrated decades of economic disaster. Despite its oil riches, 80 percent of the population lived in poverty. Corruption was endemic. Powerful business leaders dominated Congress, the Supreme Court, and the media. Yet, the *Times* charged Chavez with being antidemocratic and economically incompetent when he tried to transfer some of the income and power to those excluded and impoverished by previous administrations. The Venezuelan economy had failed prior to Chavez. Yet his effort to change the institutional structure using the electoral process was portrayed as the action of a leftist demagogue. In the absence of the Cold War fearmongering that was the driving guilt by association in Iran, the *Times* associated Chavez with Castro's dictatorial socialism.

As was the case in Iran, the *Times* was eager to attribute poor economic results to policies with which it did not agree, ignoring other obvious sources of instability. In Iran it ignored the impact of the British blockade. In Venezuela it glossed over the fact that privileged interests did everything they could, from strikes to a coup, to cause economic unrest. This was not a test of whether the Chavez government could efficiently and equitably run the Venezuelan economy but how it could insulate the economy from those who refused to share the wealth or invest it productively.

The *Times'* metric for democracy for Iran and Venezuela was measured by corporate autonomy. Government policy, no matter how broadly supported by elections, that limited the freedom of business was seen as inefficient and tyrannical. In these foreign policy cases, the *Times* demonstrated a strong, conservative perspective.

CHAPTER 5
THE *NEW YORK TIMES* AND REGULATION

The economic debate between ideologies also manifests itself about the extent of the regulatory role of the government. Conservatives argue that competition between firms in the market will protect people from dangerous, unhealthy, or shoddy commodities because firms need to produce quality fare at attractive prices in order to attract customers. With regulation largely unnecessary in a functioning market economy, conservatives inevitably decry the costs it imposes on firms as wasteful. Liberals are a little more cautious, arguing that while this is the case in most instances, in some special cases, the government may be required to oversee particular industries and prevent or encourage certain activities.

History is not kind to the conservative position. The inevitable quest by society to protect itself from the debilitating effects of the free market was most famously outlined by Karl Polanyi in his book *The Great Transformation*, in which he coined the term "the double movement" to describe this phenomenon.[1] The horrific tales told about the squalid conditions in Chicago's famous stockyards in Upton Sinclair's *The Jungle* created a movement that led to the inspection of food-processing facilities and the Food and Drug Administration (FDA). Sinclair himself was attempting to expose the terrifying conditions workers had to endure, a concern that eventually led to the creation of the Occupational Safety and Health Administration (OSHA) in the early 1970s. Unease over the environmental consequences of many production activities led to the Environmental Protection Agency (EPA).

The post-war North American economy had witnessed a dramatic expansion of the regulatory role of the state, but starting in the late 1970s, regulatory bodies came under increasing attack. With the decline in the profitability of U.S. corporations outlined in Chapter 3, conservative economic theories about the unwelcome costs associated with regulation gained considerable traction. In an effort to recover profits from the decreased levels prevailing in the late 1970s, firms not only attempted to control their wages but all other costs as well, including their portion of the costs of regulatory compliance. If U.S. firms were uncompetitive internationally, could it not be because of the punishing bureaucratic costs of the regulatory state? If U.S. firms were technological laggards, was it not because regulations forced them to invest in safety machinery rather than more productive technology and product innovation?

The protective regulatory agencies like OSHA were dramatically pared back. A number of crafty methods were developed to shackle them without taking the drastic, and perhaps politically dangerous, step of eliminating the entire organization. Agencies were populated with political appointees, especially during the Republican years, which usually resulted in a head ideologically opposed to the very mandate of the organization. During the Reagan revolution, agency budgets were slashed, limiting their ability to monitor and enforce their regulations. Between 1981 and 1984, the budgets of regulatory agencies in the United States fell by 11 percent overall. The EPA's budget fell by 35 percent. The staff of the EPA was reduced from 14,075 to 10,392. Its referrals to the Justice Department for the prosecution of violators fell by 84 percent and the number of enforcement orders fell by 33 percent. The FDA budget was cut by 30 percent over this period and its enforcement orders declined 88 percent. "Between 1981 and 1984, the absolute number of regulations in the Federal Register declined by 25 percent, and since 1984, no new permanent regulatory department has been authorized or established by the federal government."[2] The decreased funding of these agencies and their new mandate to undertake a more collaborative (as opposed to the previous, presumably, confrontational) approach to their corporate clients have resulted in a regulatory environment in which businesses that are the subject of the regulation have considerable influence on the making and enforcement of the rules by which they are supposed to abide.

The same trend affected many industry-specific regulations designed to correct for problems particular to a specific sector. This was true in a wide variety of industries including accounting, energy, the media, and transportation, to name only a few. Chapter 7 provides more detail on the 2008 crisis, but it is crucial to point out that the deregulatory moves that led to the financial collapse were not single-sector anomalies but a much broader trend. *Consumer Reports* (*CR*) evaluated deregulation in several U.S. industries. Predictably for a magazine dedicated to customer satisfaction, its evaluation was based solely on criteria that would matter to consumers like prices, consumer rights, safety, choice, and innovation. Its conclusion was that, on balance, consumers have lost ground since deregulation began in the telephone, banking, electricity, television, and airline industries. Overall consumer prices often fell after deregulation, but they were falling for decades before, typically at a faster rate. In industries like telephones and electricity, where they have fallen, it was due to demands for price cuts by regulatory boards, not the actions of the free market. There has been a decrease in consumer choice in the airline, banking, and television industries, where fewer companies control a larger share of the market than prior to deregulation. Banking has been a disaster, with 1600 bank failures in the United States even before the financial crash of 2008 with its massive and growing cost to taxpayers. Deregulated airlines have given customers more connections, delays, cramped seats, and uncomfortable planes. According to *CR*, the marketplace has become more adversarial toward consumers. The absence of strict rules has inspired aggressive tactics and enabled sellers to gain disproportionate power over buyers. *CR* recommended more regulation and vigorous anti-trust enforcement in order to protect consumers from increasingly rapacious business practices.[3] Lack of industry-specific regulation has proved to be a problem even from the narrowly defined world of consumers, supposedly the ultimate beneficiaries of deregulation. If we expand this to include the decline in protective regulation that has led to pollution problems like global warming and occupational disease and injury, the accounting becomes even grimmer.

Government regulation, pilloried by conservatives as an overprotective state intervening between the firm and its clients to the detriment of corporate profitability and consumers' interests, can actually protect the profits of firms and the legitimacy of the economic system. There are many instances when the unrestrained pursuit of profits by one firm can actually damage the profitability of other firms. For example, if energy deregulation led to higher prices, this would help energy companies but would harm energy-using industries. Regulation may also foster long-term profitability even while it constrains short-term profits. For instance, the SEC is supposed to regulate the financial system in order to protect investment and maintain fair and efficient markets. As part of its job it attempts to ensure that corporate statements are truthful and accurate so that investors have confidence that they are not being swindled by corporate shenanigans. This certainly constrains short-term profitability by not allowing corporations to take advantage of investors, but it ensures long-term profitability by ensuring that people will continue to put money into the stock market. Less obviously, environmental protection regulations may reduce short-term profits by constraining the activity of firms, but if deregulated production creates environmental problems so costly and severe that they reduce the public's confidence in the economic system as a whole, regulation becomes necessary to maintain the long-term viability of the system. Of course, regulations must be limited in order to ensure profitability and corporate autonomy. Regulations that increase workers' power in the labor market by making it easier to form unions, or for unions to use their power, can constrain profits. The *Times* should have considerable sympathy for regulation of the first two forms, which are usually characterized as liberal policies. However, it should have a much more ambiguous attitude towards the third. While the *Times* may see unions as important in spreading the wealth, and therefore, vital to the long-term popular support of the economic system, if unions act in a manner that unacceptably decreases profits, the *Times* would be much less supportive. We have seen in Chapter 1 that it was eager to rid itself of its own union "burden" when profits were threatened and was highly critical of the powerful unions in Sweden.

We have chosen three examples of regulatory activity. The first is the California energy crisis in which industry deregulation provided an opportunity for companies to manipulate prices. This example will test the *Times'* coverage on an issue in which deregulation facilitated short-term profits for a small group of firms, but caused hardship for business more generally. It is also an interesting precursor to the economic crisis of 2008 in that industry pressure for deregulation produced catastrophic results. The second is the evolution of OSHA in the United States, which created a regulatory agency designed to ensure worker safety. This example was chosen to examine how the *Times* treated regulation in which the benefits went to American workers and the costs were born by business. Finally, we will look at how the *Times* reported on firms that broke the regulatory rules by examining its coverage of corporate crime. The purpose of this example is to examine the extent to which the *Times* covers corporate violations of all types of rules and regulations as a systemic problem, endemic to firms operating as profit-maximizing entities, as opposed to the individual malfeasance of a few rogue criminals in the boardroom. As we have done in previous chapters, we will begin with an introduction to the three issues.

Enron and the California Energy Crisis

From the summer of 2000 to the spring of 2001, the news was full of California's energy crisis. Rolling blackouts around the state forced production to shut down and households to temporarily come to grips with just how many of life's necessities depend on a properly functioning power grid. As California residents continued to struggle with an unreliable power supply and rising prices, the debate about just what caused this crisis got underway. The immediate response from the Republican White House was that this was evidence of a supply problem; specifically, that government's commitment to environmental protection and regulatory oversight was constraining the power industry from building new generating plants. The solution, logically enough, was to create incentives to increase supply, from removing environmental and regulatory hurdles to offering generous tax incentives for developing power sources.

As time went on, though, it began to appear as though the cause was more complicated. It eventually became clear that the energy crisis was less a result of government regulation than a consequence of deregulation. To make matters worse for the presidential line, it appeared as though the energy shortage was, in part, deliberately created by corporations with close ties to the White House, who, in fact, had lobbied for deregulation.

The market for energy in California was very complicated as a result of a previous partial deregulation. While wholesale prices (the price at which an energy utility buys) were not capped by the government, there was a ceiling on the retail price (the price that the utility could charge the consumer). This permitted proponents of deregulation, such as Vice President Dick Cheney and Jeffrey Skilling, who became CEO of Enron in February 2001, to argue that the problem was the remnants of the regulatory regime. This was Skilling's view of the causes of the crisis: "They have fixed prices to consumers and they've got a regulatory system that basically prohibits you from building new facilities. This is a deregulated market? Come on. Deregulate the market; open it up."[4]

To make matters worse, as part of the deregulation process, public energy utilities were forced to sell off their power plants to private owners. This was also done in other states that were implementing deregulation in the energy sector. However, these other states required the firms who bought this generating capacity to sign an agreement stipulating that a significant portion of the energy would be sold back to the utility or the consumers at a reasonable price. This did not happen in California.

The weather in 2006 exacerbated the problem. Electricity generated by hydro power depends on powerful river flows. When rivers are high, much more power is generated than when rivers are low. In past years, when Californians needed power, they could purchase it from neighbors in the northwest, but this was impossible in 2001 because low water levels led to a decline in hydroelectric power generated in these states, so there was little surplus available for export to California.

Notwithstanding the convoluted, partially unregulated electricity market and the unusual weather, there appears to be little question that energy companies, especially Enron, were manipulating the supply of energy during the "crisis," actually creating the blackout problem, in an effort to increase prices and their profits. Enron traders were actually caught on tape ordering power plants to shut down production. In addition, they bought energy inside California at capped retail prices, routed it outside the state, and then sold it back to California utilities at much higher "free market" prices. These practices led to the conviction of Tim Belden, head of Enron's trading office in Portland. He argued that he was merely doing his job: "I did it because I was trying to maximize profits for Enron."[5] According to U.S. Attorney Kevin Ryan, the question of whether the energy crisis was due, in part, to criminal activity on the part of energy companies could be answered "with a resounding yes."[6]

Contrary to what one would expect if the "few bad apples" theory were correct, price gouging was not an exclusive tactic of Enron. Employees of companies like Duke, Reliant, and Williams were also caught on tape ordering power stations to shut down and using more subtle techniques to withhold supply and increase prices. The lesson here is that when profits can be made from inconveniencing or harming others, neither altruism nor the competitive forces of the market are likely to protect the consumer.

Enron was active in influencing the political process to further its profit-maximizing objectives. Tellingly, Enron's contribution to the energy crisis and its resultant massive profits were made possible by deregulation, for which Enron itself had successfully lobbied. The energy sector has been very active in the political arena. Although donations have gone to both big U.S. parties, the Republicans and George

W. Bush have been the beneficiaries of most of the money, surely reflecting Bush's pro-industry policy stance, and perhaps reflecting Al Gore's tendency to write pro-environmental books. Seventy-five percent of Enron's $2.3 million political donations in 2000 (and 78 percent of the oil and gas industry's contributions) went to the Republican Party. While Enron CEO Kenneth Lay claimed that this involved no quid pro quo, he did get invited to private meetings with Vice President Dick Cheney, who headed the president's National Energy Policy Development group, and was touted as a favorite to become the secretary of energy.[7] Enron executives also met with Energy Secretary Spencer Abraham, who received campaign contributions from Enron in his former career as a senator.[8]

Lay was not alone in getting input into the president's energy policies. Other industry executives were also invited to meetings to discuss energy policy, although the vice president refused to make public the details or the participants. It is standard government practice to involve "stakeholders" in any decision-making process. It would have been surprising if a U.S. administration had implemented sweeping changes to its energy policy without consulting the industry. What makes this administration's industry meetings so remarkable is that it made virtually no effort to involve any other stakeholders such as consumers or environmental groups. The predictable result is that the federal energy policy reads very much like an industry wish list of regulatory changes. The National Energy Policy certainly focused very strongly on increasing the supply of traditional energy sources and claimed that regulation "has become overly burdensome."[9] According to Democrat Henry Waxman, "The policies in the White House energy plan do not benefit Enron exclusively. And some may have independent merit. Nonetheless, it seems clear that there is no company in the country that stood to gain as much from the White House plan as Enron."[10]

The Occupational Safety and Health Administration

People who claim "this job is killing me" may not know how right they are. According to the International Labor Organization, in the United States an average of more than 6000 workers a year died in work fatalities in the decade between 1992 and 2002.[11] This statistic only documents sudden violent deaths, like a mine collapse. Workers also die in much slower, more insidious ways, like black lung disease or exposure to asbestos. To provide some idea about the prevalence of this problem, one study found that in 1992 more than 60,000 disease fatalities could be traced to occupational causes. When injuries and illnesses were combined, the total cost in 1992 was estimated at $171 billion.[12] Workers have consistently lobbied the government for various forms of legislated protection from a variety of workplace hazards.

Conservative economists usually argue that government intervention to protect worker safety and health is unnecessary. The labor market represents a free exchange between the firm and the worker. In this context of free exchange, workers willingly undertake varying degrees of risk and are rewarded accordingly. Since workers are less likely to queue up for dangerous jobs, firms have to pay a higher wage to compensate for the more life-threatening nature of the work. The difference in the wage between a safe job and a dangerous job is called the "compensating differential" and it represents the cost of danger to the workers. If this compensating differential were greater than the cost of safety equipment that would eliminate the danger of the job, it would pay the employer to install the safety equipment. In a competitive labor market, where firms are competing for workers, regulating safety and health should not be necessary.

Other economists argue that this is not a particularly realistic model of the labor market. First, it neglects the fact that many workers may not accurately know what risks face them on the job, especially at the point when they are first taking the job and have not yet been fully exposed to their work environment. This asymmetry of information gives the employer the upper hand in the bargaining over employment conditions. Second, it also neglects the power relationship that exists in the labor market. Unless unemployment is very low, workers will have a justifiable fear of being without a job. Most workers have little in the way of savings to fall back on and no real source of non-work income other than whatever the state provides in terms of temporary unemployment insurance benefits. Firms, on the other hand, can usually choose from a substantial pool of reasonably similarly qualified applicants, even for dangerous jobs. If the market failures of information asymmetry and power are realistic features of the labor market, workers may well take jobs that put their safety at risk, either because they are not aware of the risks or they have little alternative if they want to put bread on the table, creating a logical case for regulatory intervention.

These two very contrasting models of the labor market yield very different conclusions about the usefulness of safety and health regulation. The performance of OSHA has been criticized from both of these perspectives. From the free-labor market conservative standpoint, OSHA is an "onerous ogre," which imposes costs on business with little benefit for workers. For example, a study by John Morrall found that the OSHA regulations on asbestos cost $89.3 million for every life saved and a proposed regulation on formaldehyde would cost an astronomical $72 billion per life.[13] Even for those who view each human life to be uniquely precious and "priceless," $72 billion might seem a little steep.

From the market-failure, more liberal, point of view, OSHA is a "toothless tiger," which fails to conduct sufficient monitoring and punishment to act as a suitable deterrent.[14] With its limited staffing levels, state-run OSHA enforcement could, on average, only inspect each workplace once every fifty-five years. The average federal fine for a "serious" violation in 1995 was $763 and the maximum fine was only around $7000.[15] The cost of violating OSHA rules is therefore remarkably small even in the unlikely event that a firm is caught, making it improbable that companies will abide by the regulations.

While they have very different opinions about the extent to which workers would benefit from a more vigorous OSHA, they do both agree that it would cost firms money. This fact would seem to be supported by the casual observation that firms almost universally oppose the introduction of safety and health rules, arguing that they will decrease profits and, therefore, investment and employment in a region. Take the lead industry, for example. Despite knowledge that lead probably caused serious health problems, the lead industry waged a six-decade-long battle to avoid regulatory oversight. Health problems associated with lead were discovered as early as 1908, when it was observed that workers in the lead industry were suffering unusually high incidences of a variety of horrible illnesses and premature deaths. Workers also found that their children had an alarming rate of birth defects. Painters, especially those working on interiors, also were frequently ill. Labor unions, especially craft unions in the painting trades, lobbied governments to ban the use of lead. In an effort to counter the growing pressure for a ban, the lead industry funded scientific studies to discredit the mounting evidence about the harmful effects of lead and lobbied governments not to intervene.[16]

From the perspective of society as a whole, these kinds of regulations may well be efficient in the sense that the overall benefits, in terms of reduced health care costs and lost incomes associated with workplace illness and injury, are greater than the costs. But businesses bear the costs and workers receive the benefits. To argue in favor of OSHA-type regulation is almost invariably to argue in favor of reducing the profitability of firms, at least in the short run.

Corporate Crime

When people think of crime they automatically think of theft and murder. After all, this is certainly the regular fare of the nightly news, on which a veritable procession of dangerous thugs and police tape are trotted across the nation's TV screens and newspapers. However, this sort of conventional crime is only one type of illegal activity. Occupational crime occurs when the law is broken in the activity of a legitimate profession. Because it is often committed by more affluent business people or professionals, it is commonly referred to as "white-collar" crime. Examples of this kind of crime would be an executive embezzling money from his corporation or a lawyer defrauding a client. Organizational crime, as the name implies, is carried out within a large organization. This often makes it difficult to pin on a single criminal, since the offense is often not carried out by one individual, but by an entire group of people from boards of directors to a large number of executives. Although unions and other organizations can commit this type of illegal activity, it has become synonymous with corporate crime.

Despite the public's growing concern with conventional crime, evidence suggests that corporate crime does far more societal harm. People are rightly frightened about the shocking violence of homicides, and the popular imagination is fueled by high-profile gun rampages. According to the U.S. Department of Justice, there were 17,000 homicides in the United States in 2005, which at almost 50 a day, is fairly alarming (although this is down from murder's early 1990s heyday of almost 25,000 in 1991).[17] Yet compared to the almost 70,000 deaths traced to workplace disease and injury (although obviously not all of these are criminal in the strictly legal sense), this seems relatively minor. The corporate death toll would mount if we added to this the number of people killed or harmed at the consumption end of the production process. Ford knowingly manufactured the Pinto when executives knew that its gas tank would be punctured with even the slightest rear impact. C.R. Bard pled guilty to conducting illegal experiments on people when it tested its unproven heart catheters, forcing at least ten patients into emergency surgery. In his testimony before the United States Senate Committee on finance, Dr. David Graham of the FDA estimated that the drug Vioxx had led to "excess" heart attacks in somewhere between "88,000 to 139,000 Americans. Of these, 30–40 percent probably died."[18] Worse, the maker of Vioxx, Merck, and management at the FDA knew about these potential dangers and attempted to cover up the scientific evidence that eventually led to it being pulled from the market in 2004. Finally, pollution erodes people's health, sometimes fatally. Two economists estimated the gross annual damages in 2002 from air pollution alone at somewhere between $71 and $277 billion in the United States.[19]

When people think about theft, they usually think about mugging or perhaps Bonnie and Clyde-style bank heists. The FBI estimated that the value of burglary and robbery in the United States was the not-inconsiderable sum of $3.8 billion.[20] However, corporations have a number of less dramatic ways of stealing money, including price fixing, issuing false accounting reports, unfair labor practices that reduce workers' wages, restraint of trade, and false or misleading advertising, to name but a few. In 1999, E F Hoffmann-La Roche was fined $500 million and BASF $225 million when they pled guilty to price fixing vitamins.[21] In 1996, the Daiwa Bank paid a $340 million fine when it pled guilty to defrauding bank regulators and covering up heavy securities losses. When Enron went bankrupt after massive accounting fraud, it wiped $63 billion off the stock market, including $800 million that was invested from its own employees' pensions.

Death and theft are not the only means through which corporations harm society with illegal activity. Pollution also imposes massive costs even when it has no direct impact on human health. Although the Exxon Valdez oil spill did not actually kill anyone or lift money from people's wallets, it did cause tremendous damage. The cost of cleanup and damage compensation was $3.8 billion (although in 1998 the U.S. Supreme Court slashed the punitive damages on the company from $2.5 billion to $500 million). Despite this disaster, in 2008 Exxon was still using the more spill-prone single-hulled tankers for many of its shipments rather than the safer double-hulled ships because they are about 20 percent cheaper, resulting in a savings of around $18 million in 2008.[22]

We have so far documented a few high-profile, big-money crimes. But these are not isolated events. Rather it is habitual behavior. Clinard and Yeager conducted a survey of 582 of the largest publicly owned companies in the United States to determine whether or not they had violated the laws of the land. Only counting those violations for which official government action was taken (which the authors argue is "the tip of the iceberg" since most violations are addressed without formal action), 60 percent of the firms had at least one violation and 42 percent had multiple charges. This is especially remarkable since the survey only accounted for a two-year time period between 1975 and 1976.[23] To put these numbers in perspective, imagine how busy the police would be if 60 percent of the general population were arrested and charged at least once every two years.

This is not due to the pathology of a few criminally negligent villains but is rather the inevitable result of the normal functioning of the economic system. In a particularly nice analogy, some years ago Bertholt Brecht's *Threepenny Opera* was playing at the Vivian Beaumont Theatre at Lincoln Center in New York. The opera basically puts the question "who is the bigger criminal, the bank robber or the bank owner?" in musical form in a dramatic critique of capitalism. Brecht wanted the villain of the piece, Mack, to look ordinary because, for Brecht, ordinary capitalism was criminal and pathological. However, the director ignored Brecht's instructions and had the Mack character look like a monster, to give the impression that he was different from a typical businessman. Speculation has it that this was a deliberate attempt to alter the opera to mollify corporate patrons like the Rockefellers who were likely to be in the Lincoln Center audience.

Enron was an excellent example of conservative deregulatory activity harming the corporate sector as a whole. While deregulation yielded tremendous short-term gains for specific energy companies that were politically very well connected, for California business more generally, the deregulatory policy was an absolute disaster. We would predict that in this situation the *Times* should favor the liberal regulatory policy. However, there would be nothing inevitable about this preference. If deregulation did, in fact, reduce costs, the *Times* would favor more conservative policies on this issue. The interesting issue is how the *Times* treats the misbehavior by energy corporations. Does it portray these firms as "bad apples," in some way exceptions from the general behavior of the corporate community, or does it interpret their actions in a more structural manner, linking them to the inherent logic of the economic system? This is particularly interesting given that the Enron story bore so many striking similarities to the financial industry crisis that will be discussed in Chapter 7, demonstrating that it was not an isolated event, but rather a recurring deregulatory tale.

The OSHA example was chosen to examine the *Times*' interpretation of regulation that explicitly favors workers over firms. The conservative position would be that this kind of regulation is unnecessary. Liberals would counter that because of some unique characteristics of the labor market, regulation can help protect workers.

In this case the liberal policy is more damaging to the broad interests of corporate America than the Enron example. While it is true that the liberal policy may be in corporations' long-run interests if the results of not having safety and health regulation are so catastrophic that workers begin to question the legitimacy of the economic system itself, we would hypothesize that the *Times* should take a fairly conservative stance on this issue.

Corporate crime can be portrayed in three ways. First, conservatives would likely downplay the extent of corporate crime, pointing out that the market can take care of the problem. Second, liberals would portray it as Brecht's director envisioned—the deviant behavior of a few monstrous individuals who need to be exposed for the villains they are in order to maintain the public's faith in the rest of the upstanding corporate community. Finally, it could be illustrated as Brecht himself wanted, as the regular functioning of a private, for-profit economic system. Our hypothesis about the *Times* as a gatekeeper of the long-term interest of U.S. business would imply a liberal perspective on this issue, castigating those who bring the system into disrepute with their misbehavior but insisting on the overall solidity of the economic structure despite the frequency of these violations.

The *Times*, Enron, and the California Electricity Crisis: News

Just prior to the crisis, the *Times*' reporting of the energy deregulation was very much in line with the conservative economic analysis of demand and supply. According to this theory, interventions in the market to control price will reduce supply, creating shortages and putting upward pressure on prices. The logical solution to this problem is removing government price controls and providing other incentives, like reduced environmental controls, to make supplying energy more profitable. The *Times* praised Germany's rapid deregulation from its previously inefficient state-controlled energy system, which it reported had resulted in consumer savings of 30 to 50 percent. Its new open market had also attracted new private companies, including Enron, looking to compete.[24] But deregulatory theory and the experience of other nations took a back seat to the events in California in 2000.

The commitment to deregulation and an emphasis on the lack of supply were constant elements of the *Times*' analysis as problems with California's energy system began to emerge. The *Times* reported that although politicians were backing away from deregulation because of soaring electricity prices and consumer backlash, this was a mistake because power companies and many economists argued that "price controls are a misguided and shortsighted measure that will increase the risk of blackouts both in the short run and the long run"[25] and that "most people believed that competition would lower prices for consumers and businesses alike."[26] If California was suffering in the summer of 2000, it was really just a case of rising demand outstripping an antiquated supply system.[27] Fortunately, "thanks to deregulation help is on its way," as privately owned companies rushed into the market to take advantage of the increasing prices.[28] Ironically, the *Times* held Enron to be one of the companies best positioned to take advantage of the new deregulated marketplace since they "have market intelligence that is second to none."[29] The *Times* later quoted an energy research associate who argued: "The greatest impediment to fixing its power problems were tough environmental problems and other regulatory hurdles."[30]

Even while admitting that there were problems with the California experiment in deregulation, the *Times* argued that this was a flaw in execution rather than concept. Texas was planning its own deregulatory move with more confidence since it supplied much more energy, in part because it did not impose California's tough environmental regulations.[31] What is interesting about the early days of the *Times*' reporting on this issue is that its default assumption was that there must be a flaw in the regulatory process rather than any wrongdoing by the corporate sector. Clearly there were flaws in the California partial deregulation, but even without these flaws, the market manipulation by energy firms would have created the crisis.

The *Times* did report that at least part of the problem was that there was a temporary reduction in energy supplied by power stations in California. Unfortunately, it was incorrect about the reason for the reduction. The original explanation for the decrease was that an unusually large number of the state's power generators were shut down for maintenance or to comply with air quality standards. On some days up to one-third of the power the state needed during peak wintertime hours was not available.[32] Loretta Lynch, president of the California Public Utilities Commission, was quoted as saying "We have the power, the question was why it was not available?"[33]

As the search for the cause of the crisis expanded beyond a few generating stations, two opposing explanations began to emerge. The first, which the *Times* reported through the views of economists, the White House, and the Republican Party, continued the conservative line that regulation caused the shortage. The second, which the *Times* associated with the views of consumer groups; the Democratic governor of California, Gray Davis; and the Democratic Party, made the liberal argument that it was elimination of price controls, lack of monitoring by federal agencies, and power company supply manipulation that were to blame. To provide just one example of an article that presented both perspectives as valid possibilities, when Davis complained of federal government unwillingness to enforce price controls to constrain the companies from charging unwarranted rates, the White House–appointed chairman of the Federal Energy and Commerce Committee (FERC) responded by saying price caps would "do nothing, not one single thing, to get one additional watt of electricity to California when it needs it most."[34] From the conservative perspective, the *Times* quoted then Vice President Dick Cheney, who argued that the only way to solve energy problems was to create incentives for companies to increase supply. Any impediments to supply, or demand reduction policies, would be ineffective: "Conservation may be a sign of personal virtue, but it cannot be the basis of a sound energy policy." The *Times* presented this quote as symbolic of the Republican Party's claim that there was no real reason for the energy crisis other than regulatory constraints to oil, gas, and coal exploration.[35] Representing the more liberal perspective, Davis accused Enron and other power companies of manipulating supply, stating at one time that Lay "should serve jail time."[36] The point here is that the news stories were not choosing between these competing explanations. Both were presented as equally convincing explanations of the crisis by people with conflicting ideas.

By the spring of 2001, the *Times* started to give more credence to consumer groups who were claiming that the real problem was not excess demand, but price gouging by energy companies.[37] However, even though prices during the emergency were an astonishing fifteen times higher than prior to the crisis, and the operators of California's power grid reported some evidence of overcharging, the *Times* was still unwilling to present this as anything more than a possibility, quoting one official as saying, "we can't say what amount is truly an overcharge."[38] The state of California certainly felt that it was being overcharged. In May 2001, it sued five power genera-tors and considered criminal charges against fourteen executives because they had "gouged the state by billions of dollars." In reporting this issue, the *Times* gave industry representatives ample opportunity for rebuttal. One of the firms called the lawsuit, "false, defamatory and without merit." A spokeswoman for Duke Energy added, "The people of California should know their politicians can't sue their way into additional power supply."[39]

After a federal judge ordered energy corporations to refund California for over-charging,[40] the *Times*' reporting on price gouging took a much more definitive turn, no longer requiring equal time for the energy companies' or the White House's conservative perspective. An article in November 2001 reported that despite the fact that California was using less electricity than it did in 1999 it was costing them $35 billion more. The reason, according to the *Times*, was that energy companies had shut down up to a third of their capacity, creating artificial shortages during which a desperate California locked itself into high-price long-term contracts that had nothing to do with the actual costs of production. The result was that Duke Energy charged the state $3,880 for a single megawatt hour that had cost about $30 a year earlier.[41] The *Times* had also changed its opinion of industry leaders like Enron, who it now accused of using its influence to corrupt the industry.[42]

This became even more the case after a Congressional hearing heard testimony that Enron was "engaged in sham transactions in late 2000 that drove up electricity prices and helped worsen the energy crisis."[43] As evidence mounted, and it became increasingly clear that the shortage was caused by deliberate, nefarious, illegal activ-ity, the *Times* became more critical, reporting that Enron "created the illusion of congestion on power lines by moving power back and forth across state lines."[44] It also followed the slew of charges and convictions of Enron traders closely. It left little doubt that the company was committing illegal acts and being justifiably punished.

It ran headlines like "Manipulated California Power and Lied to Investigators"[45] and ran the now infamous "Grandma Millie" transcript in which Enron traders joyously boasted about "screwing'" California.[46]

The energy industry quickly attempted to distance itself from Enron in an effort to portray the company as a lone "bad apple." The *Times* covered an industry conference in which companies worried that they would suffer guilt by association and claimed that "Enron was the failure of integrity at one company."[47] Of course, this theory became increasingly difficult to maintain as one company after another was accused of the same activities. In the words of Davis, it was "an industry-wide pattern of cheating and stealing,"[48] making the "Traders Deny Roles in California Power Crisis" headlines appear increasingly tongue in cheek.[49]

While it was the energy companies that were the common criminals, deregulation made for a less-than-vigilant police force. According to Joe Lieberman, "better investigation may well have exposed the cracks in Enron's foundation sooner."[50] Regulatory bodies were accused of lacking "bite" and being unwilling to impose sufficiently severe penalties to protect consumers.[51] In one particularly memorable quote, FERC "was supposed to be the cop on the beat here and they were off getting doughnuts."[52]

By this point the *Times* was no longer satisfied with treating the Democrat and Republican explanations as equally valid. Since it was patently deregulation that permitted companies to engage in their illegal activity, some explanation was needed about why such a harmful policy was pursued. The answer was partly that it dovetailed nicely with the economic ideology of the White House, but perhaps more importantly Enron and other energy companies had inside access to the president. The *Times* reported that the Democratic senator for California, Dianne Feinstein, had questioned the intimate relationship between the federal regulator, FERC, and Kenneth Lay of Enron.[53] The paper also claimed that Enron "enjoyed unalloyed lobbying success in Washington."[54] But it was not only in the nation's capital that Enron was successfully banging on government doors. "When it came to lobbying the Enron Corporation and Kenneth Lay, its former chairman, were about as persistent as anyone had ever seen in California—or Texas, Tennessee, Oregon and Pennsylvania."[55]

The failure of a deregulatory regime that was the result of heavy lobbying by an industry with a vested stake in the outcome gave the logic for regulation renewed credibility in the *Times'* reporting. According to Democrat Edward Markey, "We can't leave energy products in the regulatory shadows."[56] In fact, the take-home message of the Enron-California debacle became that "starchy government regulators" were in, while "blow dried, hipster capitalists" were out, as "an unrestrained power industry isn't so appealing anymore."[57] Even price controls, much maligned as a disincentive for energy production prior to the Enron scandal, received a new lease on life. The *Times* credited price controls with halting the price increases caused by Enron's energy manipulation and blamed federal regulators for not imposing controls more quickly.[58]

Finally, the *Times* managed to hit on the appropriate lesson from this debacle. The normal functioning of profit maximizing corporations in a deregulated energy industry was disastrous. "Energy markets remain susceptible to manipulation at the hands of traders doing what traders do—exploiting loopholes and inefficiencies to maximum gain."[59] In a remarkable turnaround from its reporting in the early part of the crisis, economists were derided for being the cheerleaders of deregulation. One article quoted an economist's claim that "unfettered competition achieved through deregulation tends to lower prices and promote efficiency and innovation" only to take the reader on a tour through the devastation and inefficiency wrought by deregulation in a variety of industries including telecommunications and accounting.[60] A subsequent article nicely summed up the *Times'* conclusion on energy regulation with a quote from George Akerlof, "If you let your toddler out of the playpen, you need to watch her more carefully."[61]

The evolution of the *Times'* reporting on this issue demonstrates that it is not wedded to either a conservative or liberal position. Prior to the crisis, it suggested that the United States might benefit from deregulation. In the early days of the blackouts, it argued that the cause was a textbook economic case of demand exceeding supply, at least in part because of a regulatory anchor holding back investment in generating facilities. Given its reputation for investigative journalism, it is remarkable that the *Times* accepted this conservative line so uncritically in the early days of the crisis. Only when California politicians and consumer groups started to claim that the cause of the crisis was corporate misbehavior permitted by deregulation did the *Times* start to question the White House's regulatory supply-side explanation. Indeed, it stuck by its "balanced" approach even as evidence against the power companies mounted. However, once the "smoking gun" was produced, the *Times* became a fervent supporter of a return to a more regulated environment and wanted the corporate criminals appropriately disciplined.

This nicely reflects the *Times'* role as guardian of the overall interests of the business class. Their interest in increasing power supply in a deregulatory context lasted until they became convinced that this policy was in fact harming business. They ran several stories highlighting the difficulties for companies as diverse as Land O'Lakes,[62] dot.com firms,[63] and small businesses[64] during the peak of the crisis. When it became clear that what was happening was a specific group of companies profiting through illegal means, at the expense of the rest of the business community, the *Times* demanded strong disciplinary action and a return to a more regulated industry.

The *Times*, Enron, and the California Energy Crisis: Op-eds

As we have noted elsewhere, starting in the late 1990s the *Times* moved away from having outside experts contribute its opinion pieces to a more in-house style, where its own columnists take center stage. Of the thirty-five articles, twenty-five were written by staffers, with Paul Krugman featuring especially prominently. In contrast to many of the other issues covered previously, there was no column space dedicated to industry representatives looking to present their side of the story.

As was the case with the news articles, the *Times* columns on this subject presented deregulation as a possible, although hardly guaranteed, improvement on a regulated market. Staff writer Alex Berenson argued that although California's deregulation had produced shortages and price spikes, deregulatory proponents argued that this was a difficulty unique to California due to its lack of investment in power plants and rapid economic growth. Further, deregulation would solve this problem when planned private investment in generating facilities came on line. According to Enron boss Skilling, "Within two or three years the problem will be fixed." However, Berenson also presented the skeptic's view that the structure of the energy industry, which has no substitutes, wildly fluctuating demand, and an inelastic supply, makes it susceptible to price gouging through market manipulation, "with the possibility of windfall profits every time there is a hot summer."[65]

Early on in the crisis, the *Times*' columns gave considerable space to the proponents of deregulation. The deregulatory cause was taken up by William Safire in his typically bombastic style. He argued that "left coast" Californians were to blame for their energy problems after years of "not in my backyard" environmental concerns had caused a lack of generating capacity. Given this source of the problem, re-regulation may "please some new breed of dot-communists, but such populist pap destroys the private incentive to invest." Rather the state should "get out of the way of stimulating supply."[66] In a more guarded tone, University of California professor and author of a very widely used microeconomics text Hal Varian took up the excess demand tale. "The reason for the California electricity crisis can be summed up in four words: demand grew, supply didn't." The solution was logically "increased attention to conservation and bringing more supplies online."[67] If California's move to a free market seemed to have produced unfortunate results, the problem was its particularly chaotic implementation, not deregulation, which was not "some harebrained scheme." Rather it was built on solid economic theory and the positive experience of Britain in the 1990s.[68] This argument was made plausible given California's partial deregulation discussed earlier, but it did not fit well with the final evidence of price manipulation, which was the real culprit.

On the other hand, Paul Krugman was quick to speculate that the real culprit was energy company exploitation of a deregulated environment. "You don't have to be a conspiracy theorist to wonder whether there are some perverse incentives when an industry dominated by a few large players finds it hugely profitable not to invest."[69] By the spring of 2001 Krugman was convinced the California crisis was the product of corporate larceny aided and abetted by FERC's free-market ideology. He argued that given the structure of the deregulated industry, "to believe that the generators didn't engage in market manipulation you have to believe that they are either saints or very bad businessmen because they would have been passing up an obvious opportunity to increase their profits." In direct opposition to conventional economic theory, price caps "might actually increase supplies because power companies would no longer have an incentive to withhold electricity."[70] He even took pains to point out that this was much more than a case of a single immoral firm. "The great risk now will be that this will be treated as purely as an Enron story."[71] The summer of 2001 did not produce a repeat of the energy problems in California, something that probably should have happened if the conservative "demand outpacing supply" theory had been correct. Krugman argued that the reason for the pleasantly uneventful summer was that more of California's generating capacity had remained on line in 2001 compared to 2000 due to "the recent decision by federal regulators to impose price caps."[72]

The White House insistence on the benefits of deregulation despite all evidence to the contrary was the result of both personal connections and successful industry lobbying, a point Krugman repeatedly hammered home, arguing that energy companies "wrote Mr. Cheney's energy plan."[73] As the extent of the price manipulation became clear in 2003, Krugman wrote a column in which he admitted he was "patting myself on the back for getting it right." He also took time to mock the now thoroughly discredited White House, which concluded that the crisis was caused "by meddling bureaucrats and pesky environmentalists who weren't letting big companies do what needed to be done." This conclusion could only come from a man "who drew his advice about how to end the energy crisis from the very companies creating the crisis."[74]

While Krugman was certainly the point man for the price-gouging theory, as the crisis wore on the *Times* marshaled others who argued for a return to price caps and a more regulated industry. According to Michael Weinstein of the Council on Foreign Relations, respectable economists argued that because it is impossible to store electricity it is prone to market manipulation, so price controls will force more of the available electricity onto the market.[75] Even Davis was granted column space to say "I told you so" after the Enron smoking gun memos came to light. "A year ago, we in California stood virtually alone when we charged that Enron and possibly others were ripping off California consumers. The energy industry scoffed, saying the charge was paranoid."[76]

The op-eds followed roughly the same trajectory as the news stories. Deregulatory advocates received ample opportunity to tell their supply constraint story in the early days. However, mostly due to the influence of Krugman's writings, the op-ed section gave more credence to the price manipulation accusations at an earlier date.

The *Times*, Enron, and the California Energy Crisis: Editorials

The *Times*' editorial page did not wade into the energy crisis until well after its newsroom. While the newsroom was still giving equal weight to Davis' allegations of corporate supply manipulation and Bush's regulatory burden explanation, the editorial page took the line that deregulation was not the problem, but that California's particular style of partial deregulation certainly was. "While other states had embarked on deregulation plans with initially favorable results," California's policies were "colossally wrongheaded," featuring "gross miscalculations of the likely demand of electricity and a failure to build any new generating plants."[77]

The editorial page was, however, fairly quick to jump on price caps as at least a temporary solution to the crisis. Even while still under the misapprehension that it was the "imbalance between supply and demand that lies at the root of the crisis," the editorial page called for a cap to relieve California of its massive energy bills.[78]

Unlike the news section, editorials rapidly dismissed the White House interpretation of the crisis. A January 2001 editorial argued that using the energy crisis as an excuse to roll back environmental regulations on energy production, including restrictions on Arctic drilling, was "wholly specious."[79] When Enron was finally caught red-handed manipulating power, the *Times* used the California energy crisis to demonstrate the flaws in the White House energy plan, which it described as "nonsense."[80] According to the editorials, the Bush energy plan seemed tailored to satisfy the ambitions of the oil, gas, and coal industries, either by easing environmental rules or by opening public lands for aggressive exploration.[81] The editorial page argued that one of the lessons of the Enron mischief was that "in Washington it is considered perfectly 'appropriate' for officials to grant access to a company that used vast campaign donations to influence policy."[82]

Armed with overwhelming evidence that companies manipulated the energy market, the *Times*' editorials demanded justice. California should not only be "fairly" compensated for the overcharges but penalties should also be "big enough to send a message about energy suppliers' responsibility to play fair."[83]

Federal policy should be dramatically reversed. "It is Washington's duty . . . to devise the necessary safeguards. Electricity is a public necessity that must be managed wisely, not entrusted blindly to the markets."[84] In 2004 the *Times* called for a unified national policy on energy and conservation to prevent companies fleeing regions of high regulation for those with lax environmental policies.[85]

In one sweeping editorial the *Times* publicized a study by the "anti-regulatory" Office of Management and Budget that demonstrated that over the ten years 107 different government regulations produced between $100 and $200 billion more in benefits than costs. With billions saved in terms of fewer premature deaths, hospitalizations, emergency room visits, and lost work days, this evidence conclusively demonstrated the error of Bush's deregulatory ways.[86]

Again, we see the now familiar trajectory of the *Times*' coverage of this story. The supply constraint story gave way to a realization that there were corporate shenanigans, leading to a call to punish the energy company offenders. Unlike the news stories, the *Times*' editorial page was a pulpit from which to denounce the

White House's energy policy in general and their hypothesized connection between environmental regulations and California's energy crisis in particular.

The *Times* and OSHA: News

The *Times* consistently reminded its readers that the workplace was an unnecessarily dangerous place. One prominent voice for this concern was Ralph Nader, who, as early as 1971, criticized the safety record at U.S. firms, claiming that there were "14,000 traumatic fatalities on the job" compared to "7,000 nonkinship homicides."[87] The *Times* was concerned that "toxic industrial chemicals, dust, radiation, heat, and cold kill 100,000 persons a year and are responsible for the development of occupational diseases in 390,000 more."[88] In another rather remarkable story, the *Times* reported on the dramatic increase in cancer rates in the 20th century. "Somewhere between 60 percent and 90 percent of these cases, scientists now believe, are triggered by substances in the environment of America, many of which originally are generated in the workplaces regulated by OSHA." "The human anguish behind these statistics is impossible to quantify."[89] This concern is consistent throughout the thirty years of reporting on OSHA. In 1996, the *Times* ran a story documenting the tragedies of workers who were killed under the attention-grabbing headline "One Day's Death Toll on the Job."[90] The *Times* also frequently reported on the dangers in specific occupations, from migratory farm workers[91] to meatpacking[92] to the federal government, where "the costs of worker sickness and injury are skyrocketing."[93] It also constantly reminded its readers of the specific dangers that plague broad sections of the working population from on-the-job hazards of chemicals[94] to repetitive strain injuries.[95]

An indication of the *Times*' support for a more vigorous OSHA was its favorable reporting on Dr. Eula Bingham, who ran the agency between 1977 and 1981 under Carter, or as the *Times* dubbed her, "The woman who turned OSHA around." When Charles L. Schultze, "the influential chairman of the Council of Economic Advisers" wanted "to regulate industry through economic incentives rather than through specific rules and standards" the *Times* was supportive of Bingham's opposition to his position. "The idea of using workers' bodies to drive the wheel is a philosophy untenable to me. I am in the business or preventing sickness and injury, not using bodies to drive up the cost so that business will find it more profitable to comply."[96] Similarly, when the *Times* reported that the progress in reducing job-related injuries and illnesses was sluggish despite stepped-up federal efforts to protect worker safety and health, it quoted Dr. Bingham, who argued that is was time for OSHA to "commit ourselves to an all-out effort to assure working men and women no longer must trade their lives, limbs or health for a paycheck."[97]

If the workplace was a minefield of unknown dangers for the American worker, OSHA was supposed to keep the problems from exploding. Unfortunately, it was never really up to the task. The *Times* almost constantly viewed OSHA as a toothless tiger rather than an onerous ogre. In 1971 it ran a story in which Nader blamed the limited implementation of OSHA for the prevalence of workplace disasters and suggested that the agency should levy substantially heavier fines on dangerous companies. "The least we can do is pull such companies down to the zero profit level to stop this."[98] Later, the Reagan administration was described as "anti-regulation" by the Brookings Institution for its failure to use good scientific analysis in making regulatory rules on health and safety.[99]

The reason for OSHA's lack of bite was attributed to opposition from an obstinate business community and its Republican allies. In the early days of the agency, the *Times* quoted Nader's claim that the OSHA Act was being "turned into a farce" by providing "maximum relief for employers."[100] OSHA's efforts to protect workers were made considerably more difficult by the numerous obstacles strewn in their path by determined Republican actions to undermine the agency. The *Times* suggested that Republicans were exaggerating the cost of complying with OSHA regulations, including false charges that companies were being forced out of business by the new safety regulations.[101] The paper also criticized the Nixon White House for placing the blame for worker health problems on the carelessness of workers themselves. "Scientists now believe that 90 percent of cancer is caused by conditions in the environment but the White House blames accidents on the workers."[102]

This is not to say that the concerns of business were always dismissed as "crying wolf." The *Times* did frequently place the potential costs of safety and health regulation alongside its potential benefits, especially in the late 1970s and early 1980s when regulation was frequently scorned as one of the causes of the American stagnation. The most commonly cited dangers of regulatory oversight were "inflation,"[103] a decline in "industrial capacity,"[104] or violating companies' rights.[105] However, these articles were all balanced in the sense that they presented both the labor and business perspective on the issue. Even when the cost concerns of business were reported, the *Times* pointed out that OSHA had a small impact on "companies' overall expenditures for worker health and safety."[106] Further, the headlines of these articles often leaned towards labor instead of business. For example, one headline read: "Senator Is Outraged by Proposal to Ease Job Safety Efforts,"[107] another "Panel Urges Strict Regulation of Perilous Chemicals."[108]

The emphasis on the costs of OSHA gained temporary prevalence in the late 1970s and early Reagan years. Cutbacks in OSHA oversight were celebrated as "taking the shackles off business."[109] Under a headline proclaiming that "the heyday is over" for OSHA, the *Times* ran a quote from the director of the National Federation of Independent Business claiming, "OSHA is the worst four letter swear word in small business's vocabulary" because of its excessively bureaucratic regulations.[110] Soon after, the *Times* ran an article on Reagan's efforts to trim regulatory agencies that cited Murray Weidenbaum, the chairman of the Council of Economic Advisers, who conducted a study while at Washington University that concluded all government regulations cost the economy $125 billion. What is interesting about this unqualified reporting is that this same study was harshly criticized by Nader and the *Times* only a few years before.[111]

This pro-business, anti-regulation trend quickly returned to a more balanced approach that gave more or less equal weight to Reagan's desire for a more cost-competitive regulatory regime and labor's argument for worker protection. Articles headlined "Pressure Grows to Alter Rules on Worker Safety"[112] and "Safety Agencies Find Their Common Ground Eroding"[113] were carefully structured to present "for" and "against" arguments on Reagan's plan to "streamline" OSHA regulations. Similarly, a *Times* article on the debate about regulating cotton dust, which causes brown lung, in the textile industry reported Democrat Al Gore's claim that the "great weight" of scientific evidence supports regulatory protection. The story also gave equal space to business claims that the regulation would be too costly at "more than $380,000 for each case of brown lung disease avoided."[114]

After a few years of Reagan regulatory cutbacks the *Times* returned to its more unequivocal support of a stronger OSHA. Headlines like "Nader Says OSHA Shackled Now,"[115] "Reagan Plan on Labeling Hazards Is Drawing Fire,"[116] "Study Links Workplace Deaths and Lax Criminal Prosecution,"[117] "Who's Making the Rules?"[118] "Are Federal Regulators Falling Down on the Job?"[119] and "Study Faults US on Safety Effort"[120] underscored reporting about the dangers of regulatory retrenchment. A story about Boyden Boyle, whose job in the Reagan administration was to get "Government off the backs of the people," quoted Joan Claybrook, president of Public Citizen, who claimed "I think he's a fine example of the fox guarding the chicken coop."[121] That same year the *Times* quoted Congressional Democrat David Obey's criticism of Reagan's OSHA director: "If he's telling us that he knows that workers are going to die, and yet he is not moving because OSHA doesn't have enough money, and then he stays within his current budget. That's outrageous."[122] By 1985 the *Times* was reporting critically on the low morale of OSHA employees forced to work under Reagan appointees who cared little for its safety mandate and who felt that the agency was "full of commies."[123] The *Times* also reported on a study very critical of OSHA for substantially reducing fines for firms found violating job safety rules, blaming lax enforcement for "9,115 worker fatalities."[124] Another story quoted a Chamber of Commerce economist who credited the Reagan OSHA because it, "really for its first time, has acceptance in the business community" but countered by quoting a former Republican head of OSHA who warned that "there's very little enforcement going on," and another critic: "Regulatory reform doesn't have to mean regulatory euthanasia."[125]

Clinton's ascendancy to the presidency marked a brief period of optimism, during which the *Times* hoped for a more rigorous OSHA. The paper celebrated with the headline, "Breathing New Life into OSHA," which had high hopes for an organization that was "orphaned during the Reagan years," but "the agency now gets support from the top."[126] The *Times* supported its hope for a new, stronger OSHA by exposing the misinformation that was being spread about OSHA regulations by conservative members of Congress, calling them "stories stranger than truth, because there's little truth in them." One of the more outrageous claims, made by "anti-regulation crusader" Republican David McIntosh, was that OSHA was forcing dentists "to confiscate all of the teeth that they pull."[127] However, the Clinton version of OSHA proved to be little different from the previous Republican administrations', a trend that did not escape the notice of the *Times*. As early as 1995, a year and a half into his presidency, the *Times* ran a story criticizing the Clinton administration for balking on regulations to protect workers from repetitive strain injuries because of pressure from business groups and the Republican Congress.[128] Four years later, the *Times* charged Clinton's OSHA with conducting the fewest inspections since the agency's inception in 1971.[129]

One important indication of the *Times*' pro-labor position on health and safety was its position on cost-benefit analysis, the favorite defense of business. Cost-benefit analysis is frequently used to demonstrate that the costs to business of any proposed regulation will exceed the benefits in worker health. Of course, these sorts of studies are very sensitive to the assumptions chosen by their authors—a point that did not escape the *Times* when it came to health and safety in the workplace. In one article, entitled "Did Industry Cry Wolf," the *Times* reported that when industry was forced to comply with health and safety rules, "not one of their doomsday predictions had proved accurate."[130] The *Times* repeatedly favored labor's cost-benefit accounting over that of business on this issue. When the *Times* reported on a Nader study that concluded that government health and safety regulations provided Americans with $35 billion in benefits in 1979 and would produce $80.6 billion in 1985, it took the opportunity to dismiss rival studies by business groups as "ideological arithmetic." One such study (uncritically cited by the *Times* two years later) was written by the Center for the Study of American Business, which "received almost $700,000 in a single year from business and corporate foundations cast(ing) doubts on the independence of [Nader's] research."[131] When proposed OSHA regulations were delayed in 1992 because of a cost-benefit finding that regulations might result in lower incomes for workers and therefore lead to worse health outcomes, the *Times* quoted a past president of the American Public Health Association, Dr. Anthony Robbins, who said that he would like to close down the cost-benefit office so that "the economists who daily manipulate data and revel in mischievous speculation could be sent to work on ships, constructing buildings, and harvesting crops."[132]

Many articles presented both sides of the health and safety story. Business seemed to gain a more favorable hearing in the late 1970s and early 1980s. However, the overwhelming tone was that workers were dying on the job. Two articles sum up the *Times*' news stories on the issue. The first was a report on a study done at MIT on workplace danger, which "is more widespread than almost anyone had thought." "A significant proportion of heart disease, cancer and respiratory disease may stem from the industrial process," according to Dr. Nicholas A. Ashford. Unlike previous studies, which were largely a recounting of "horror stories," the MIT book presented the "sober analysis of the technical, legal, economic and political sides of the problem." In response to critics who argued that the costs of ridding the workplace of chemical, biological, and stress hazards outweigh the benefits, Dr. Ashford argued that "the occupational setting can be made much safer and much healthier than it presently is—in my view at small long-term costs."[133] The second article was a story on the history of worker health and safety. The *Times* argued that not only were industry's claims of onerous compliance costs usually way off target, but that even OSHA tended to overestimate the costs of implementing its rules. Case after case indicated that business was able to make workplaces safer for a fraction of the costs that were anticipated because when they were forced to innovate by a regulatory push, firms pared "millions of dollars off the estimated compliance costs."[134]

The *Times* and OSHA: Op-eds

A simple examination of their choice of op-ed contributors does reveal a slight preference for the pro-regulation perspective. Thirteen articles were written by authors who could be assumed to be in favor of the regulatory approach (Democratic politicians, union representatives, and liberal think tanks like Public Citizen). On the other hand, seven were written by those who would be assumed to approve of a lighter regulatory touch (Republicans and business executives).

Mirroring the trajectory in its news reporting, *Times'* op-eds were much more critical of OSHA's regulatory role in the late 1970s and the very early years of the Reagan administration. A column in 1979 by the president of the American Cyanamid Company argued, "No one is against truly beneficial regulation. However, we must all be wary of allowing our regulatory agencies to demand that we spend enormous sums in return for very slight improvements in health or environment." "I do not think it is too much to ask that our regulatory agencies present us with convincing figures so that we can fully support those programs that give us the greatest return in benefits."[135] A 1980 op-ed argued that the weight of regulations was dragging down U.S. business. For example, OSHA standards on benzene cost "$300 million to save one life."[136] Aside from this brief two-year time period, there was only one more example of this type of column, when an op-ed headlined "Who Will Regulate the Regulators" expressed fears of a return to a stricter regulatory environment under Clinton.[137]

Before and after this period, even articles portraying regulations as overzealous pointed out that a deregulated environment would be deadly. In 1976 *Times'* writer

Steven Rattner documented the growing dissatisfaction with the burden of government regulation that was influencing "virtually every facet of public life." His *Sunday
Magazine* article quoted deregulatory enthusiast Weidenbaum who claimed that the
overall bill for regulation was over $100 billion, contributing substantially to infla-
tionary pressure. The column was also peppered with pithy examples of nonsensical
regulations like this gem from Maryland: "State law requires hospitals to keep hot
water in patient's rooms at no less than 110 degrees while a federal regulation requires that it be kept at no more than 110 degrees." Despite the very critical nature
of the article, Rattner was careful to point out that what was needed was regulatory
reform, not deregulation. After all, the reason that OSHA was founded in the first
place was the "failure of business to protect its workers" without regulation. As a
result he was delighted with the regulatory reforms brought in by Bingham, whom
he credited for getting rid of many of the overly officious rules while imposing stiff
penalties on serious corporate offenders.[138] Similarly, when the Reagan administration was weakening OSHA rules on chemicals in order to reduce compliance costs,
a column was careful to point out that "one in every four workers (is) exposed daily
to 8,000 identifiable chemical hazards."[139]

One strategy was to have two opposing views square off in adjacent columns to
present balance on the regulation issue. In 1982, William Winpisinger, president of
the International Association of Machinists and Aerospace Workers, wrote "never
before has an Administration stacked a Labor Department (in which OSHA is
situated) so heavily against labor and so mightily in favor of management." Immediately below, the vice president of industrial relations at Asarco Inc. (a mining and
smelting company) responded that Reagan's deregulatory move has been done in
an "evenhanded and judicious manner while eliminating waste and duplication and
emphasizing greater cost effectiveness."[140]

The *Times'* columnists certainly left their readers in no doubt that the world of
work was fraught with hazards. A 1974 op-ed on the history of the battle waged by
public health experts and unions against corporations and their hired research guns
claimed that "the World Health Organization estimates that 75–85 percent of all
cancers are triggered by environmental agents such as industrial chemicals. Since
1945, these agents have increased dramatically." "Even the families of some workers
are endangered by occupational diseases."[141] A later column accused the asbestos
industry of "disabling and killing thousands of people."[142] New School economist
David Gordon described the increased incidence of workplace injuries since 1965 as
an "epidemic."[143] *Times'* columnist Bob Herbert depicted UPS as a "grim and often
dangerous place to work."[144]

Given the overwhelming dangers at work, even seemingly sizeable regulatory
costs can be overwhelmed by the benefits of reducing worker injuries. According to
the director of the American Labor Education Center, "employers have been unable
to keep workplaces safe," resulting in an estimated direct cost of workplace injuries
of $21 billion in 1978. Business opposition to OSHA was a "smokescreen for more

fundamental objections to paying the cost of preventing work-related injuries and illnesses."[145] A year later, John B. Richer Jr., the president of the Continental Corporation, argued that complaints by the Chamber of Commerce about the costs of OSHA did not stand up to close scrutiny. Although the cost of OSHA's regulation was about $2.5 billion a year, this was only about 11 percent of the estimated "$23 billion that workplace accidents cost the United States in the form of lost wages, medical expenses, insurance claims, and diminished productivity during 1978." "Spending $2.5 billion to reduce a $23 billion problem does not seem excessive." He also dismissed the argument that OSHA's regulations contributed to inflation. "To the extent that OSHA has helped to prevent accidents, it has thereby served as a check on inflation" by keeping costs down.[146]

As was the case with the news articles, a couple of years of Reagan's deregulatory push resulted in a renewed appreciation of the old regulatory days at the *Times*. Two Nader researchers lamented that safety and health regulations were being dismantled by "OSHA, industry's new friend."[147] Later in 1983 a lengthy piece in the *Sunday Magazine* claimed "the child-labor laws would never have passed a cost-benefit test" that the Reagan presidency had imposed on regulators as a condition to establish new rules. A large sidebar in the column proclaimed Al Gore's opinion that "this administration's No. 1 priority is to make certain that no industry is in any way displeased or even slightly disconcerted by any action of government."[148] The next day, Mark Green of Democracy Project accused Reagan of "comforting the comfortable and afflicting the afflicted." According to Green, under Reaganomics OSHA citations for violations fell by 49 percent, follow-up inspections by 55 percent, and fines by 77 percent.[149] *Times'* columnist Anthony Lewis also indicted the Republican Congress for cutting OSHA's budget and forbidding it to "enforce job safety rules disliked by home builders."[150]

The *Times* and OSHA: Editorials

The editorials were perhaps a little more sensitive to the regulatory burden than either the regular reporting or the op-eds. "More Safety, Less Government" headlined an article that claimed OSHA was "federal bureaucracy at its worst," dedicated to enforcing ridiculously inappropriate regulation about the "shape of toilet seats." The editorial went on to endorse making employers responsible for accidents through the full cost of accident insurance rather than using the more conventional tools of regulation.[151] A couple of years later an editorial moderated this claim slightly, arguing that although OSHA had "squandered most of its resources on identifying safety hazards" that could be dealt with using financial incentives, direct regulation was necessary for health issues in the workplace because the link between workplace hazards and human health is so difficult to prove.[152] When a John Birch Society member used the Supreme Court to keep OSHA inspectors out of his shop, it was called "a symbolic triumph."[153] An editorial titled "So It's a Carcinogen, But How Bad?" asserted that hundreds of millions of dollars were spent to meet regulations that "might save two lives every six years." The problem, according to the editorial, was that "some regulators mindlessly treat any exposure to carcinogens as intolerable."[154] The Carter administration was credited for reigning in overzealous regulatory agencies, making them "far less likely to be a drag on productivity or prosperity."[155] A slightly more cautious editorial argued that "when inflation and safety collide" profits should not necessarily triumph over the health of the most vulnerable workers. However, regulators should be very explicit about how much improvement in health has cost in terms of inflation.[156]

This is not to say that the perspective of the editorial page was in sharp conflict with the other sections of the paper. The editorial page was quick to draw attention to the health consequences of a toothless OSHA. The Ford administration was chastised for ignoring the health of workers. Ford's government had "been disgracefully negligent up to now in enforcing the law; to worsen that miserable record in the interest of winning corporate campaign support is an insupportable sacrifice of employee health as well as a breach of legal obligation."[157]

As was the case with the other sections, the benefits of regulation became increasingly clear to the *Times'* editorial page after a few years of Reagan's animosity to the agency. Editorials placed much of the blame for this with the Reagan appointees in charge of OSHA. Thorne Auchter was flogged for "undoing" the job of protecting workers. His lax, business-friendly environment "imperiled lives and particularly [the] health" of American workers, according to the *Times*.[158] Reagan's "hostility to health and safety regulation" was "inexcusable."[159] OSHA was compromised by its desire to "burden business with few regulations." It may have been "too much to expect the Administration to show zeal for the agency, but how about honorable professionalism?"[160] "Perhaps the best that can be said of Robert Rowland's performance as the head of the Occupational Safety and Health Administration is that he knew when to leave." Hopefully, his departure would pave the way for a "conscientious professional dedicated to enforcing the law."[161]

The editorial page was also not shy about fingering specific companies and industries as examples of corporations' willingness to sacrifice people for profits under a lax OSHA regulatory environment. When grain elevator explosions killed 50 and sent 50 more to the hospital in one week, the editorial page proposed a remedy: "Perhaps steeper fines would be an inducement to putting safety first."[162] A 1979 editorial exposed Cyanamid for operating a plant where women of childbearing age were barred because of the toxic chemicals prevalent in the workplace (although later in 1979, a Cyanamid executive received op-ed space to defend the company).[163] The limited enforcement budget at OSHA resulted in twenty-one deaths "in explosions at a fireworks factory that OSHA didn't even know existed."[164] Whirlpool was chastised when two workers refused to work on a wire mesh platform twenty feet high where only a week earlier another employee had fallen to his death; "Workers could have been left to choose between risking their lives and their jobs."[165] An editorial exposed Union Carbide when its workers were assigned to sniff for phosgene gas (in World War I it was known as mustard gas) after alarms indicated a leak.[166] The plight of migratory agricultural workers was particularly galling to the editorial page. It pleaded for OSHA to set standards that would guarantee farm workers basic human dignity at work. According to one editorial, one third of workers had no toilet access, one fifth no place to wash the pesticide residue off their hands, and one half did not have access to drinking water.[167]

On those few occasions when OSHA actually passed stronger rules or penalized firms, the editorial page was unanimously positive. When OSHA imposed a $1.5 million fine on Chrysler and an official claimed that the agency was "approaching its duties with a new vigor" an editorial greeted this turn of events as "good news."[168] Given OSHA's largely toothless history, even the merest hint of stronger regulatory action was portrayed as a step toward greater worker protection by the *Times*. According to one editorial, a bill to establish a panel to identify workers most likely to be exposed to hazardous substances "could ease the minds and maybe lengthen the lives of thousands of American workers."[169]

The overall consensus of the editorial page was perfectly epitomized in a column that declared in a moment of utopian fervor: "In no case can the health of workers be sacrificed to profits."[170]

The *Times* and Corporate Crime: News

The search for corporate or white-collar crime generated only 116 articles over a fifty-year period, far fewer than most of the other topics. For the purposes of comparison, a quick search for the term "street crime" returned 2230 articles between 1950 and 2000. The *Times* certainly dedicated more space to specific examples of individual corporations behaving badly. In our Enron energy example of corporate malfeasance we found 206 news stories, op-eds, and editorials in a five-year search. A quick search for another famous bit of corporate mischief, when the oil tanker *Exxon Valdez* ran aground off the coast of Alaska in 1989, resulted in 1310 hits. This relative paucity of articles responding to corporate crime perhaps reveals a tendency to eschew a more systemic explanation. Articles including the words "corporate crime" are inherently more likely to suggest a broader, more systemic examination of legal violations by firms. So the disparity of articles on the more general search of corporate crime as opposed to any of our more firm-specific violators suggests that the *Times* was not shy about exposing and demanding punishment for corporate rogues, but dedicated far less time and effort to discovering a more systemic explanation. In this sense, our search terms of "corporate crime" and "white-collar crime," which will generate articles with a more systemic explanation, will overstate the *Times'* commitment to this perspective.

As was the case with the Enron example, the *Times* was eager to expose firms undertaking a variety of underhanded schemes to profit by breaking the law. In 1974 it reported that airlines were paying illegal kickbacks to travel agents who were willing to funnel passengers in their direction. The case was broken after a travel agent was discovered with "more than $80,000 concealed in his sock."[171] A year later the *Times* indicted New York supermarkets and Iowa beef processors for similar violations when purchasers from the supermarket received payoffs for buying meat from Iowa. The *Times* reporting in this article placed the blame firmly on the shoulders of Moe Steinman, an executive for the Daitch-Shopwell supermarket, who "corrupted all the meat buyers."[172] Later articles expose firms for Medicaid fraud in nursing homes,[173] illegal environmental violations,[174] arms sales to South Africa's apartheid regime,[175] fraud,[176] price fixing,[177] insider trading and manipulating stock prices,[178] tax evasion,[179] check kiting,[180] bribery of foreign officials,[181] and racial discrimination at Texaco.[182] These types of "firms behaving badly" articles fingered a number of companies and industries. In these stories the corporate miscreant was treated as a bad apple, without referring to the widespread nature of these crimes.

This is not to suggest that the *Times* insisted that corporate crime was not prevalent. Its reporting on corporate and white-collar crime included many articles that stressed the frequency of criminal activity in the boardroom and traced the cause to the light touch of legal sanctions. As was the case with OSHA, it was Nader's rabble rousing, by calling for tougher penalties on "white-collar" crime like fraud and corruption, that first attracted the paper's attention. The *Times* reported Nader's complaints about Vice President Agnew's sentence of three years unsupervised probation and a $10,000 fine for failing to pay taxes on $13,551 of alleged bribes. (Who knew bribes counted as taxable income?) Nader contrasted this penalty with that handed down to a wayward angler who received seventy days in jail for fishing without a license and possessing seven striped bass under the legal size.[183] In the late 1970s the *Times* reported that "the top law enforcement officials of New York and New Jersey told a Congressional committee today that white-collar crime was so pervasive it was destroying the moral fabric of American society."[184] Occasionally the *Times* did suggest that crime was prevalent among the biggest names in corporate America. The *Times* ran a list of alleged corporate criminals compiled, again, by Nader, that was a veritable who's who of American business, including Citicorp, Du Pont, Eli Lilly, US Steel, and Winn-Dixie stores.[185] A decade later a *Times* article investigated offshore banking as a means of evading taxes for much of corporate America.[186] It also exposed corporate heavyweights IBM, Lockheed, and AT&T for possible regulatory violations and suggested that without government oversight other industries would also be tempted to stray down the criminal path: "If Wall Street appears to be more honest, though, it is largely a function of increased surveillance by brokerage firms and by regulators."[187]

According to the *Times*, without very severe financial penalties and even jail time for guilty executives, firms would not have a sufficient deterrent to avoid corporate crime. When U.S. prosecutors sought increased penalties for corporate crime in the late 1970s, the *Times* was very supportive of prison sentences for executives under headlines like "Jail the Boss,"[188] "Leniency Decried in Business Crime,"[189] and "US Aide Urges Jail in Antitrust Crimes."[190] The *Times* lamented the toothless nature of current penalties as "a minor fine that can be written off as a cost of doing business."[191] During the sentencing of infamous white-collar criminals like Ivan Boesky, who was convicted of insider trading, the *Times* claimed that "the public needs to see that even white-collar crimes are punished."[192] The overall problem according to the *Times* is that the legal code and judges are simply unsure about how to deal with corporate crime, since the defendants are often so different from "common" criminals. As a result, punishment is usually limited to a "judge's lecture and a fine that, while the maximum often prescribed by law, is relatively small."[193]

In 1988 the Reagan administration's U.S. Sentencing Commission proposed a "scientific" proposal to punish corporate crime based on an "optimal" punishment theory developed by conservative Chicago School economists like Gary Becker. In practice, this proposal meant a noticeable decrease in penalties, and the *Times* stressed the position of critics who charged that the proposal took a quantum step backwards "by making punishment so insignificant as to make it impractical to pursue corporations for environmental or securities law violations." "It trivializes many offenses and minimizes and undercounts the losses caused by crime."[194] The *Times* later reported on Democratic accusations that the Bush Sr. administration caved to Business Round Table lobbying against Justice Department proposals for stronger financial penalties on corporate America.[195]

Despite its need to generate ad revenue from fellow members of the corporate community, when guilty firms were let off lightly, the *Times* called for stronger penalties. In 1985 the Department of Justice failed to file felony charges when drug company SmithKline caused the "death and injury of hundreds of innocent people worldwide," instead opting for a $100,000 fine. The *Times* ran several stories on this issue, frequently citing criticisms from Democrats that this penalty was "lenient" and "disturbing."[196] A 1992 story on the savings and loan debacle criticized the failure to sufficiently punish the hucksters that, through a variety of fraudulent activities, stole approximately $100 billion, lamenting that "for the real smart guys, white-collar crime does pay."[197] Later that year the paper reported on the failure to prosecute the manufacturer of a defective heart valve that killed "around 300" people because the statute of limitations had expired.[198]

The *Times* supported what others described as overly punitive sentencing of white-collar crime. When famous junk bond dealer Michael Milken received ten years in prison, the judge handing down the sentence was criticized by some for imposing a penalty that exceeded the crime. The *Times*, however, wrote that the judge had "accomplished her stated goal of achieving general deterrence."[199]

A common theme running through much of the *Times*' reporting on this issue was the stark contrast between penalties for corporate and street crimes. "Corporate executives who might plot in their boardrooms to defraud the public of millions of dollars demanded criminal sanctions against some kid who steals their Cadillac."[200] Even when penalties for corporate crime became much stiffer in the 1980s, the *Times* still stressed their lenience compared to street crime, quoting Nader: "The more you steal the less time you do, as long as you do it on the 20th floor."[201] When Reagan implemented his "get tough on crime" policies in the 1980s, the *Times* again quoted Nader, who pointed out that the government may have been cracking down on drug dealers and organized crime, but the "Justice Department has continued to ignore far more serious crime" such as pollution and bank fraud.[202] By 1985 the *Times* even pondered whether a corporation could be charged with murder. It sounded a bit of a warning to corporate wrongdoers by quoting a judge who claimed that just because corporate executives had never before stood trial for murder "doesn't mean it can't happen now."[203] When Steven Hoffenberg was defrauding hopeful investors by claiming to run a healthy company, promising conservative, secure, long-term returns, but instead funneling the income into his own lavish lifestyle, the *Times* printed letters from his now destitute victims. It highlighted one particularly, although understandably, irate correspondent: "Hoffenberg hurt more people in a brief five years than a jail full of street criminals in their lifetimes."[204] It is noticeable that these articles emphasize that corporate crime is let off lightly compared to street crime, especially when the much greater social harm resulting from white-collar criminals is factored into the equation. There was no suggestion that corporations or their executives should be treated any differently than other criminals or that their punishments should be in any way be more lenient.

Only one article suggested that punishments might actually be too severe. After the Ivan Boesky insider-trading scandal, defense lawyers started to argue that prosecutors were becoming overzealous in seeking maximum penalties even for fairly innocuous crimes. However, even this claim was disputed in the article, which quoted government officials saying that "criminal prosecutions have a greater deterrent effect than the fear of civil penalties such as fines."[205] A later article on the same topic was even more unequivocal. After reporting on complaints that "inflexible negotiators" were requesting stiff punishments for "marginal crimes," the *Times* countered with a quote from Bruce Baird, the former heard of the securities fraud unit: "Every poor kid who goes though the criminal courts on an average day gets a fraction of the due process given to the average white-collar defendant with the best of defense council."[206]

While the state's hands-off approach to enforcement was partly responsible for corporate crime, lack of moral fiber in the executive suite also played an important role. When seventeen companies were charged for making illegal campaign contributions in 1975, the *Times* portrayed an SEC executive who claimed that his organization starts "with the premise that American business is run on a very high level of morality" as hopelessly naïve.[207] In 1985, Rudolph Giuliani, a U.S. attorney at the time, claimed "There's a serious ethical problem in American business."[208] An article tracing the renewed prevalence of white-collar crime suggested that the causes were that "economic pressures, a new permissiveness and simple greed are eroding corporate morality." The cure? "Ethical leadership."[209] According to a Merrill Lynch executive, the new Roman Catholic catechism included fraudulent accounting as a sin. "We can only hope that will have a positive impact going forward."[210] This is a telling interpretation of the cause of corporate criminal behavior. Rather than locating the cause of illegal activities in the regular day-to-day logic of profit-maximizing firms weighing the costs and benefits of breaking the law, these articles stressed the moral shortcomings of executives who succumb to the lure of short-term, ill-gotten gains rather than playing by the rules. Further, they do not take the next logical step and explicitly identify the profit motive that is a fundamental aspect of privately owned firms as the driving motive behind corporate criminality.

The *Times* and Corporate Crime: Op-eds

The most common op-ed contributors were university academics. To the extent that professors from business schools could be expected to grant firms a more favorable hearing on this issue than those from less business-friendly social sciences departments (sociology, for example), the *Times* balanced their op-eds on this issue by selecting equal numbers of authors from these different areas of academia. It also ran seven op-eds from think tanks and research institutes, but unlike its academic mix, these came exclusively from organizations that would brand themselves as "progressive" as opposed to "free market," and Ralph Nader and his organization were allotted three articles in which to state his case. The remaining op-eds were written by a combination of staff reporters, freelance writers, elected officials, and even a couple of representatives of the business community.

Compared to its news section, the *Times* did provide a little more space in its op-eds for those who felt that the state was being too tough on corporate crime. When the unlawful business political contribution scandal was broken during Watergate, Weidenbaum, who appears to be the *Times* conservative voice of choice, argued that this was not so much a case of business paying for unjust government favors as it was "the demands from the representatives of a powerful government which was in the position to do great harm to the company." The solution, logically, would be to "curtail the vast authority of government agencies."[211] In a later column, a self-identified teacher of Marxian economics argued that prosecutors had abandoned "due process when it comes to dealing with members of the business community." Far from being too lenient on white-collar crime, "the plain wealth of some members of the business community . . . have led to their being treated as second or third class citizens."[212] A business school dean argued that corporations "do as much, if not more than, all forms of regulation" in keeping criminal fraud out of the securities market since they need to demonstrate their trustworthiness to a skeptical investing public.[213]

Despite a slightly higher emphasis on a more conservative, laissez faire attitude to boardroom criminality, the *Times* was still willing to name and shame corporate miscreants in its op-eds. In a seven-page *Sunday Magazine* article, James Traub covered the 1988 trial of the president and vice president of the Beech-Nut Nutrition Corporation. The two executives received prison terms of one year plus a day and $100,000 fines for knowingly selling apple juice that contained only "sugar, water, flavoring and coloring." The anger over this horrid misuse of the word "apple" was exacerbated because the juice was marketed for babies.[214] This case was portrayed as an outrageously unnecessary lapse in judgment by executives who proceeded to bungle even their attempts to cover their own tracks by refusing to destroy the apple-free juice that was the prosecution's smoking gun.

The *Times* also contained stories that suggested that crime was a little more endemic. A lengthy *Sunday Magazine* spread on the widespread use of the Cayman Islands as "the location of choice for the wise-guy businessman who wants to hide a few hundred thousand dollars" lamented the regulatory freedom that made this kind of tax avoidance possible. Although the article reported that businesses both large and small were using offshore banking to avoid paying their rightful share of taxes, those who did so were not upstanding citizens. Apparently one of the main advantages of the Caymans over alternative tax-free havens for businessmen was that "it was close and they could party while they hid their money there."[215]

Op-eds also continued the *Times'* trend of stressing the need for government oversight to provide the appropriate deterrent for executives who might be tempted down the wrong path. A law professor stressed the need for "prompt, uniform and consistent application of criminal sanctions including jail sentences, because it is so infrequently imposed it is not a credible threat."[216] Op-eds also continued to contrast corporate with street crimes. In 1985 Nader accused a wide variety of industries and specific firms of criminal activity and argued that "by almost any measure crime in the suites takes far more money and produces far more casualties and diseases than crime in the streets." He urged stronger penalties for executives, since "an effective enforcement strategy has to target the big fish in the corporate sea."[217]

Of course, the counterpart of encouraging stronger penalties is to discourage any move to reduce punishment. Headlines like "Keep the Teeth in White-Collar Law,"[218] "Don't Hinder the Pollution Police,"[219] and "Don't Water Down the Anti-Fraud Law"[220] all pleaded not to further dilute the already gruel-thin protections in place at the time. An editorial crediting the SEC for restoring confidence in America's financial system after the scandals that caused the stock market crash of 1929 argued that its continued vigilance is necessary. "Investors must believe all wayward capitalists have a real chance of being caught by the SEC enforcers."[221]

Finally, one columnist provided a more systemic explanation of corporate crime. Richard Barnett of the Institute of Policy Studies argued that "the most serious problems posed by the multinational corporations stem not from their all too frequent scandals but from standard business practices." "By acting within present law . . . the multinational corporation, in pursuit of its own interests, constitutes a clear and continuing threat to the interests of people around the world, including the people of the United States." The global corporation "is a social institution and our laws must reflect that reality."[222]

The *Times* and Corporate Crime: Editorials

As was the case in its news section, the *Times* dedicated less editorial space to a discussion of broader corporate or white-collar crime than it did many of our other subjects. The search only returned seventeen articles, which is less in an entire fifty-year period than Enron produced in five. While this suggests that the *Times* was less interested in treating corporate crime as an endemic problem as opposed to particular businesses or industries behaving badly, the editorial page remained steadfastly consistent with its news reporting in insisting that the legal system treated corporate crime with kid gloves.

The issue first started cropping up in the mid-1970s and the tone of the first editorial on the subject formed the template for almost all the articles that followed. In September 1975, the *Times* argued "it is time to begin working urgently to limit the extent and the effect of corporate crime." "The harm to society from such wrongdoing is substantially less obvious than street crime against people, but it is no less real and every bit as damaging." "Tolerance of corruption in high places in industry, labor or government is bound ultimately to foster lawlessness throughout society." "Wrist slapping is the usual and anticipated response to corporate criminality . . . firms paid off their fines with about six seconds of corporate activity."[223] Jail might be an ideal deterrent for white-collar criminals, since for them "prison is much more jarring than to criminals who live at society's economic and social margins."[224] In fact, the *Times* argued that since white-collar crime "subverts the political and economic system, destroys competitors, sabotages social services, plunders the public treasury and, in extreme cases, even creates international conflict" "a free society cannot let a socially or professionally privileged group enjoy preferred treatment before the bar of justice."[225]

On those rare occasions when corporate criminality was punished more severely, the *Times* was complimentary. When a judge sentenced a slumlord to live in his own building for fifteen days, an editorial concluded, "Creative and enforceable alternatives to prison exist, for poor criminals as well as rich."[226] Two years later an editorial praised junk bond fraudster Michael Milken's ten-year prison sentence. "Only the new decade can tell whether Judge Wood's justice is a new model of equal treatment of white-collar felons. If so, the nation won't miss the cynicism and demoralization that goes with disparate sentencing."[227]

In keeping with their view that corporate crime is badly under-punished, the *Times*' editorial page criticized any attempt to reduce the already lenient punishments meted out by the courts. When the U.S. government was considering rewriting the Racketeer Influenced and Corrupt Organizations Act (RICO) to make it less puni-tive, the *Times* portrayed the proposed change as the "latest attempt to gut a law that is proving to be especially useful in a period of rampant white collar crime."[228] A 1984 editorial mocked the SEC penalty for insider trading—a fine equal to the illegal gain and a promise to never do it again—as "no more severe than making a child return a chocolate bar to the counter from which it was filched."[229]

The editorial page also singled out prestigious members of the corporate com-munity if they crossed the legal line. When the editorial page did this, however, it also attempted to distance the specific actions of the bad apples with the general good behavior of the corporate community as a whole. When Gulf Oil, and many other companies, made illegal contributions to the Nixon campaign, an editorial claimed: "Some of the most successful companies have found that cleanliness ulti-mately worked as a benefit, not as a cost, to their business. However, the reputation of all business suffers from the excesses of those executives who behave in flagrant disregard for the laws and the principles that they pretend to respect."[230] Later, when General Electric defrauded the Air Force by forging workers' time cards, the *Times* simultaneously chastised the specific action and managed to praise the broader company. "They surely operated in a culture of sleaze and borderline morality" but "that's not the culture of General Electric."[231] If it was not in the culture of GE, it was certainly in the culture of many of the other weapons suppliers. The Reagan administration's precipitous military buildup set off a virtual crime wave among defense contractors. "The Pentagon's Inspector General had 59 of its 100 largest contractors under criminal investigation." The editorial placed the blame for this crime spree less on the firms themselves than on the Pentagon's "negotiated cosseting of defense contractors" instead of allowing more open competition.[232] Again, it is clear that the *Times* did not consistently place the desires of its corporate advertisers above its role as gatekeeper of the long-term interests of the business community, which needs to maintain the trust and confidence of the general public.

Conclusion

Regulation is usually characterized as a liberal policy while deregulation has been broadly associated with conservative economics. However, we would argue that a more telling distinction for the *Times* is whether either regulation or deregulation would affect business profits. In the Enron case, deregulation was a disaster for firms in California, providing an opportunity to analyze the *Times'* perspective when a conservative policy may help the short-term profits of a small section of business, but is detrimental to overall corporate interests. The *Times* did not develop a hypothesis about corporate behavior that anticipated the possibility of collusion, corruption, and malfeasance. Only Krugman was able to see that this particular market was ripe for exactly the kind of manipulation that people like Davis were claiming. The *Times'* initial inaccuracy about the cause of the crisis was caused by its choice to give credence to the energy policy of the Bush administration, overwhelming corporate support for deregulation, and the casual application of conventional economic theory. The conservative claim that price controls distort markets, ensuring less investment in new plants and equipment while encouraging more demand, was as widespread as it was wrong. Yet this was the *Times'* original perspective on the crisis.

When the Feds finally imposed price controls the energy crisis ended. No longer able to maximize profits by sabotaging supply and raising prices, the industry had to provide the electricity that actually existed to make money, which was more than enough to meet California's demands. As the evidence became incontrovertible, the *Times* did become liberal, concluding that for-profit, privately owned electric and natural gas companies were sabotaging California. As the gatekeeper for responsible corporate behavior and the overarching interests of the broader business community, the *Times* portrayed this behavior as reprehensible, called for the offenders to be punished, and demanded regulatory oversight to ensure that this type of behavior was less likely in the future. The paper had no obvious hesitation about condemning misbehavior, even from potential advertisers, that was inimical to the public interest. It is perhaps no coincidence that in this case, the public interest and broad corporate interests dovetail nicely.

This was not the case in the OSHA example. Liberal regulation to protect workers does cost corporations money, which provided an interesting test of the *Times'* perspective when regulations favor labor at the expense of business. Whether the topic was macroeconomic or foreign economic policy, the *Times* consistently favored rules that enhanced the profitability of American business. Eschewing conservative and liberal dogmatism, the *Times* preferred economic policies that often came at the expense of the U.S. general public or foreign democracy. OSHA was significantly different. The editorial page may have been slightly more concerned with the costs of the regulatory burden than either the op-eds or its news reporting but the overall message was clear: workers needed regulatory protection in a dangerous work environment. It might be possible to argue that the *Times* believed regulation might pay for itself with reduced health- and injury-related business costs or that the short-term costs of regulation were small when the long-term legitimacy of the wage labor system might be jeopardized by a mounting toll of death and disaster on the job. An uncharitable interpretation of the *Times'* stance on OSHA might be that workers were the canaries in the coal mine. Perhaps the paper was worried that health hazards spread from the factories to the executive suite. It is possible that a pesticide that poisoned farm workers would also kill the well-heeled consumers of designer endive on which it was sprayed. It would then be in everyone's interest to support worker safety in much the same way that public sewers and water reservoirs did not only benefit the urban poor, but their more affluent neighbors as well. However, this would be uncharitable. Even when health and safety problems were unlikely to spread from the workplace, as was the case with grain elevator explosions, the *Times* came out clearly on the side of the worker, often in opposition to the stated interests of the business class as a whole. What was good for America in this case, unlike all the other cases we have so far studied, was what was good for the health and safety of its working class.

The *Times* favored regulation in both the Enron and OSHA examples, indicating a preference for more liberal policy options. The final case was selected to determine whether the *Times* treats corporate violations of society's rules and regulations as unlikely events that scarcely need to be punished, deviations from normal business behavior that must be prosecuted, or a systemic inevitability for profit-maximizing firms. The *Times* was consistent on corporate crime in its op-eds, editorials, and news stories. The op-ed page may have given slightly more credence to the idea that punishing corporate crime could lead to negative side effects and the editorial page may have leaned a little more heavily on the bad apple explanation, but all three sections were consistent in calling for more punishment of corporate crime and equality of punishment with the day-to-day street crimes of the working class. The *Times* was outraged at the inconsistency of treating street criminals more harshly than corporate criminals, demanding not just stiffer financial penalties but more jail time for executives. It is clear that the *Times* cannot be confused with apologists for corporate crime or those that deny the issue is significant. The free market and individual corporations were sacrificed for the principled stand that corporations have a responsibility to not kill or steal from their fellow Americans. The *Times* saw itself as a watchdog with respect to the corporate criminal activity it believes inimical to the credibility of its business class.

However, the *Times* seemed able to maintain continuous outrage at the level of immorality in the boardroom without recognizing the systemic character of corporate crime. Breaking the law is sufficiently habitual that it should be seen as just another way of doing business, not, as the *Times* frequently argued, as a lack of ethics or morals. It is simply another arrow in the corporate quiver, like cutting labor costs, clever marketing, and reducing taxes. Of course, this is purely a cost-benefit calculation by profit-maximizing firms. Considering the usually small penalty even in the unlikely event of being caught, the costs of violating laws and regulations are likely to be much lower than the benefits. Given the recidivism rate for corporate America, criminal prosecutions would require a construction boom for luxury minimum-security prisons just to hold the executives convicted of the deaths of thousands of their fellow citizens and the theft of billions of dollars.

A more systemic approach would not have analyzed the California energy crisis as a one-off, but as a cautionary tale in the context of sweeping withdrawals of government oversight taking place since the late 1970s. It would have treated corporate violations of even these weakened sets of rules as inevitable consequences of the economic prerogatives of a profit-driven system. This perspective would have provided the *Times* with a stronger background with which to analyze the looming specter of deregulation in the banking and finance industry that would ignite the economic crisis of 2008.

CHAPTER 6

THE *NEW YORK TIMES'* STAR COLUMNISTS

Attentive readers will have noticed that the mid-1990s marked a change in the *Times'* opinion section. Rather than relying on outsiders from academia, the business world, or government to provide insightful commentary on current events, the *Times* moved to develop its own stable of experts. If its goal was to associate its news brand with a group of influential writers who would be experts and celebrities in their own right, it was very successful.

The *Times'* columnists are a veritable who's who of household names in U.S. intellectual circles, most often promoted from the reporting corps of the paper, but occasionally pinched from other professions. Their roster includes luminaries like novelist and Pulitzer Prize–winner William Safire. Nicholas Kristof has won two Pulitzers, among a slew of other awards. Maureen Dowd is famous enough to be satirized by *Saturday Night Live*'s Tina Fey and, of course, she won a Pulitzer in 1999. Frank Rich has not managed to bag a Pulitzer thus far, but can console himself with the George Polk Award for commentary in 2005. All of these columnists are sought-after intellectuals, much desired on the talk show and speaking circuit. The point here is not to pat the *Times* on the back for its excellent journalistic standards, but to emphasize that not all written work in the *Times* has equal weight. The columnists pack a political punch that is more powerful than mere reporters.

For this chapter we could have selected any of these leading lights of U.S. journalism, but have opted for Paul Krugman and Thomas Friedman for two reasons. First, even among the famous *Times* columnists, who could spend their work downtime shining up their collective Pulitzers, these two stand out. Second, these two writers, more than their colleagues, focus particularly on the economic issues that we have so far addressed in the book.

Friedman began his career at the *Times* as the Middle East correspondent, moving on to posts reporting on economics and Washington. He became a bestselling author with the publication of *The Lexus and the Olive Tree*, *The World is Flat*, and *Hot Flat and Crowded*. He has won three Pulitzers while at the *Times* and was named their foreign affairs columnist in 1995. Krugman, unlike most of the other columnists, was not a staff writer, but an academic economist from Princeton University and frequent op-ed contributor. He was awarded the Nobel Prize in economics in 2008 for his work on international trade and finance. With the possible exception of Joseph Stiglitz (author of *Globalization and its Discontents*), Krugman is likely the most famous currently practicing economist in the world.

The differing backgrounds of these two writers make for an interesting contrast in styles. Friedman is a trained journalist but amateur economist. His research relies much more heavily on interviews and personal anecdote than a professional economist would be comfortable with. In addition, his interview subjects are selected from the upper echelons of economic privilege. He reports from the WEF in Davos and tours businesses with their CEOs. This creates a view of the global economy from the heights of those who are in control of it. By contrast, Krugman is a professional economist but an amateur journalist. As a result, his prose is often not quite as quote-worthy, but his research techniques are considerably more careful. He has a professional reputation to maintain and his opinions are formed much more by academic literature and empirical research than are Friedman's. Krugman must pay attention to an underlying theoretical coherence in his writing. He has a body of academic work from which he draws his reputation that he should not contradict in his life as a columnist. The contrasting professional backgrounds of these two star columnists and the "focus groups" from which they draw their information create important distinctions between them in terms of the topics they choose to address and the manner in which they do so.

By necessity, this chapter will have a slightly different structure than the previous chapters. Thus far, news reporting, op-ed columns, and editorials have been separated in order to determine whether there was any difference in the economic ideas expressed in the different types of articles. Since this section focuses exclusively on the opinion-setting ideas of the *Times*' name brand writers, it will only contain op-eds from Krugman and Friedman. In addition, previously each topic has been introduced by a brief, factual introduction that provides the background necessary to evaluate the *Times*' reporting on the issue. Although this chapter analyzes the ideas of individuals rather than particular issues, there are two themes that run through both writers' work that do require some introduction.

The first is how macroeconomic and labor market policy has created growing inequality in the United States, particularly between the labor force and those who own businesses. This topic was covered extensively in the section on monetary policy in Chapter 2, so a quick reminder about the trends should suffice. Real wages for the average worker in the United States are less than they were thirty years ago, while labor productivity—the value of what they produced—has increased. The only real income gains have come at the very top of the income spectrum. Even the top 20 percent of earners have had wage gains that were very modest. The real gains are to those in the top 1 percent of the population.

There are several reasons for this wage stagnation. In the 1980s, monetary policy was used deliberately to increase unemployment and to create future expectations of unemployment as a means to reduce workers' bargaining power. As unemployment fell in the 1990s and wages still failed to increase, it became clear that there were additional factors at play. This was Greenspan's traumatized worker. Changes in the U.S. domestic labor market (for example, making it more difficult to form unions and decreasing unemployment insurance payments) reduced workers' bargaining power even at lower levels of unemployment. This was the legacy of political leaders and Fed chairmen predating the financial crisis of 2008. An additional factor traumatizing workers was international competition. Competing with cheap overseas labor puts downward pressure on wages. According to Josh Bivens, trade agreements reduced the annual real income for a full-time median-wage earner in 2006 by about $1,400. For a typical household with two earners, the loss was more than $2,500.[1]

While we have discussed the impact of trade on American workers, there has not yet been any discussion on the broader impacts of trade or globalization. Conservatives argue that unfettered free trade must benefit all countries involved. This is due to the famed theory of comparative advantage, which states that if nations specialize in what they do best and then trade with each other, they will be better off than if they attempt to produce everything that they consume. The logic behind this is that if Guyana is better at growing pineapples than building cars and the United States is better at making cars than pineapples, Guyana should not waste resources building cars or the United States growing pineapples. Making what each can do at its relative lowest cost and trading will result in more lower-priced goods for both nations. In addition, conservatives argue, the competition from imported goods will increase innovation and lower consumer prices. Conservatives admit that there will be some transition costs in moving to a more free-trade world. The U.S. workers who were previously employed picking pineapples will be put out of work and will require some time and retraining to find employment in the expanding automobile sector. However, the temporary losses to these unfortunate few will always be overwhelmed by the gains to the many.

These arguments, like other conservative claims surrounding macroeconomic policy and deregulation, have won the day since the late 1980s. As a result, governments around the world have been signing free trade agreements like the World Trade Organization (WTO) and the North American Free Trade Agreement (NAFTA), which put the theory of unimpeded free trade between nations into practice. As a result, the last thirty years has seen a dramatic lowering of the barriers to the movement of trade and finance between nations. This provides an interesting test of the conservative theory of free trade. Is the world, and especially the poorer nations, better off as a result of this free-market version of globalization?

To justify these theories in the real world, conservative economists point to the success of countries that have grown rapidly on the back of dramatic increases in manufactured exports. East Asian countries like South Korea and Taiwan have been transformed from impoverished developing nations into high-income industrial economies. Further, it has been done with broad-based income gains and driven by a deliberate strategy of export-led growth. Now it appears that China and India are following that same path. Both countries have experienced prolonged periods of extraordinary economic growth of almost 10 percent a year. The growth in these nations has also been export-driven, with exports as a percentage of GDP increasing steadily during their boom. The fact that poorer countries have enjoyed some of the highest growth rates appears to support the conservative claim that, while all participants benefit from trade, it is the less-developed countries that will benefit the most because labor-intensive industries will find their low-wage economies particularly attractive. As these firms relocate, the demand for workers will increase in impoverished regions, forcing wages closer to those prevailing in developed countries.

Unfortunately for the conservative argument, there is only a superficial resemblance between free trade and the policies followed by any of these nations. While South Korea aggressively sought to increase its exports, it did so under a set of very protectionist rules. Unsatisfied with simply exporting goods in which it had a comparative advantage, the government deliberately targeted income-elastic, high-productivity industries for growth. The government forced mergers between firms to develop economies of scale and make them more internationally competitive. It banned foreign technology if domestic suppliers were available. It used reverse engineering, which plays a little fast and loose with intellectual property laws, to play technological catch-up. Finally, it maintained strict rules for its financial sector and used state-controlled banks to extend credit to firms that the government was looking to aid.[2] All of these policies, which were crucial so South Korea's successful development, run counter to the prescriptions of free trade. In fact, all of them are now outlawed under various provisions of the WTO.

Broader studies also find little support for a causal relationship between free trade and growth. In one survey of the economic literature, Francisco Rodriguez and Dani Rodrik found "little evidence that open trade policies—in the sense of lower tariff and non-tariff barriers to trade—are significantly associated with economic growth."[3] Perhaps even more damning is the historical inconvenience that not one nation in the modern age has successfully developed without protectionist policies. Britain was one of the most protectionist nations in the world when it developed, only moving to a more open trading policy when it had become the world's leading industrial power. The United States developed its industrial capacity behind a 40 percent manufacturing tariff at the end of the 19th century.[4] Japan and Germany also industrialized behind tariff walls. To a developing nation it must appear somewhat

perplexing that free trade is often advocated by economists and politicians from nations that successfully rejected that very route.

Further, the idea that the last thirty years of globalization has narrowed the gap
between rich and poor is not quite the undisputed fact that conservative economic
theory would suggest. According to a very careful survey of several studies on the
subject, "it is not possible to reach a definitive conclusion regarding the direction of
change in global inequality over the last three decades of the twentieth century" but
"the one point of agreement among all studies is that the level of global inequality
is very high."[5] While China increased its per-capita income from about 10 percent
of that in the United States to just below 20 percent between 1990 and 2000, the
developing world as a whole has not closed the income gap at all, remaining at below
20 percent of U.S. per-capita GDP. Latin American and African countries are, in
fact, further behind U.S. incomes than they were in 1990.[6] An ILO report found
that income inequality within developing world countries increased during the
globalization period. For fifty-one out of seventy-three countries in its study, the
share of wages in total income declined over the past twenty years. Importantly,
the report concluded that much of this growing inequality was caused by financial
liberalization, which has eroded the bargaining power of employees and contributed
to the trend of declining wage share in income.[7]

Even in terms of absolute poverty the results have been more nuanced than
globalization advocates would suggest. A World Bank study on poverty trends
concluded that there were 400 million fewer people living on less than $1 a day in
2001 than in 1981. However, the entire gain was due to the experience in China;
in other countries there has actually been a slight increase in people living on less
than $1 a day. Further, about half of the improvement in China occurred very early
in the 1980s, before China's rapid growth in exports.[8] Despite the income gains
in China, conditions remain abysmal for the average worker. In an article that
documented the rapidly rising labor costs in China, *Business Week* reported that
one manufacturer was having its profits squeezed by wages of $160 per month,
about $2,000 per year. Further this was a region in which wages had been rising
faster than in the rest of the country because of relative labor shortages.[9] Even
with the stagnant wage gains for U.S. workers documented in the monetary
policy section of the macroeconomics chapter, the median weekly wage of a U.S.
wage or salary worker was $738, or $38,000 a year.[10] The Chinese workers cited
in *Business Week* earned about 5 percent as much, yet China's GDP per capita is
just a little below 20 percent of that in the United States. The inevitable conclusion is that the income from Chinese production is not going to its workforce. In
fact, the share of wages in total income declined from 53 to 41 percent between
1998 and 2005.[11]

The condition of workers in India provides even less cause for optimism. According to an ILO report, the real manufacturing wages in India have declined 22
percent between 1990 and 2001. This decrease came despite an increase in labor

productivity of 65 percent.[12] Unlike in China, Indian workers were actually worse off in absolute terms.

In both of these countries it is not only low wages that attract firms, but also lax environmental regulations. The rapid growth of production, especially in manufacturing, coupled with limited environmental protection has had disastrous consequences. China's pollution problems are notorious. When it hosted the 2008 Olympics, the most common concern was how the athletes could compete under the smog of air pollution in major cities despite the fact that the government took the drastic steps of keeping half the cars in Beijing off the road and shutting down nearby factories. A World Bank report on pollution in China warned that "the resources that such growth demands and the environmental pressures it brings have raised grave concerns about the long-term sustainability and hidden costs of growth."[13] The study was an ambitious attempt to calculate the cost of air and water pollution in China in terms of human health, water scarcity, and reductions in production. Although any study such as this must make some heroic assumptions (the value of life is important here), the final tally is a truly remarkable 781 billion yuan, 5.8 percent of GDP in 2003.[14] According to an article in the *Times*, China is an environmental disaster. Only 1 percent of people living in cities breathe air that would be considered safe by European Union standards. China became the world leader in greenhouse gas emissions in 2008. China's great lakes, the Tai, Chao, and Dianchi, have water quality so poor that it is ranked unfit for industrial or agricultural use. The World Health Organization concluded that the death toll from water and air pollution had reached 750,000 a year.[15]

India has similar problems. The water in India's Ganges River may be sacred but it is not very pure. By Indian government standards, bathing (not drinking) in water containing more than 500 faecal coliform bacteria per 100 millilitres is considered unsafe. Some sections of the Ganges contain 60,000 bacteria per 100 ml and this figure rises to 1.5 million where untreated sewage is pumped directly into the river. It is no wonder that an estimated 1,000 Indian children die of diarrhoeal sickness every day.[16]

Free trade advocates (including Friedman and Krugman) argue that the international interconnections created by trade are a force for democracy. It is true that during the period in which globalization has expanded, the number of democracies in the world has increased. However, attributing this to the need for entrepreneurs to operate in an environment that includes civil liberties is more problematic. In fact, businesses appear to be shunning democracies. Despite the fact that there were more developing countries that could be counted as functioning democracies in 1999 than in 1989, the share of exports from developing country democracies fell from one-half to one-third during this period.[17] The crude correlation here is precisely the opposite of what free trade advocates suggest. Global exporting firms seem to be growing more rapidly in dictatorships than democracies.

Finally, even on their own free-trade terms, the WTO and NAFTA contain provisions that are far more about the exercise of bargaining power than they are commitments to genuine free trade. Any argument that WTO- or NAFTA-style free trade will benefit the poor most of all has to deal with some very awkward rules. For example, the North American Free Trade Agreement required the Mexican government to remove restrictions on corn imports. The result has been a flood of cheap corn into Mexico from the United States, partly because of the more productive industrial agriculture practiced in the United States, but also because the American corn industry is heavily subsidized. The result has been massive hardship for the traditional Mexican small-scale farmer. One and a half million Mexican farmers have been forced into the low-wage labor force because of NAFTA. On the other hand, farming interests in the United States have proved very capable lobbyists, maintaining an impressive array of import restrictions on agricultural products.

The WTO is plagued with similar problems. In 2001 the WTO declared that the Doha negotiations (so named because the talks were held in Doha, Qatar) were to be a development round in which the trading interests of the developing nations would be given first priority. The pressure for a development round came from the fact that the previous set of negotiations, the Uruguay Round, left many of the developing-nation participants very disillusioned with the lack of progress on issues that they felt were important, like reducing trade barriers on agricultural exports to the United States and EU. Instead, the Uruguay Round passed agreements on investment (TRIMS) and intellectual property (TRIPS), which were on the agenda of the developed countries. TRIMS limited the conditions that countries were allowed to place on foreign investment. TRIPS committed countries to strict rules protecting patents and other intellectual property. Both of these provisions benefit the developed nations, whose firms do most of the foreign investing and hold most of the intellectual property. Unfortunately, the Doha Round negotiations quickly descended into acrimonious bickering with the developing nations accusing developed countries of abandoning their promises of concentrating on policies that would benefit developing nations.[18] After a bitter breakdown in negotiations in Cancun in 2003, there have been several attempts to restart the Doha Round but all have so far ended in frustration. The fact that so many developing countries are so unhappy with current state of the WTO must provide some pause for those who want to argue that it truly helps the poor.

Unfettered free movement of trade and finance is a conservative position, while a more interventionist approach involving some protectionist measures is usually associated with liberal policy. The current WTO or NAFTA version of free trade contains elements of both, with developing nations opening their markets while the United States maintains agricultural subsidies and protection. The current rules may borrow from liberal and conservative menus, but they are very consistent in benefiting the U.S. business class. The TRIPS and TRIMS measures were particularly sought after by U.S. firms. As with all of the chapters so far, the writings of Krugman and Friedman—not just on globalization, but on all other economic issues—will be examined to determine where they stand when it comes to the long-term interests of U.S. business.

Thomas Friedman

The cornerstone of Friedman's economic analysis is that the global economy is a socially beneficial but cutthroat environment in which dynamic and innovative entrepreneurs drive each other to invent and market new technologies. It is the dynamism of the entrepreneurial class that is responsible for a country's success. Tragically, the United States is falling behind on this score. America "has a huge set of challenges if it is going to retain its competitive edge." With an "administration in denial" and "Congress off on Mars" Friedman was concerned that when he looked for "the group that has the power and the interest in seeing America remain globally focused and competitive—America's business leaders—they seem to be missing in action."[19] Fortunately there was still hope for the United States. Although New York was a technological backwater compared to Hong Kong, Americans still "generate new ideas with speed and . . . implement them through global collaboration (which) is the most important competitive advantage."[20]

Entrepreneurs must bear the heavy burden of the nation's progress. When they lived up to this responsibility, as Friedman argued has been the case in India and China, Friedman celebrated their accomplishments. When they failed to do so, as Friedman felt was the case with U.S. green technology, he was very critical. He was, accordingly, outraged when outgoing Exxon Mobil Chairman Lee Raymond was paid $400,000,000 while his company ran misleading ads aimed at convincing Californians to vote against Proposition 87, a law that would increase extraction fees on oil companies in California.[21] It is telling that the Exxon ads were not portrayed as a logical move by a profit-maximizing firm attempting to maintain a lucrative policy environment, but the lack of vision of a single man. Friedman was especially critical of the U.S. automobile industry and particularly GM for its promotion of gas-guzzling SUVs and general animosity to energy efficiency.[22] Friedman's solution was to have the head of Apple, Steve Jobs, run a car company for a year. "I'd bet it wouldn't take him much longer than that to come up with the GM iCar."[23]

While the heads of the auto industry were constantly chastised for falling behind their foreign competitors in terms of green innovation, the leaders of the financial sector were also criticized for ruining the American economy. Friedman argued that the infamous Madoff scandal, in which a smooth talker convinced Hollywood millionaires to invest in his house of cards, must be seen "as the cherry on top of a national breakdown in financial propriety, regulations and common sense." While the United States must be careful not to "kill the animal spirits that necessarily drive capitalism" it should not "be eaten by them either." Interestingly, he puts forward China, which has moved increasingly to a market economy, as a role model.[24]

While, for Friedman, it is the entrepreneurial class that drives a dynamic economy, it is up to the state to provide the right policy framework within which innovation can flourish. Unlike extreme free market conservatives, Friedman argued that this requires an excellent civil service. He was very critical of George W. Bush's contempt for the role of the federal government. "Much of America's moral authority to lead the world derives from the decency of our government and its bureaucrats, and the example we set for others. These are not things to be sneered at by a president. They are things to be cherished, strengthened and praised every single day."[25]

According to Friedman, the most important economic role of a well-functioning state is to foster innovation. He recommended a variety of policies in this vein, from regulating Microsoft[26] to public technology infrastructure. He recommended that New York should follow the lead of Philadelphia, "which decided it wouldn't wait for private companies to provide connectivity to all. Instead Philly made it a city-led project—like sewers and electricity."[27] These liberal policy prescriptions, which encourage an active state to promote R&D, obviously do not benefit all businesses— Microsoft might be especially aggrieved by these recommendations. However, these policies do provide important subsidies and supports for overall business profitability.

He constantly worried about gaps in U.S. technology. In 2000, he claimed that Japan was "a glimpse of America's future because it was a year or two ahead of America in the deployment of wireless internet surfing phones."[28] A typical Friedman column highlighted the technological advances of China. He was amazed that he could call his wife back in Maryland, static free, from an island off Hong Kong using a friend's Chinese cell phone. Landing at Kennedy Airport from Hong Kong was like "going from the Jetsons to the Flintstones." The contrast made him wonder, "If we are so smart, why are other people living so much better than us?" To transform the sluggish U.S. economy into the more dynamic Chinese model, the government should "stop the tax cuts we can't afford, the bailouts of auto companies that have become giant wealth-destruction machines, energy prices that do not encourage investment in 21st century renewable power systems or efficient cars, (and) public schools with no national standards to prevent illiterates from graduating." Although he was not specific about how this should be done, Friedman encouraged the state to eliminate the perverse incentives that channel the most creative minds in the country to financial engineering "rather than designing cars, phones, computers, teaching tools, Internet programs and medical equipment that could improve the lives and productivity of millions."[29]

According to Friedman, the U.S. workforce was also not sufficiently skilled to support innovation. American education was lagging in math and science compared to "Ireland, Finland, India or dozens of other nations whose economies are growing." He was concerned that U.S. twelfth-graders "performed below the international average for 21 countries in math and science."[30] Friedman was especially taken with the dynamism of the newly emerging economies of India and China, which were superior to the United States in terms of educational achievement, work ethic, and technological advances.[31]

In a competitive world, it is up to the government to provide firms with a skilled workforce. Friedman continuously advocated for an improved public school system, recommending strict standards for students, and removing teachers' federal income taxes, "so more people would choose these careers." He also recommended skimming the best and the brightest technical (as opposed, presumably, to fuzzy-thinking social scientists that are unlikely to provide much of a productivity boost) minds from other countries. The United States should "staple green cards to the diplomas of foreign students who graduate from any U.S. university in math and science—instead of subsidizing their education and sending them home."[32]

With the publication of *Hot, Flat and Crowded* Friedman became a convert to a particularly entrepreneurial version of ecological modernization declaring: "green is the new red, white and blue, pal. What color are you?"[33] Friedman did not share the free-market conservative economists' belief that allowing the market to determine prices is the key to economic success. Rather government must influence prices to alter the behavior of consumers and firms in order to protect the environment, especially from global warming. One of the biggest industrial villains was the American auto industry. Since the executives of GM, Ford, and Chrysler refused to go green on their own initiative, Friedman recommended using the leverage of the 2009 industry bailout to force the auto companies to produce hybrid electric cars as part of a move to reduce emissions and improve mileage. As was so often the case in Friedman's writing, he predicted that green cars were the automotive wave of the future and feared that American companies were losing ground to manufacturers from Europe, China, and Japan. In order to wean Americans off their love of gigantic cars, he also recommended a gasoline tax. "Every time the price of gasoline went down to $1 or $2 a gallon the consumers went back to buying gas guzzlers."[34] Maintaining a high price for gasoline was one of Friedman's most popular themes. He repeatedly called for a price floor for gasoline of $3.50 to $4.50. Less frequently he wanted to force the auto industry to produce cars with an average gas mileage of 35–40 miles per gallon.[35] He argued that there was really no downside to this unpopular policy. Far from slowing down economic growth and creating economic stagnation, this price floor would trigger massive investments in renewable energy, like wind, solar, and thermal.[36]

The future of America should be found in a "Green New Deal." "The next great industrial revolution . . . is going to be energy technology."[37] The coming century will belong to the nation that most quickly creates the conditions for green innovation. "So, we're toast, right? I mean, that's pretty much the pervasive global assumption these days: The 19th century belonged to England, the 20th century belonged to America and the 21st century will belong to China. Tell your kids to study Mandarin." Against this pessimism, Friedman sounded a rallying cry: "The major industrial country that gets the greenest the fastest, with the smartest technologies—that's the country that will lead the 21st century. We've got the innovators; we've got the venture capitalists. If only we had the government that would create the right market conditions and then get out of the way."[38]

Unfortunately, the Bush Jr. administration, and the Republican Party more generally, failed miserably in this respect. "A deep pessimist, Mr. Cheney has an utterly impoverished view of what American technologists can do when asked to do the impossible and an utterly impoverished view of what the American people would do post-9/11—if summoned to the great national cause of energy independence."[39] Friedman's assessment of the Bush energy plan that we have previously examined in the Enron section was "get more addicted to oil."[40] During the 2008 presidential election, Friedman was very critical of the Republican "drill, baby, drill" policy and John McCain's suggestion to build more nuclear power plants. His objection was not that nuclear power was inherently wrong but that Republican policies of lowering taxes, banning abortions, borrowing from China, or having Sarah Palin "reform Washington" were unlikely to pay for the $10 billion-per-plant price tag.[41] During the 2008 presidential election, McCain's energy policies were the target of many Friedman barbs. He was critical of McCain's unwillingness to subsidize wind turbines while supporting government money for nuclear power[42] and his plan to cut the federal excise tax on gasoline during the period when the prices were skyrocketing. "This is not an energy policy. This is money laundering: we borrow from China and ship it to Saudi Arabia and take a little cut for ourselves as it goes through our gas tanks."[43]

Friedman provided an excellent summary of his overall views on the importance of government in a 2008 editorial. He was scornful of Ronald Reagan's line, "The nine most terrifying words in the English language are: I'm from the government, and I'm here to help." Friedman argued that, "In the age of globalization, government matters more than ever." It saved the United States from economic disaster by bailing out Fannie Mae, Freddie Mac, and AIG. (As an interesting aside, his limited vision of the role of the government is also nicely highlighted by his endorsement of Henry Paulson: "I am impressed with his handling of this crisis," which, as the next chapter will demonstrate, is a horribly naïve analysis of the causes of and cures for the financial crisis.) In fact, government needed to do more. It needed to have the fiscal capacity to promote the next industrial revolution: "E.T., energy technology" and mandate a forty-miles-per-gallon car fleet by 2015.[44]

Friedman argued that a supercompetitive global world requires an active state, but the kind of intervention he recommended was remarkably pro-business. America may have been losing ground to Chinese and Indian entrepreneurs, but its policy framework was vastly superior to that of the absurd Europeans. For Friedman, the ideal policy package for the global economy was a "flexible, educated workforce and low corporate taxes," in order to attract investors from America and elsewhere, a fact that seems lost on the Europeans. "There is a huge debate roiling in Europe today over which economic model to follow: the Franco-German shorter-workweek-sixweeks'-vacation-never-fire-anyone-but-high-unemployment social model or the less protected but more innovative high-employment Anglo-Saxon model preferred by Britain, Ireland, and Eastern Europe. It is obvious to me that the Irish-British model is the way of the future, and the only question is when Germany and France will face reality: either they become Ireland or they become museums. That is their real choice over the next few years—it's either the leprechaun way or the Louvre."[45] The French are the worst of a bad European lot. "Ah, those French. How silly can they be? The European Union wants to consolidate its integration and France, trying to protect its own 35-hour workweek and other welfare benefits, rejects the E.U. constitution. What a bunch of antiglobalist Gaullist Luddites! Yo, Jacques, what world do you think you're livin' in, pal? Get with the program! It's called Anglo-American capitalism, mon ami."[46] "French voters are trying to preserve a 35-hour workweek in a world where Indian engineers are ready to work a 35-hour day." "Yes it is a bad time for France and friends to lose their appetite for hard work—just when India, China and Poland are rediscovering theirs."[47]

Friedman's invective against Europe was not due to an irrational hatred of berets and *lederhosen*. Rather it was a cautionary tale about what governments should absolutely not do—side with workers in the labor market by implementing a protective social welfare policy. The problem with Europe was that business was held back by a lazy workforce protected by the state's generous unemployment benefits, mandatory vacation time, and reduced workweek. However, Friedman's analysis of economic history is abysmal. European workers once faced the same conditions currently being endured by the Chinese and Indian labor force. They too worked twelve-hour days six days a week for the privilege of starvation wages, miserable housing, and an early death. The difference between workers in Europe and China is that the former have managed, through a century of industrial and political action, to carve out some protection from the ravages of the free labor market, like an actual weekend. It is interesting that despite the supposedly coddled labor market in places like France, Germany, and Sweden that labor productivity in Europe exceeded that in the United States between 1975 and 1995. It is true that the European economy slowed in the late 1990s and early 2000s. It is also true that much of this has been due to a decline in the European manufacturing sector, which makes up a larger part of its economy than in the United States and is losing market share to India and China.[48] However, the cosseted European workers seemed to be soldiering on quite effectively before being forced to compete with their superexploited colleagues from China. Friedman's solution to this problem is indicative of the conservative side of his policy prescriptions—create more exploitative, business-friendly labor market conditions in Europe.

Europeans were not only lazy, but also had an unhealthy distrust of innovation. Friedman was amazed and dismayed when he discovered a warning on a European menu that the food may contain genetically modified organisms (GMO). "Europeans, out of some romantic rebellion against America and high technology were shunning US-grown food containing G.M.O.s." Friedman viewed European concerns about the negative impact of GMOs on human health and the environment as ludicrous because "there is no scientific evidence that these are harmful." Rather than lend any credence to European fears about this new technology he attributed their reluctance to "being weak after being powerful," which "can make you stupid."[49] This conclusive opinion about an ongoing scientific debate reflected Friedman's love of technological advance and predisposition to trust the corporate world.

Despite Friedman's mockery of Europeans' desire to protect their health, it appears as though in many indicators they are faring much better than Americans. A study by Ken Thorpe of the Rollins School of Public Health at Emory University compared older adults in Europe and the United States. He found that those in the United States were twice as likely to have heart disease and arthritis. They also had higher rates of cancer, diabetes, and obesity.[50] Perhaps the Europeans know what they are doing in applying a more cautious approach to potential hazards to human health.

A logical extension of Friedman's commitment to innovation and global competition was his advocacy of a conservative, business-friendly version of globalization that had been institutionalized over the last several decades under the WTO. "I just spent a week in Germany and had to listen to all these people telling me how globalization is destroying India and adding to poverty, and I just said to them, 'Look if you want to argue about ideology, we can do that, but on the level of facts, you're just wrong.'"[51] Citing a report by consulting firm AT Kearney, Friedman argued that, "the fastest globalizing countries have enjoyed rates of economic growth that averaged 30 to 50 percent higher over the past 20 years. The same countries also enjoyed greater political freedom . . . more social spending and received higher scores on the U.N. Human Development Index, an indicator of longevity, literacy and standard of living." The report added that while some 34 percent of the world's population lived in absolute poverty in 1980, by 1990 that number had dropped by more than half. "In other words, 1.4 billion people escaped absolute poverty as a result of economic growth associated with globalization."[52] This nicely reflects how Friedman's views are colored by his sources. A.T. Kearney is a global management consulting firm, which, according to their website, "have been trusted advisors on CEO-agenda issues to the world's leading corporations across all major industries."[53] These supposed "facts" were declared without the qualification or nuance necessary, considering the contradictory data from the ILO presented earlier in this chapter.

The free flow of finance and trade not only produced the competitive world that created innovation and prosperity, it also fostered world peace, according to Friedman. When Russia invaded Georgia he asserted that "the Russian stock market has been hammered as a result." It was not the old world of politics that prevented countries from shooting at their neighbors, but the requirement to maintain a stable environment for investment.[54] Similarly, he claimed that the reason that India refused to react to Pakistan's military provocations in 2002 was because the huge Indian software and information technology industry "told the nationalist government to cool it."[55]

Conversely, countries that closed themselves off from the outside world were breeding grounds for terrorists. Saudi Arabia, Yemen, Afghanistan, and northwest Pakistan had all rejected external economic links. As a result they had an impoverished population with little to lose by violent activity and lacked entrepreneurs who required peaceful relationships with other countries.[56] It was this insularity that accounted for the prevalence of terrorism in Islamic countries, which made up "20 percent of the world's population, yet only 4 percent of the world's trade."[57]

Globalization and international competition also promote democracy. According to Friedman, China's lack of free speech was a costly obstacle in its attempt to become globally competitive. "China may have great airports but last week it went back to censoring *The New York Times* and other Western news sites. Censorship restricts your people's imaginations. That's really, really dumb."[58]

If globalization is a force for peace and democracy, if it lifts people out of poverty, those who oppose it must be badly misinformed, according to Friedman. His pen was certainly sharpened when it came to describing the protests against the WTO in Seattle. In a column entitled "Senseless in Seattle," Friedman called the protesters "ridiculous," "crazy," "a Noah's ark of flat-earth advocates, protectionist trade unions and yuppies looking for their 1960's fix," who if they only "stopped yapping" long enough to think "would realize that they have been duped by knaves like Pat Buchanan."[59] According to Friedman those who protest globalization are against so many things, "from cell phones to trade in Big Macs—that it connotes nothing." "Which is why the anti-globalization protests have produced noise but nothing that has improved anyone's life." These well-meaning but misguided people failed to comprehend that properly managed globalization was the "poor's best ladder out of misery."[60]

A year later Friedman took a slightly more nuanced approach to the WTO protesters, which he divided into two groups. The first, more reasonable, group understood that globalization had benefits and costs. Their goal is to improve globalization by "agitating for the World Bank to be more sensitive to the environment in its building projects, by urging rich countries to write off the debts of the poorest countries, and by urging the I.M.F. to be more open to alternative, possibly less harsh remedies for rescuing countries in financial distress. All worthy issues." He also identified a second group for which he had less sympathy. This group is made up of "economic quacks peddling conspiracy theories about globalization; the anti-free-trade extremists, such as Ralph Nader's group, Public Citizen; the protectionist trade unions; and the anarchists. These groups deserve to be called by their real name: 'The Coalition to Keep the World's Poor People Poor.'" "This coalition is supported by U.S. unions that have launched a protectionist jihad against more free trade with the developing world, for fear of competition. The unions don't want to say that out loud—so they tell you they are for free trade with countries that get their worker standards up."[61]

Questions could be raised about whether there was any contradiction between Friedman's advocacy of globalization, especially as it has been practiced in China, and desire to see a greener energy policy. This illustrates Friedman's fundamental misunderstanding of the Chinese model. Although the Chinese certainly structured their economy better than some other countries by investing early on in a modern infrastructure, spending on education, and investing in public health, this was only part of what drove Chinese success. The Chinese miracle was based far more on cut-rate labor costs, repression of workers, and environmental destruction than it was high-tech innovation. Further, it was precisely the globalization that Friedman so covets that created pressure on those more comfortable, like the Europeans, to compromise the gains that have struggled to achieve over the years. Of course, this was precisely what the WTO protestors objected to, not cell phones and technology, as Friedman suggested.

Friedman turned China (or Hong Kong) into a cartoon TV sitcom like the *Jetsons*, where residents enjoyed all of the wondrous technological innovations created by vibrant entrepreneurs. By comparing their ultra-modern airports and infallible cell phone access to U.S. technological malaise, he provided Americans with a chilling warning of the second-class economic status that awaits them if they fail to follow the Chinese example. Perhaps if he had stepped out of his five-star hotel or guided CEO tour long enough to rub shoulders with those at the sharp end of the Chinese miracle he might have had a slightly different perspective.

Paul Krugman

Krugman has been the *Times*' most important economic columnist over the last decade. While other columnists, like Friedman, spent much of their time opining on economic policy, they are "merely" journalists, reporting on a field in which they may be remarkably talented observers, but have little formal training. In contrast, Krugman can boast impeccable academic credentials. His columns continuously returned to a few common themes: the macroeconomy, free trade, and the appropriate role of state intervention in the U.S. economy.

Krugman's macroeconomic columns have been largely dedicated to analyzing the relationship between monetary policy, economic growth, and income distribution. His opinions on this relationship have evolved considerably since a remarkable column in 1999, when Greenspan warned that "steadily depleting the pool of available workers" in the United States would create conditions for wages to outpace gains in labor productivity. "To a normal human being—Greenspan's concerns might sound very peculiar." "After all, what's wrong with giving jobs to the jobless and higher wages to the employed?" But according to Krugman, "Greenspan is probably right to be worried" because maintaining a large "reserve army of the unemployed" keeps workers from asking for large pay increases that might stoke inflation. It was not Greenspan's policy of keeping people out of work that irked Krugman, but his transparency about doing so. "It's not that he is mean-spirited or a tool of capitalist oppression: he's just doing his job. But you still have to wonder whether it was a good idea to describe that job so explicitly and so honestly."[62] At this early stage, Krugman mirrored the opinion of many other columns and news stories at the

Times on this topic. Macroeconomic policy should ensure that workers do not gain at the expense of profits.

By 2003, however, Krugman started to criticize the niggardly gains of workers during the George W. Bush-era boom of the early 2000s. "Real G.D.P. rose at an annual rate of 8.2 percent. But wage and salary income, adjusted for inflation, rose at an annual rate of only 0.8 percent." In an economy in which the vast majority of the gains were going directly to corporate profits "the big question is whether a recovery that does so little for most Americans can really be sustained."[63]

According to Krugman, static incomes for so much of the population had greatly reduced social mobility in the United States, meaning that people's prospects in life depend mostly on the wealth of their parents. "For years, opinion leaders have told us that it's all about family values. And it is—but it will take a while before most people realize that they meant the value of coming from the right family."[64] He responded to those who attempted to dismiss the income inequality problem as "the politics of envy," as did Republican Mitt Romney, with this analogy. "A liberal and a conservative were sitting in a bar. Then Bill Gates walked in. 'Hey, we're rich!' shouted the conservative. 'The average person in this bar is now worth more than a billion!' 'That's silly,' replied the liberal. 'Bill Gates raises the average, but that doesn't make you or me any richer.' 'Hah!' said the conservative, 'I see you're still practicing the discredited politics of class warfare.'"[65] While he was concerned about the outcome of rising inequality, as late as 2005 he was still searching for a cause, declaring that "at this point the joylessness of the economic expansion for most Americans is a mystery."[66]

What was particularly perplexing for Krugman was that unemployment had fallen so dramatically that it could no longer play the wage-moderating role that he recommended in 1999. "The official unemployment rate is low by historical standards, but workers still don't seem to have much bargaining power."[67] He rightly dismissed the theory, put forward by Fed Chair Ben Bernanke, that growing income inequality stemmed from increasing gains to educated workers. Krugman argued that the income gains were concentrated so far up the income spectrum that this explanation could not be accurate. "Between 1972 and 2001 the wage and salary income of Americans at the 90th percentile of the income distribution rose only 34 percent, or about 1 percent per year. But income at the 99th percentile rose 87 percent; income at the 99.9th percentile rose 181 percent; and income at the 99.99th percentile rose 497 percent." If the reassuring tale of education gains did not explain income inequality, what did? "The idea that we have a rising oligarchy is much more disturbing. It suggests that the growth of inequality may have as much to do with power relations as it does with market forces. Unfortunately, that's the real story."[68]

In other columns he was more explicit. "But it seems likely that government policies have played a big role in America's growing economic polarization—not just easily measured policies like tax rates for the rich and the level of the minimum wage, but things like the shift in Labor Department policy from protection of worker rights to tacit support for union-busting."[69] In fact, labor market policy "seems intended to accelerate our march back to the robber baron era."[70]

Krugman was scathing in his criticism of how George Bush Jr.'s income tax changes worsened an already unequal income distribution. When "key conservative ideologues" declared support for a tax increase on those with lower incomes, the lesson, according to Krugman, was "how relentless and extremist today's conservative movement really is."[71] As we shall see, Krugman could be very critical of Nader, but after watching "Senate Democrats waffle over what should be a clear issue of justice and sound tax policy—namely, whether managers of private equity funds and hedge funds should be subject to the same taxes as ordinary working Americans," in 2007 he agreed with Nader's claim that both Democrats and Republicans were "equally subservient to corporations and the wealthy."[72]

As we pointed out in the macro chapter, the issues of increasing inequality, monetary policy, and free trade are intertwined. While tight monetary policy that caused unemployment, stifling workers' wage gains, was part of the wage stagnation story in the 1980s and early 1990s, it could not explain why the growth in wages remained low as unemployment decreased. At least part of the reason for this later stagnation was downward pressure on wages from international competition. As was the case with macro policy, Krugman's views on this subject have changed considerably since the late 1990s.

In the late 1990s, Krugman was an advocate of what might be called "compassionate globalization," which acknowledged that there would be an unfortunate minority in the developed, high-wage countries who would lose out from free trade and needed to be compensated in some way (say retraining allowances). However, on balance, free trade was a massive force for good. "What you will discover is that life in that pre-globalization society was nasty, brutish and short; for example, in 1975 only one rural Thai in six had access to safe drinking water. Today it's four out of five."[73] In discussing the progress made by South Korea, China, India, and other "export-led" East Asian countries, he marveled, "I'm not talking about arid economic statistics; what we've seen over the past generation is an enormous, unexpected improvement in the human condition." "Every one of those development success stories was based on export-led growth."[74] In perhaps his strongest statement, Krugman claimed, "Globalization, driven not by human goodness but by the profit motive, has done far more good for far more people than all the foreign aid and soft loans ever provided by well-intentioned governments and international agencies."[75] As was mentioned in the free trade introduction, there can be no question that several East Asian countries have done remarkably well using the strategy of export-led growth. However, the kind of free trade globalization that Krugman was discussing was very far removed from the actual policies that were followed in these nations.

Krugman argued that free trade was only a minor source of job losses for U.S. workers. In 2000 he claimed that although "globalization makes the world a richer place," two groups of people gain the most. The first "are those who benefit from vastly improved access to technology and capital—which is to say, workers in developing countries." The second are those who "have technology and capital to sell—which means the rich and the highly educated." On the downside, free trade was one, "though probably not the most important, of the reasons that real wages of many American workers have stagnated or even declined over the last 25 years."[76]

During this early period Krugman was concerned that all of the bad press for free trade might do irreparable economic damage. First it might encourage protectionism. "If the job gap doesn't start closing soon, protectionist pressures will become irresistible. The point is that free trade is politically viable only if it's backed by effective job creation measures and a strong domestic social safety net."[77] Second, the fallacy that free trade constrains domestic policy created an excuse for abandoning liberal policies. "None of the important constraints on American economic and social policy come from abroad. We have the resources to take far better care of our poor and unlucky than we do; if our policies have become increasingly mean-spirited, that is a political choice, not something imposed on us by anonymous forces. We cannot evade responsibility for our actions by claiming that global markets made us do it."[78]

As did Friedman, Krugman argued seriously that free trade and globalization were forces for openness and democracy. "China—for all its ham-handed repression—has become a far freer, more open society than anyone could have imagined 25 years ago, mainly because all-out totalitarianism and a market economy don't mix."[79] For Krugman, open markets create two important avenues that promote democratic expression. "When a nation opens to the world, its businesses become less dependent on government favor, its citizens become more aware of how politics is conducted in advanced countries. The result, repeatedly, has been a peaceful transition to true democracy."[80]

Although Krugman's language was slightly less derisive than that used by Friedman, he shared his colleague's assessment of the limited intellectual capacity of globalization critics. When protestors took to the streets at the Summit of the Americas in Quebec City, Krugman was not impressed. "Anyone who thinks that the answer to world poverty is simple outrage against global trade has no head—or chooses not to use it. The anti-globalization movement already has a remarkable track record of hurting the very people and causes it claims to champion."[81] He claimed that the protestors at the WTO meetings in Seattle thought that free trade was "simply a way for capitalists to exploit the world's workers." They did "not believe that most of the world is still poor because development is hard to do" but because of the villainous behavior of multinational corporations.[82]

Globalization protestors were certainly not capable of nuanced "fine distinctions" in international economic policy. "They are as opposed to free trade in goods as they are to speculative movements of short-term capital; they view the longer-term trends in the world economy, not just the short-term crises, with dismay."[83] "Real experts, you see, tend to have views that are not entirely one-sided. For example, Columbia's Jagdish Bhagwati, a staunch free-trader, is also very critical of unrestricted flows of

short-term capital. Right or not, this mixed stance reflects an honest mind at work."
"You might think that hacks would at least try to simulate an open mind—that
simply for the sake of appearances . . . the Economic Policy Institute (EPI) [would]
find some trade liberalization it favors. But it almost never happens."[84] Choosing to
ally oneself with Bhagwati against the EPI is the academic equivalent of siding with
Goliath against David. While the EPI and so many other opponents were against
the WTO or NAFTA version of free trade, we have shown in the introduction that
there were many problems with these agreements, even from the standpoint of
the internal logic of free trade. Moreover, as the problems with the Doha Round
demonstrated, the developing nations themselves appear to be of the opinion that
globalization should proceed on a vastly different basis than that which currently
exists under the auspices of the WTO.

Krugman argued that the fundamental mistake made by those who oppose free
trade was confusing the low absolute living standards in the third world with the
rising trend. While working conditions were abysmal by U.S. standards, they nonetheless represent a real improvement for the sweatshop employee. When Bangladeshi
textile factories stopped employing children, Oxfam found that the "displaced child
workers ended up in even worse jobs, or on the streets—and that a significant number
were forced into prostitution." The fact is that low wages were developing countries'
advantage in international trade. "The same factors that make poor countries poor—
low productivity, bad infrastructure, general social disorganization—mean that such
countries can compete on world markets only if they pay wages much lower than those
paid in the West."[85] Krugman's explanation for poverty in the developing world was
not incorrect. Bad infrastructure and social disorganization are factors. However, it
was a remarkably incomplete analysis. It crucially, and probably not coincidentally,
focused on sources of poverty internal to developing world countries, while ignoring
those that were imposed from outside their borders by powerful, developed nations.
A closer reading of history, including Chapter 4 of this book, on U.S. foreign policy,
would reveal that many of the causes of developing country difficulties can be laid
at the feet of external, often U.S., forces.

At this stage of Krugman's career at the *Times* his opinions closely mirrored
those of Friedman on free trade. Both argued that it benefited the poorer nations
of the world. Both were cutting in their criticism of the flat-earth Luddites who
opposed WTO-style globalization. Krugman differed from Friedman primarily
in his insistence that a global free trade regime should not mean that workers in
wealthy nations should have to give up their hard-fought gains. He argued that
the decline in state protection of the American worker should be laid at the feet of
domestic political decisions, not increased competition U.S. labor was facing due
to free trade. Friedman, of course, argued that this kind of competition was inevitable in a global free-trade regime, but that stripping developed country workers
of their comfortable safety blankets would induce harder work, more education,
and greater productivity.

By 2007, Krugman was starting to rethink his position on the impact of free trade on American workers. "Fears that low-wage competition is driving down U.S. wages have a real basis in both theory and fact. When we import labor-intensive manufactured goods from the third world instead of making them here, the result is reduced demand for less-educated American workers, which leads in turn to lower wages for these workers. And no, cheap consumer goods at Wal-Mart aren't adequate compensation." However, since free trade still benefited the developing world, U.S. protectionism was not a policy option. Although Krugman admitted that he did not have an ideal solution to this dilemma, domestic pro-labor policies like "universal health care, paid for by taxing the economy's winners, would be a good place to start."[86] Later in 2007 he dramatically changed his assessment of the critics of free trade. "I'm not a protectionist. For the sake of the world as a whole, I hope that we respond to the trouble with trade not by shutting trade down, but by doing things like strengthening the social safety net. But those who are worried about trade have a point, and deserve some respect."[87]

In addition to broad macro and international economic policy, Krugman also paid considerable attention to the structure of the domestic economy, especially the role that the state should play. He paid special attention to three areas: the labor market, the extent to which Social Security and health care should be delivered by the government, and regulation. His opinions on labor market policy followed the trajectory of his ideas on both macroeconomics and trade. In 2000 he was Friedman-like in his mockery of the Europeans. Although European "policies that slow down the rat race: high tax rates, generous health and unemployment benefits, long mandatory paid vacations, maybe even a limit on individual working hours" may appear attractive, "France has an unemployment rate more than twice as high as America's, largely because of those same government policies. . . . I'd say that given the alternatives, the American system, though not beautiful, still takes the prize."[88] But by 2005, he was more complimentary of Europe. Although the average French citizen does have less income than in the United States, "Government regulations actually allow people to make a desirable tradeoff—to modestly lower income in return for more time with friends and family."[89]

On most other domestic issues Krugman has remained a steadfast liberal. He objected to conservative free market policies that, he felt, amounted to little more than "crony capitalism" in which a particularly well-connected industry benefited at the expense of the rest of society and even other businesses. Krugman was particularly galled by two of Bush Jr.'s economic policies: the move to privatize Social Security and the refusal to offer public health care.

One of the early policies floated by the George W. Bush administration was to privatize Social Security. Broadly speaking, this meant having people invest for their own retirement during their working lives rather than having government pay retirees out of tax revenue. While the alluring logic of this proposal is that returns from the stock market would increase retiree income, its dangers should be all too apparent after the stock market crash of 2008. What this would, unquestionably, have done was provide a huge windfall for finance and investment firms that would cash in on the sudden increase in private investment money.

Krugman was opposed to this policy from the beginning, arguing that it had more to do with helping Republican friends on Wall Street than any rational economics. "The administration economists who claim that privatization will strengthen Social Security are, more than ever, revealed as quacks."[90] According to Krugman, a crucial part of the political strategy of the pro-privatization lobby was to create the false impression that Social Security was in crisis. "The revenue lost because of the Bush tax cut will be more than twice the sum needed to secure Social Security without any reform at all for the next 75 years." "The truth is that the only serious threat to Social Security comes from those who want to panic us into junking the system, when all it needs are minor repairs."[91] Krugman argued that, ironically, experience in the UK suggested that privatization might actually increase government spending on retirees in order to "avoid the return of widespread poverty among the elderly—a problem that Britain, like the U.S., thought it had solved."[92]

Krugman was equally enraged about American unwillingness to institute universal public health insurance. He argued that public health care could deliver better results at a fraction of the price than the current private system. "In 2001, we spent $4,887 on health care per capita, compared with $2,792 in Canada and $2,561 in France. Yet the United States does worse than either country by any measure of health care success you care to name—life expectancy, infant mortality, whatever." "Does this mean that the American way is wrong, and that we should switch to a Canadian-style single-payer system? Well, yes."[93] Although doctors in the United States were paid more than those in publicly run France, and drug prices are higher in a private system, the largest problem was that "administrative costs took 31 cents out of every dollar the United States spent on health care, compared with only 17 cents in Canada," according to the *New England Journal of Medicine*.[94] In fact, the savings from a public system would be so great that they would be "far more than the cost of covering all of those now uninsured."[95]

In mustering support for his public health care position, Krugman argued that it would increase the profitability of all U.S. businesses except those in the health care industry. "In Canada, respectable business executives are ardent defenders of 'socialized medicine.' Two years ago the Conference Board of Canada—a who's who of the nation's corporate elite—issued a report crediting public universal health care for its 'economic contribution to the competitiveness of Canadian businesses.'"[96] A year later Krugman quoted a study by consultants A.T. Kearney, who found that "last year in the US General Motors spent $1,500 per vehicle on health care" but "Toyota spent only $97 in Japan." "If the United States had national health insurance, G.M. would be in much better shape."[97]

A significant difference between Krugman and Friedman is in the degree to which the former explicitly supports government-only-run programs like social security and public universal health care. Friedman certainly favors a well-run state bureaucracy setting the broad policy framework through things like price controls, tax policy, and public education, but he is clear that the economy should be driven by the entrepreneurial private sector. He has no qualms about government subsidizing the right kind of business, but is no advocate of state-run institutions.

Krugman's opinions on the regulatory role of government have always been liberal, but they have become more so in recent years. During Ralph Nader's run at the presidency in 2004, Krugman declared him unfit for the office because of Nader's supposed anti-corporate bias. One of his criticisms was due to Nader's advocacy of tighter FDA oversight of the prescription drug industry, particularly Feldene (piroxicam), an anti-inflammatory Krugman used to help treat his arthritis. "Mr. Nader now apparently believes that whatever is good for General Motors, or Pfizer, or any corporation, must be bad for the world." "To block opportunities for corporate profit he is quite willing to . . . prevent patients from getting drugs that might give them a decent life."[98] As it turned out, Nader may not have been preventing patients from having a decent life, but protecting them against some fairly nasty side effects. In 2007 the European Medicines Agency (EMA) recommended restricting the use of piroxicam because of "gastrointestinal side effects and serious skin reactions," which doesn't sound pleasant.[99]

However, only one year later Krugman admitted that Nader's more general concerns about the prescription drug industry might just have been justified after the painkiller Vioxx was found to increase the risk of heart attacks. To make matters worse, the manufacturer, Merck, deliberately attempted to suppress evidence in medical journals that would publicize these risks. "The point is that the whiff of corruption in our medical system isn't emanating from a few bad apples. The whole system of incentives encourages doctors and researchers to serve the interests of the medical industry."[100] Of course, this was exactly the point that Nader had been making all along.

It is useful to contrast how Krugman analyzed the Vioxx case with Friedman's criticism of GM. Friedman pinned GM's problems on its executives, arguing that the U.S. automobile industry's problems were generally down to a lack of visionary leadership. His solution was to trade those at the top for the supposedly more visionary Steve Jobs of Apple. Krugman's treatment of Vioxx explicitly rejects the personal explanation, locating the problem instead in the system of incentives in the drug industry that would inevitably lead to this type of scandal. For Krugman, it is the system itself that must be structured properly and appropriately insulated from the kinds of perverse incentives that might result in social problems if the market is left unregulated.

Krugman required no Vioxx moment of conversion in his discussions of the regulatory efforts surrounding finance. The accounting scandals of Enron and Worldcom in the early 2000s provided evidence that regulatory oversight of accounting and investment was both necessary and neglected. "When things are going well there is a strong tendency to suppose that financial markets can take care of themselves. Well, they can't."[101] Unfortunately, the SEC's ability to regulate the finance industry had been compromised by budget cutbacks. "The SEC is ludicrously underfinanced." "Officials say there are investigations that they should pursue but can't for lack of resources."[102] When the extent of the accounting violations became clear as Enron went bankrupt and the stock market crashed, among populist calls for punishment of executives there were also hopes for a restructuring of financial regulation. On the latter score Krugman was overoptimistic. "I predict that in the years ahead Enron, not Sept. 11, will come to be seen as the greater turning point in U.S. society."[103] Krugman's prediction that the 2002 financial scandals would lead to a groundswell of popular support clamoring for a return of regulation may highlight his limitations as a political crystal ball gazer. However, his analysis of the problems in the accounting scandal and the California energy debacle served him very well in his analysis of the financial crisis that is covered in the next chapter.

Krugman argued that rigorous food safety inspection was beneficial for both consumers and the industry itself, despite the assurances of conservatives that regulation was unnecessary. According to Krugman, strong regulation is in businesses' best interests in an industry in which consumers are largely unaware of the quality of the merchandise they are purchasing. "The president of the United Fresh Produce Association says that the industry's problems 'can't be solved without strong mandatory federal regulations': without such regulations, scrupulous growers and processors risk being undercut by competitors more willing to cut corners on food safety. Consumers have no way of knowing whether the food they eat is contaminated, and in this case what you don't know can hurt or even kill you."[104] "Failure to regulate effectively isn't just bad for consumers, it's bad for business."[105]

Much to Krugman's dismay, the FDA's inspection and enforcement powers have been whittled down over the last three decades. As we have seen with other regulatory examples, this was done in a number of ways, including under-funding, and "the systematic appointment of foxes to guard henhouses." In 2003, during the mad cow scare in the United States, "the Department of Agriculture was headed by Ann M. Veneman, a former food-industry lobbyist." "The ironic thing is that the Agriculture Department's deference to the beef industry actually ended up backfiring: because potential foreign buyers didn't trust our safety measures, beef producers spent years excluded from their most important overseas markets."[106]

Krugman also expressed liberal opinions on tax policy. He was incensed when corporations were permitted to violate tax law by a lax IRS. "We're losing revenue because profitable U.S. companies are using fancy footwork to avoid paying taxes." "In other words, this isn't about competition; it's about tax evasion."[107] As was the case with the FDA and SEC, the problem was the constant whittling away of the agency's ability to do its job. "Since 1995 Congress has systematically forced the Internal Revenue Service to shrink its operations; the number of auditors has fallen by 28 percent." This was especially remarkable since increasing the budget of the

IRS would actually generate revenue for the government. "So starving the I.R.S. isn't about saving money, it's about protecting affluent tax cheats."[108]

Krugman's insistence that both corporations and the affluent pay what he sees as their fair share of taxes reflects both his opinions on equitable after-tax income distribution and the need to fund important social programs. This liberal policy of "tax and spend" placed him in direct ideological conflict with the administration of George W. Bush, who Krugman saw as dangerously, or deliberately, irresponsible on the matter of fiscal policy. "By pushing through another huge tax cut in the face of record deficits, the administration clearly demonstrates either that it is completely feckless, or that it actually wants a fiscal crisis." "How, then, can the government pay for Medicare and Medicaid—which didn't exist in the 1950's—and Social Security."[109] Krugman rightly pointed out that cuts to taxes and social programs have brutal distributional consequences. The Bush tax cuts go to the rich, while a tight budget will "squeeze programs for the poor and middle class."[110]

Again, there is an obvious contrast to be made on tax policy between Friedman and Krugman. Friedman's reliance on the innovative power of the entrepreneur inevitably leads to a policy of lower corporate taxes. By permitting visionary innovators to keep more of the returns of their entrepreneurial skill, those at the forefront of the economy will take more risks to the benefit of all. Krugman argued that taxation of society's wealthier members is desirable because it creates a more equal distribution of after-tax income and funds important social programs.

Conclusion

Friedman and Krugman started the new millennium with a fair amount in common. Their opinions on Europeans and free trade were remarkably similar. They also both had little tolerance for ill-gotten profits, especially when they came at the expense of the broader corporate world, calling for increased regulatory oversight from agencies like the SEC. However, eight years later they were very different. Krugman reconsidered many of his earlier positions, especially on free trade and the labor market. As the economic catastrophes of the late 2000s continued to mount, Krugman became increasingly social democratic in his outlook.

Friedman was neither consistently conservative nor liberal, but had a vision of the long-run interests of the U.S. business class as a whole. He advocated the conservative WTO version of free trade and railed against the liberal social welfare policies of Europe. However, he also proposed liberal measures of industrial policy, regulation, tax increases, and price floors. Both his liberal and conservative policies have a common thread. His overarching goal was to foster innovation, acknowledging that a strong state was necessary to do so, but in a manner that is supportive of its business entrepreneurs. While Friedman did not want the state to directly bail out failures like GM, he did want the state to subsidize R&D, reduce corporate income taxes, and attract a skilled workforce. It is clear that for Friedman the road to prosperity is creating the broad public policy framework for promoting innovation and then allowing the entrepreneurial private sector to take over.

In addition to subsidizing businesses' innovative activities, government should also encourage profits by ensuring that the labor market is tilted in favor of employers. This was reflected in his vilification of European workers as coddled and lazy. It was also reflected in his misreading of the costs and benefits of globalization generally and the Chinese and Indian examples in particular. The role of the worker in Friedman's economy is long hours of toil while continuously remaining technologically tooled up in order to compete with those who have not yet been able to protect themselves from the cutthroat global labor market.

Friedman's glorious utopia of high-tech innovation may be superficially appealing, but like the Chinese miracle that he so admires, a closer inspection reveals some serious problems. While the planet may be a little better off should his energy recommendations be implemented, his advocacy of globalization makes it less likely that these kinds of policies will see the light of day at the national level. His competitive and innovative economy favors owners and executives at the expense of the vast majority of working people. Friedman's world is built not on technological wonder but on human misery. His insensitivity to the condition of the general population was highlighted by his claim that the Chinese were living better than "us" because of their advanced technology. Even a casual glance at the living standards of the average person in the two countries would show this comment to be ludicrous, but from a perspective that only focuses on the top end of the entrepreneurial class it becomes more coherent, if not defensible.

Until the latter half of the 2000s, Krugman was both liberal and conservative. He was liberal in his insistence on strong regulatory agencies. He also recommended public ownership when he felt it could prove cost effective in the case of health care and Social Security. He has constantly favored taxing high-income Americans and business to pay for a well-funded social safety net. However, he was also quite conservative in his opinions on free trade. He argued forcefully that free trade was an overwhelming force for good in the developing world and that it did, at worst, modest and easily reparable harm in the high-wage countries like the United States. He was just as scathing as Friedman about the Luddites and Utopians whose knavish intellect failed to grasp globalization's obvious benefits. If free trade was his only conservative foible, it could perhaps be viewed as an anomaly. However, his attacks on Nader's desire to protect consumers from pharmaceutical companies, support of Greenspan's efforts to create unemployment, and lack of sympathy for pro-labor policies in Europe reflected a deeper conservative streak.

By the last half of the 2000s, Krugman's opinions were considerably different. Although he maintained his insistence that globalization benefited the world's poor, he became convinced of its detrimental impacts on U.S. workers. He recognized that the very structure of the pharmaceutical industry created incentives for firms to profit at the expense of consumers. His opinions on macroeconomic policy became an attack on the growing inequality and an admittedly belated realization that wage stagnation in the context of low unemployment was being caused by very deliberate policy changes at the national and international level. He even came to appreciate the laid-back, leisure-loving lifestyle made possible by the regulated French labor market. As the senator said in the movie *Gladiator*, he may not be of the people, but he is for the people.

Krugman was also convinced that many of these liberal policies, like Social Security, universal health care, and regulation were necessary to maintain U.S. corporate competitiveness. For example, universal public health insurance would lower the wage bill for the U.S. firms that currently pay for their employees' health care. Again, this is an excellent example of one particular industry benefiting from the current conservative policy environment, at the expense of the larger corporate sector. For Krugman, there should be no debate on the issue. How many policies contribute to an increase in both equity and efficiency?

Friedman's analysis remains blithely oblivious to those that end up with the short straw in this competitive global economy, whether it is, ironically, the environment in the low-regulation developing world or workers in both developing and developed nations. Of the two, Krugman's late-blooming recognition of the longstanding limits of a maroeconomy based on squeezing the working class and his focus on the potential pitfalls of unregulated markets placed him in a considerably better position than Friedman when it came to the analyzing the economic crisis of 2008, to which we will turn in the next chapter.

CHAPTER 7

THE *NEW YORK TIMES* AND THE FINANCIAL CRISIS

Debt, Deregulation, and Disaster[1]

The economic crisis started out as a financial crisis. The spark that set off the crisis was the collapse of several large banks and insurance companies in the United States. What started as an industry-specific crisis, albeit in a particularly important industry, spread so broadly and so deeply because of the underlying weakness of the U.S. economy. Earlier sections of the book addressed wage stagnation for the average American. According to Elizabeth Warren, the median income for a fully employed American male was nearly $800 less than his counterpart of a generation ago. The only real increase in wages for a family has come from the second paycheck earned by a working mother. Even worse, when cost increases for necessities like health insurance were taken into consideration, a median U.S. family has about $1,500 less in discretionary spending than the previous generation.[2] With families facing falling wages, longer hours, and increasing economic fragility, borrowing became an increasingly attractive option. Lending firms leapt to meet the demand for credit, frequently at less than desirable repayment terms. According to Warren:

> Congress has turned the industry loose to charge whatever it can get and to bury tricks and traps throughout credit agreements. Credit-card contracts that were less than a page long in the early 1980s now number 30 or more pages of small-print legalese. In the details, credit-card companies lend money at one rate, but retain the right to change the interest rate whenever it suits them. They can even raise the rate *after* the money has been borrowed, a practice once considered too shady even for a back-alley loan shark.[3]

The result of companies eager to lend and consumers desperate to borrow was an explosion in household debt. In 2007 household debt was at its all-time high of 100 percent of GDP, up from only 50 percent of GDP in 1980.[4] This was made up of both increases in mortgage debt, which increased from about 50 percent of personal disposable income in 1991 to about 90 percent in 2003, and consumer credit, which increased from just over 15 percent of disposable income to 25 percent in 2003.[5]

People were spending a much larger portion of their income, in part because they were reassured by increases in their wealth, most importantly, their housing assets. Between 2000 and 2005 the real estate assets of U.S. households increased by an amazing $9.1 trillion.[6] House prices increased by 51 percent between 2000 and 2005, which is twice the growth of the next best five-year period for the previous thirty years.[7] So U.S. consumption was in a very precarious position. It was not being fueled by rising incomes, but by rising debt backed by increasing asset values.

With the U.S. economy hazardously propped up by increasingly indebted households, the collapse of the finance industry was the wind that blew down the house of cards. The obvious question that arises is why the banking and finance industry would continue to offer mortgages and other consumer credit to an increasingly indebted U.S. public. The quick answer might be that they didn't know what they were doing, but a more accurate assessment requires a detailed look at the evolution of the banking and finance industry in the United States. The Great Depression of the 1930s was, in part, caused by a massive wave of bank failures across the country, creating a consensus that the sector required government oversight to create an industry in which risks were minimized. The Glass-Steagall Act (or Banking Act) of 1933 prevented commercial banks, which collect deposits and loan money, from also dealing in securities. It also established the Federal Deposit Insurance Corporation (FDIC) to insure depositors' savings in the event of bank failure. The first of these provisions was designed to prevent banks from undertaking speculative investments that might cause banking collapse. The second was designed to reassure the public that in the event of a collapse they would not lose all of their hard-earned savings.

The banking industry was never happy with the legislated separation of commercial banking and investment. In the 25 years between 1975 and 1999, the banking industry unsuccessfully attempted to get Glass-Steagall overturned twelve times.[8] The industry lobby finally paid off in 1999, when the act was repealed and replaced with the Gramm-Leach-Bliley Act (GLBA). The general thrust of the GLBA was to allow banks to engage in a wider range of activities, including the previously forbidden roles of selling securities and insurance. It also eliminated many federal and state restrictions on affiliations between banks and investment and insurance firms. The new regulations were enacted in spite of a prescient warning by the Congressional Research Service in 1987: "Securities activities can be risky, leading to enormous losses. Such losses could threaten the integrity of deposits. In turn, the Government insures deposits and could be required to pay large sums if depository institutions were to collapse as the result of securities losses."

The elimination of Glass-Steagall did not come from a groundswell of popular anger against unjust and archaic legislation. The pressure for regulatory change came directly from the banking and finance industry. The bank Citigroup was especially keen on advancing this agenda. In 1998 it had merged with Travelers Insurance into exactly the kind of corporation Glass-Steagall was designed to prevent, so it needed deregulation to keep the new corporation intact. What is perhaps most remarkable about this merger is that Citigroup was so confident that it could obtain the required deregulation that it pursued the merger with Travelers despite knowing that the resulting corporate structure contravened the existing act. More generally, the industry as a whole was concerned that corporations were bypassing the traditional avenues of bank lending to raise money directly in the financial markets.[9] Getting traditional loans from commercial banks is only one avenue that firms can choose to pursue when they need to raise capital. Banks were eager to participate in the many other alternative measures but were prohibited from doing so due to the stipulations of Glass-Steagall. They further argued that the ancient Glass-Steagall restrictions disadvantaged U.S. banks and investment firms compared to their foreign competitors who were not fettered by the same regulatory requirements. Finally, they argued that the legislation was completely unnecessary since competition in the industry would ensure that firms would be careful with their clients' money.

The industry could count on some sympathetic figures in high-profile places when pressing its case for deregulation. The chairman of the Federal Reserve, Alan Greenspan, was a former director of investment giant J.P. Morgan. The secretary of the Treasury under the Clinton presidency from 1995 to 1999, Robert Rubin, was a former co-chair of Goldman Sachs, a securities firm. Perhaps more tellingly, only days after the Clinton administration (and his Treasury Department) agreed to support the GLBA, Rubin took one of the top jobs at Citigroup, where he went on to support their increasing exposure in the debt market. In the days before Citigroup announced its merger, Travelers head Sandy Weill made phone calls to Rubin (still then secretary of the Treasury) about the deal. He also met with Greenspan, who gave the merger his personal approval.[10]

The banking industry fought against any proposals to regulate its use of increasingly complex financial instruments, including the mortgage-backed derivatives that helped spark the crisis. Mortgage-backed derivatives are investments in which home mortgages are bundled into groups and then sold. The logic behind these kinds of instruments is that diversification reduces the risk of any individual default. However, because it is often difficult for investors to determine just what is in the derivative, these "opaque" investments caused concern in some quarters long before they helped cause the financial crash. In the late 1990s the Commodities Futures Trading Commission (CFTC), a federal agency that regulates options and futures trading, grew concerned about the increasingly complex nature of many of the financial instruments being traded. This unease stemmed in part from a 1994 General Accounting Office report on the growing use of exotic financial instruments in the

United States that concluded that the rapid evolution of derivatives had resulted in important "gaps and weaknesses" in financial regulation and argued for Congress to "modernize the entire U.S. regulatory system."[11] Despite these warnings, when the CFTC proposed regulating derivatives, the finance industry and its government supporters like Greenspan and Rubin lobbied successfully to have the proposed legislation quashed.

The final deregulatory piece in the financial crisis puzzle was the expansion of the subprime mortgage market. A subprime mortgage is granted to applicants whose credit rating is too poor to qualify for a traditional loan. This market extended the possibility of home ownership to many Americans who would have been unable to get a mortgage in the conventional market. However, because these applicants are a greater risk than more creditworthy customers, their interest payments were correspondingly higher. While in retrospect, offering expensive loans to marginal borrowers seems like a recipe for disaster for lender and borrower alike, it was being done in a broadly favorable economic climate. Greenspan created a prolonged period of historically low interest rates in his attempt to keep the U.S. economy bobbing along despite the turbulent waters created by large international financial crises centered on places like East Asia and Mexico. This had made debt more attractive and created a long-term increase in the value of housing. As long as housing prices continued to increase, borrowers' growing wealth would compensate for their rising mortgage payments and lenders would have a valuable asset in the event that the borrower defaulted on their mortgage and the lender foreclosed. In this environment, the value of subprime mortgage loans increased from $160 billion in 2001 to $600 billion in 2006. Of course, these high-risk homeowners might have been a little more creditworthy if their wages had kept pace with rising productivity instead of stagnating for twenty-five years.

Much of the subprime mortgage expansion was engineered by mortgage brokerage companies who, unlike banks, were not subject to government regulations. Subprime mortgage loans outside of federal oversight contained an average debt-to-income ratio of 40 percent, well above federal guidelines.[12] As the subprime market expanded, increasingly marginal borrowers were enticed with increasingly suspect interest schemes. For example, an adjustable rate mortgage offers a low "teaser" interest rate for the first couple of years and then increases to above market rates for the rest of the payback period. An interest-only mortgage delays the payment on the principal for a specified period of time, allowing the borrower to only pay the interest costs. After this period, of course, the compressed payments on the principal greatly increase the monthly payments. Because the total payments for these kinds of subprime mortgages were considerably higher than a conventional mortgage, they were very profitable as long as they were repaid. Precisely because these subprime mortgages were more lucrative than their conventional counterparts, people that would have often qualified for conventional loans were given subprimes. Of course, the higher payments increased the likelihood that they would default. This problem was exacerbated by the flexible interest rates on many of these loans. When interest rates started to rise in 2007, mortgages that were barely manageable for many people became impossible. The default rate on subprime mortgages increased from 10 percent in 2004 to 17 percent in 2007.[13] As people began to default and fewer buyers were looking for homes in a higher-interest-rate environment, housing values began to sag. The decline in housing values piled on the financial distress for many families, since often the amount of their mortgage exceeded the now decreased value of their home.

This leads to the question of why banks would find these risky loans so attractive. Part of the answer is undoubtedly that they, along with most other observers, were overly optimistic about the U.S. housing market. More compellingly, the growth in mortgage-backed securities (from $19 billion in 1995 to $508 billion in 2005) changed the incentive structure at the banks, which had traditionally used their customers' deposits to finance their loans. Banks had been careful lenders, since they were essentially loaning their depositors' money.[14] As a direct result of the repeal of Glass-Steagall, they were able to raise additional finances through the sale of a bundled package of mortgages as financial instruments on the bond market, transferring the risk from the bank to the buyer of the mortgage-backed security and reducing the incentive for banks to carefully check the mortgages that they were offering. The additional finances also had the potential to considerably increase the banks' profitability.

The replacement of Glass-Steagall with the GLBA permitted banks to create the mortgage-backed financial instruments that sparked the current crisis. The unwillingness of regulatory agencies to fulfill their monitoring and oversight mandate delayed the discovery of the extent to which financial companies had based their portfolios on risky investments. Finally, the expansion of the unregulated mortgage brokers with their subprime mortgages increased the fragility of the housing market and provided banks with the steady supply of mortgages necessary to create a stream of shaky mortgage-backed financial securities. All of this deregulation created a crisis waiting to happen. When interest rates increased slightly and housing values started to decline, the collapse began. The troubles in one industry quickly spread to the rest of the economy when precarious banks stopped lending and indebted consumers cut back their spending as their wealth contracted.

In many ways the financial crisis was similar to the Enron energy story described earlier in the book. Deregulation was sought by a particular industry keen to expand its profit-making avenues and convinced that regulation was unnecessary. Unfortunately, it resulted in the collapse of both profitability in the industry itself and the broader corporate sector. We would predict that the *Times* would take a similar line to financial deregulation as it did with Enron, unwilling to support the type of cowboy capitalism that would produce short-term speculative profits at the expense of the long-term stability of business. We would also hypothesize that it would most likely focus on this more industry-specific cause of the crisis rather than the broader macroeconomic sources of weakness that stemmed from the stagnant earnings of U.S. workers.

The *Times* and the Financial Crisis: Articles

In the immediate run-up to the repeal of the Glass-Steagall Act, the *Times* ran a number of articles that were neutral, simply describing the proposed changes to the regulation of the industry, without providing a great deal of analysis. However, by the fall of 1999 the debate about the merits of the new regulatory environment was underway. An early pro-deregulation salvo argued that it would eliminate the shady deals that banks were forced into by Glass-Steagall, "like setting up subsidiaries in Bermuda to underwrite insurance policies or buying savings and loan companies to sell bank-like products through the back door."[15] On the other hand, it also printed opinions that were solidly in favor of regulation. Glass-Steagall created a "fire wall, so that if something caught fire on the underwriting side, it would not burn the deposits away."[16]

When the reform act was officially passed, the *Times* presented the Clinton administration's rationale for the deregulation, but also provided ample space for those who predicted disaster. President Clinton claimed, "We have done right by the American people."[17] According to Summers, Clinton's treasury secretary after Rubin departed for Citigroup, "This historic legislation will better enable American companies to compete in the new economy." According to its supporters, the repeal would reduce the risks to the banking sector by allowing them to diversify their activities. Democratic Senator Bob Kerrey erroneously predicted that "the concerns that we will have a meltdown like 1929 are dramatically overblown." On the other hand, dissenters warned that "the deregulation of Wall Street would someday wreak havoc on the nation's financial system" because the separation of investment and banking prevented destabilizing speculation. Democrat Paul Wellstone claimed, "Glass-Steagall was intended to protect our financial system by insulating commercial banking from other forms of risk. . . . Now Congress is about to repeal that economic stabilizer without putting any comparable safeguard in its place."[18]

From the outset, the *Times* was concerned about the ties between the banking industry and politicians. When the new regulation was passed, the *Times* pointed out that the banking industry had spent lavishly to grease the political wheels, calling the lobbying "one of Washington's great gravy trains. In the last Congressional session alone, the industries affected by the bill poured more than $300 million into lobbying and campaign fund-raising."[19] Rubin's intimate relationship with the industry and Citigroup was also publicized. In a remarkably prophetic article, the *Times* warned its readers that the United States could end up much like Japan, whose economy collapsed because of intimate connections between the banking industry, firms, and politicians. "Its banks rose on their holdings in the Japanese stock market, which emboldened them to lend money for wildly overpriced land deals. Then the stock market collapsed, the real estate market followed, the loans went bad and the banks ceased lending—putting the Japanese economy into a seven-year-long deep freeze." The article warned that the United States could be on its way to exactly this type of scenario. "Citicorp and Travelers announce a mega-merger to extend their global reach—but first they make courtesy calls to the Treasury Secretary and the President, because the deal violates laws separating banks, brokerages and insurance."[20] Later, the *Times* ran a damning indictment by Stiglitz on the "financialization" of the U.S. economy, much of the blame for which he placed squarely at the feet of Rubin. Stiglitz characterized Rubin's mantra as "what is good for Goldman Sachs, or Wall Street, is good for America and the world."[21]

The deregulation issue surfaced again a couple of years later with the accounting scandals and accompanying stock market crash of 2002. Banks, including Citigroup and J. P. Morgan, were accused of helping Enron hide its debt. In addition, the *Times* suggested that some analysts at the new investment banks were too closely tied to the firms that they were supposed to be impartially scrutinizing. Jack B. Grubman at Salomon Smith Barney, a Citigroup subsidiary, attended Worldcom board meetings and his "relentlessly upbeat pronouncements on the company" helped shore up an important bond issue.[22] After Citigroup agreed to pay $208 million to settle an SEC case into its wrongdoing in the Enron affair in 2005, the *Times* argued that the entire scandal demonstrated "why the Depression-era legislation known as Glass-Steagall, written to eliminate the kinds of conflicts that financial supermarkets present, should not have been dismantled."[23]

As the crisis that originated in the housing and finance sector spread to the entire economy, the *Times* was not inclined to look at the consequences with rose-colored glasses, carrying stories that downplayed the likelihood of a quick recovery. "It's pretty despondent everywhere," said Dwyfor Evans, a strategist at State Street Global Markets in Hong Kong; "the traditional mechanisms by which economies come out of a recession are absent at this time."[24] It chronicled the ominous decline in obvious indicators like the stock market plunge and bankruptcies. "But what is striking is not just the magnitude of the declines, staggering as they are, but also their breadth. All but two of the 30 Dow industrials, Wal-Mart and McDonald's, fell by more than 10 percent. Almost no industry was spared as the crisis that first emerged in the subprime mortgage market metastasized and the economy sank into what could be a long recession."[25]

The paper also focused on the hardship that the crisis created for the working population. "Layoffs have arrived in force, like a wrenching second act in the unfolding crisis."[26] "It is likely to revolve around the worst slump in worker pay since—you knew this was coming—the Great Depression. . . . Income for the median household . . . will probably be lower in 2010 than it was, amazingly enough, a full decade earlier."[27] While these predictions were, indeed, dire, it is worth noting that the median household income in the United States has not increased very much over the last thirty years, in spite of the increase in hours worked. Indeed, it was the static income gains for most of the population that contributed to household indebtedness.

The *Times'* news reporting on the crisis followed two broad themes. It cast a critical eye over the emerging solutions to the crisis, from fiscal stimulus to the finance industry bailout. It also, understandably, attempted to unearth the causes of the crisis. As was the case with the Enron debacle, the *Times'* portrait of the causes of the crisis centered on an irresponsible industry under a succession of permissive political regimes.

As we highlighted in the introduction, the crisis started in the U.S. housing market. Many analysts have placed the blame at the feet of homeowners who overextended themselves in a vain attempt to live beyond their means. The *Times* placed the blame more broadly. "Many share responsibility: overextended homeowners, overly aggressive mortgage lenders, financial engineers who built exotic securities and bank executives and government regulators who underestimated the risks to the financial system."[28] The paper also rightly pointed out that although consumer debt was, indeed, at an all-time high, it was not households who were the biggest debtors. "It is the financial sector itself. The banks that made the loans proved to be much more willing to borrow than their customers, whether corporate or consumer."[29] This suggests that the banking industry was to blame on both borrowing and lending sides of the ledger. They were too willing to make unwise loans and too willing to borrow.

The *Times* displayed a populist streak in its outrage over the salaries of executives who made many of the poor decisions that led to the crisis. Under headlines like, "On Wall Street, Bonuses, Not Profits, Were Real," writers pilloried executive excess. "For Wall Street, much of this decade represented a new Gilded Age. . . . Bankers celebrated with five-figure dinners, vied to outspend each other at charity auctions and spent their newfound fortunes on new homes, cars and art."[30] News stories also pointed out that the incomes of those in the financial sector had not always been higher than other professionals. The *Times* publicized a study by Thomas Philippon and Ariell Reshef, who found that most of the time there was no real pay premium in the financial sector. The only two exceptions were "in the late 1920s to 1930 and then again from the mid-1990s to 2006."[31] Of course, it is no coincidence that the two periods in which the financial sector had the highest incomes were those that led to inflated asset values and financial crisis. Part of the reason for the financial crisis was that the stratospheric incomes of industry high fliers came from extending risky loans and selling exotic derivatives. Quoting Secretary of the Treasury Tim Geithner, "Excessive executive compensation that provides inappropriate incentives has played a role in exacerbating the financial crisis."[32]

The *Times* also reported on the close relationship between the credit rating companies and investment firms. Part of the reason for the crisis was the credit rating agencies' unrealistically optimistic assessments of high-risk derivatives, which gave investors a false sense of confidence in these assets. When the leaders of the biggest rating firms, like Moody's, were called to testify in front of Congress, the *Times* was suspicious of their claim that their inability to detect toxic mortgages was "an honest mistake," writing sarcastically that "the woefully inaccurate ratings that have cost investors billions were not, mind you, a result of issuers paying ratings agencies handsomely for their rosy opinions."[33]

The banking industry was a classic case of moral hazard, according to the *Times*. The idea behind moral hazard is that when actors are shielded from the negative consequences of their behavior, they are more likely to engage in that activity. Since bankers had some confidence that the government would not let them fail, they could engage in more risky activities, knowing that they would not have to face the worst consequences if it all went wrong. According to two economists quoted in the *Times*, investors behaved with a "'total disregard for even the most basic principles of lending,' failing to verify standard information about their borrowers or, in some cases, even to ask for that information." So, those who argued that self interest would lead a competitive banking industry to make solid loans to creditworthy customers at reasonable rates had a very limited understanding of the industry. Given the problem of moral hazard in banking, the crisis was caused by the fact that "bankers were acting in their self-interest, after all."[34]

As we have seen in the introduction, deregulation of the financial sector including, but not limited to, the repeal of the Glass-Steagall Act was crucial in providing financial firms with the rope they used to hang themselves and, by extension, the rest of the economy. The *Times*' reporting on the deregulatory trend went looking for culprits and found them at the highest levels, including Greenspan. It dedicated a feature article to a "reassessment of the Greenspan legacy," which was not particularly kind. "If Mr. Greenspan had acted differently during his tenure as Federal Reserve chairman from 1987 to 2006, many economists say, the current crisis might have been averted or muted." "Over the years, Mr. Greenspan helped enable an ambitious American experiment in letting market forces run free. Now, the nation is confronting the consequences." This less-than-flattering assessment was from Alan S. Blinder of Princeton University: "I think of him as consistently cheerleading on derivatives." The article also included some Greenspan quotes that now appear to be woefully incorrect. "I believe that the general growth in large institutions has occurred in the context of an underlying structure of markets in which many of the larger risks are dramatically—I should say, fully—hedged."[35] Greenspan was not only to blame for his deregulatory zeal; the *Times* also reported that he exacerbated the bubble in housing prices "by keeping interest rates too low for too long."[36]

Greenspan may have had the highest profile, but he was aided by a cadre of less-well-known deregulatory enthusiasts, many of whom the *Times* held accountable. Republican Phil Gramm, of the Gramm Leach Bliley Act and other deregulatory moves like opposing regulation on predatory lending, was also highlighted in a feature article. Quoting a former SEC lawyer, "To me, Phil Gramm is the single most important reason for the current financial crisis." As was the case with Greenspan, the *Times* printed quotes from Gramm that, in retrospect, look horribly wrong. After he blocked the regulation of derivatives in 2000 he claimed, "This legislation is important to every American investor. It will keep our markets modern, efficient and innovative, and it guarantees that the United States will maintain its global dominance of financial markets." The paper also pointed out that after a political career in which he sided constantly with the interests of the banking and finance industry, Mr. Gramm moved on to a lucrative position at Swiss Bank UBS, as its senior investment banker and head of lobbying.[37]

Two other figures were also fingered. The chair of the SEC, Christopher Cox, was criticized for allowing Wall Street to "load up on leverage without increasing its oversight of them."[38] The second was Rubin, whose tenure as Clinton's treasury secretary was summed up by the leading headline "Where Was the Wise Man?" The article criticized him, along with Summers and Greenspan, for successfully opposing the 1998 proposal by the CFTC to regulate many derivatives. According to one CFTC director, Rubin was vocal in his opposition: "It was controlled anger. He was very tough. I was at several meetings with him, and I've never seen him like that before or after." As was the case with Gramm, the *Times* connected his policies while in office with a lucrative post-government career in the private sector. "Since arriving at Citigroup, Mr. Rubin has been awarded compensation worth at least $126.1 million."[39]

Perhaps the most obvious guilty party was the George Bush Jr. administration, which was in power when the crisis occurred. According to Republican presidential advisor L. William Steadman, "This administration made decisions that allowed the free market to operate as a barroom brawl instead of a prize fight."[40] The paper also publicized the financial ties between Bush and the finance industry. "In the 2004 election cycle, mortgage bankers and brokers poured nearly $847,000 into Mr. Bush's re-election campaign."[41]

Perhaps it was the combination of belief in the free market and the more pragmatic concerns of campaign financing that led the Bush Jr. White House to so badly mishandle the looming crisis. In a front-page story headlined "White House Philosophy Stoked Mortgage Bonfire" the *Times* chronicled the fairly lengthy list of Bush's errors. To start with, he appointed James B. Lockhart, "a friend of Mr. Bush from their days at Andover," to head Freddie Mac and Fannie Mae, two of the largest mortgage institutions in the United States. Lockart immediately set about speculating in the riskiest sectors of the mortgage market, "gobbling up more than $400 billion in subprime and other alternative mortgages." When the financial condition of the two agencies started to worsen, Lockhart attempted to hide the problem to such an extent that one analyst accused him of "pimping for the stock prices of the undercapitalized firms he regulates." Further, when an administration official attempted to release a report exposing the troubles at Fannie Mae and Freddie Mac, "the White House tried to fire him."[42]

The administration's denial of the problems at Fannie Mae and Freddie Mac was a typical response to economic bad news in the runup to the crisis. Despite repeated warnings from many administration insiders and Democrat Rahm Emanuel, who told "Paulson in a series of phone calls that the credit crisis would get 'deep and serious,'" the White House was reluctant to intervene. According to the *Times*, Bush claimed that it would be a mistake "to say that anything short of a massive government intervention in the housing market amounts to inaction," and added that the markets would take longer to recover if the government intervened.[43]

The *Times* situated the causes of the crisis in the structure of the banking and finance industry. The incentive structure in the industry made a speculative bubble inevitable. However, it was the hands-off approach of the government that helped create that incentive system. To close the circle, the *Times* also pointed out that the deregulatory environment that created the conditions for the crisis was bought and paid for by the lobbying efforts of the industry itself.

The second component of the *Times'* coverage on the crisis was its analysis of the solutions proposed by first Bush and then Obama. There were two separate issues in the crisis response. The first was whether the government should use fiscal stimulus in an attempt to make up for the decline in economic activity by the private sector. The *Times* was consistently in favor of this liberal, Keynesian policy and was confident that Obama would be more amenable to this type of policy than was Bush. Quoting one professor from New York University, "The lesson from the 1930s and early 1940s is that the government has to do much more than it has done so far. . . . I do think the Obama team knows this and seems prepared to act on the knowledge."[44]

The second issue was the bailout of the financial sector. The *Times'* approach to this issue was fairly nuanced. On one hand, the reporting at the *Times* reflected the injustice of a taxpayer bailout for the very institutions that had created the crisis. This view was reflected in frequent reports about the absence of an appropriate degree of humility from a group of companies that had to go cap in hand to the government to ensure their own survival. The insurance firm AIG was an easy target. "Instead of sounding chastened as its second bailout was announced this week, the company was bragging about how wonderful its insurance operations are, and denying this was really a bailout at all."[45] To make matters worse, while AIG was under fire for continuing to pay lavish executive bonuses after the bailout, the *Times* reported that it had the audacity to fight "the federal government for the return of $306 million in tax payments, some related to deals that were conducted through offshore tax havens."[46]

The *Times* constantly reported concerns that the bailout would amount to little more than a blank check to financial firms, throwing taxpayer money away with little long-term plan about how to solve the crisis. According to Janet Tavakoli, a finance industry consultant, "It is not enough to throw money at a problem; you also have to use honesty and common sense."[47] It was worried that the Bush administration was handing billions of dollars over to its financial industry friends without any proper oversight. "The legislation set up an elaborate oversight mechanism, and required periodic reports. None of that is happening."[48] The Obama administration was little better. The *Times* accused his administration of a lack of vision about how to restructure the industry. "It has been putting out fires, and the apparent lack of an overall plan has created yet more issues and bailouts, engendering public consternation instead of confidence."[49]

According to the *Times*, a large part of the reason for the dangerously limited response to the crisis was that those who were put in charge of solving the problem were exactly the same characters that created the conditions that caused the meltdown. When Obama populated his economic team with "experienced" hands, the *Times* interpreted this as a bad sign for meaningful change. Geithner, for example, "oversaw and regulated an entire industry whose decline has delivered a further blow to an already weakened American economy. Under his watch, some of the biggest institutions that were the responsibility of the New York Fed—Bear Stearns, Lehman Brothers, Merrill Lynch and most recently, Citigroup—faltered." According to one financial industry insider, "all of these 'rescues' are a disaster for the taxpayer, for the financial markets and also for the Federal Reserve System as an organization. Geithner, in our view, deserves retirement, not promotion."[50]

The second experienced hand on the economic tiller was Lawrence Summers. Before heading Obama's National Economic Council, Summers spent a very lucrative time at the financial firm DE Shaw & Company. Although the *Times* did admit that this might give him some insight into the inside workings of Wall Street, it was much more worried that he would act in the interests of the industry that had paid him so well. In the words of Andrew Sabl of UCLA, "This is what might be called contamination. Did Summers spend so much time with the hedge fund, or its investors, sovereign wealth funds and so on, that he started to think like them?"[51] An article in early 2009 nicely summed up the *Times*' pessimism on this issue. The story was reporting on an exchange on the CNBC show *Power Lunch* in which the two financial guest experts refused to see any end to the crisis despite the incessant optimistic prodding of the host, because "we have the same people in charge, those who did not see the crisis coming."[52]

According to the news section, what these characters were failing to deliver was a return to sensible regulation of the financial industry. One article lambasted the populist tone of Congressional hearings on the crisis, arguing that grandstanding denunciations of executive excess may play well, but what was really needed was "hearings that might actually help us get out of this crisis. It's happened before. In 1932, Congress established the Pecora committee, named for its chief counsel, Ferdinand Pecora. It was an intense, two-year inquiry, and its findings—executives shorting their own company's stock, for instance—shocked the country. It also led to the establishment of the Securities and Exchange Commission and other investor protections."[53]

At the time of writing, Obama's plan for the industry is not yet clear. As different proposals have been announced, the *Times* supported even tentative ideas for renewed regulation. When a report surfaced proposing new regulation that would "enable regulators to impose capital and collateral requirements on companies that issue credit default swaps," the story claimed "that would make them safer investments."[54]

In a more radical turn, the *Times* also ran stories advocating nationalization for the troubled banks. The template for this proposal was Sweden's successful nationalization during its own financial crisis in the early 1990s. According to the Swedish Minister of Fiscal and Financial Affairs at the time, Bo Lundgren, "If you go in with capital, you should have full voting rights." The Swedish nationalization was a resounding success, according to the *Times*. Taxpayers actually made their money back when the government sold its nationalized assets back to the private sector. "If there is any criticism of how Sweden handled the bad bank, it is that it might have managed an even better return if (it) had sat on its assets longer."[55] The *Times* also supported economist Paul Romer's suggestion that "the federal government needs the power and the will to take over a firm as soon as its potential losses exceed its assets."[56] The *Times*' support of Sweden's banking solution reflected a pragmatic commitment to nationalization rather than a genuine, long-term policy of public ownership. Sweden's nationalization only lasted long enough to stop the weakness of the financial sector from destroying the broader economy. Once the firm returned to profitability it was returned to the private sector as opposed to remaining a public utility.

Given its discomfort with the recipients of the bailout but its desire to stabilize the banking industry, the *Times* logically suggested that the public money could be directed to alternative destinations. One of their suggestions was to send some of the bailout money directly to financially strapped homeowners rather than firms. "Preventing foreclosures could bring a double-barreled benefit. It would allow families to remain in their homes and could also help keep the housing market from spiraling out of control."[57]

The news section was never in favor of the banking industry deregulation. When the crisis arrived, the *Times* was quick to identify the irresponsible behavior of a deregulated industry as the source of the problem. In order to solve the crisis, it recommended not only liberal fiscal stimulus, but also a dramatic return to regulation in the industry and temporary public ownership of financial firms. What the *Times* news reporting did not do, however, was extend its analysis beyond the industry-specific failure of the housing, banking, and finance sectors to the broader issue of stagnant wages and growing inequality that undermined U.S. household consumption.

The *Times* and the Financial Crisis: Op-eds

As the financial crisis became increasingly grave it came to dominate political discussion in the United States and the *Times*' editorial columns. While only a couple of opinions were offered on the Glass-Steagall Act and banking deregulation prior to the crisis, these topics became part of everyday conversation in the fall of 2007.

The *Times* printed a remarkable 94 columns on the crisis in the nineteen-month period between August 2007 and April 2009. The op-ed pieces were fairly evenly split, with *Times* columnists writing fifty-one articles and outsiders contributing forty-three. As one might expect on this issue, Krugman was a major contributor with twenty-nine articles, almost one third of the total. While he was certainly the first of the *Times'* columnists to jump on this issue, and his name dominated the early days of the discussion, as the crisis deepened and it became increasingly clear that this marked an important moment in the future direction of economic policy, others weighed in. David Brooks had nine columns and Friedman a respectable seven. Of the outsiders, three featured prominently. Tyler Cowen is a professor of economics at George Mason University and director of conservative research institutes the James Buchanan Center and the Mercatus Center. The second was Robert Schiller of Yale, and the third was Alan Blinder of Princeton, an economic advisor for Clinton and John Kerry.

Prior to the onset of the financial crisis the *Times* did not dedicate a great deal of space to the deregulation of the banking industry. But those who did express an opinion on the Glass-Steagall repeal were unanimously opposed. Even from his conservative vantage point, William Safire had some serious reservations in 1998 when he wrote that Glass-Steagall prevented the "crony capitalism" that would become inevitable if commercial banks were allowed to expand into investment and insurance. This "cozy network of insider financial dealings" would create inefficiency and breed corruption.[58] The 2002 financial scandals did nothing to alleviate these worries. One op-ed railed against the lax regulatory environment that led "consenting adults to do financially awful things behind closed doors." It argued that unless Glass-Steagall–inspired legislation was passed to shine light on these murky transactions, situations in which "bank secrecy hides favors that will be repaid later with lucrative work on mergers or underwriting" would inevitably wreak havoc with the financial system.[59]

In the wake of the collapse, Krugman was quick to criticize the risky behavior of an industry that felt that its innovation in financial instruments made regulatory oversight unnecessary. "But the wizards were frauds, whether they knew it or not, and their magic turned out to be no more than a collection of cheap stage tricks. . . . Banks used securitization to increase their risk, not reduce it, and in the process they made the economy more, not less, vulnerable to financial disruption."[60] Herbert was more damning, arguing that the crisis was caused by "the people who always pretended to know better, who should have known better, the mortgage hucksters and the gilt-edged, high-rolling, helicopter-flying Wall Street financiers, (who) kept pushing this bad paper higher and higher up the pyramid without looking at the fine print themselves, not bothering to understand it, until all the crap came raining down on the rest of us."[61]

While there was little question that the financial industry had made some bad decisions, the real debate in the *Times'* op-ed page focused on the motive behind the catastrophic errors. The first salvo in the debate came in a column by Simon Johnson based on an article that appeared in the *Atlantic Monthly* magazine. He argued that economic policy in the United States had been captured by the finance industry resulting in a U.S. crisis that had a great deal in common with those that afflicted emerging countries in South East Asia and their fledgling financial systems in the late 1990s.[62] Krugman supported Johnson's "greed" or capture narrative of the financial system. "Elite business interests—financiers, in the case of the U.S.— played a central role in creating the crisis, making ever-larger gambles, with the implicit backing of the government, until the inevitable collapse. More alarming, they are now using their influence to prevent precisely the sorts of reforms that are needed, and fast, to pull the economy out of its nosedive."[63] While Brooks was also convinced that mistakes were made in the financial sector, he did not agree with the greed explanation, opting instead for an "ignorance" justification. The problem was that "overconfident bankers didn't know what they were doing. They thought they had these sophisticated tools to reduce risk. But when big events—like the rise of China—fundamentally altered the world economy, their tools were worse than useless."[64] As we shall see, this is not just a meaningless debate about motivation. It has important implications for the appropriate corrective policy.

As was the case with its news reporting, the *Times*' columns stressed that it was deregulation that created the casino-like atmosphere in which the finance industry could make its overly speculative gambles. According to Krugman, "false beliefs in the political arena—the belief of Alan Greenspan and his friends in the Bush administration that the market is always right and regulation always a bad thing—led Washington to ignore the warning signs."[65]

Op-eds also stressed that the finance industry had lobbied heavily for the lax regulatory environment. "I would like to see the self-proclaimed conservative, small government, anti-regulation, free-market zealots step up and take responsibility for wrecking the American economy." Chief among these zealots was Phil Gramm, who was rewarded with a comfortable position at UBS. In the words of Herbert, "Would you believe that he's the vice chairman of UBS Securities, the investment banking arm of the Swiss bank UBS? Of course you would. Toadying to the rich while sabotaging the interests of working people was always Mr. Gramm's specialty."[66]

Op-ed contributors agreed that the economic crisis required fiscal stimulus to decrease the length and depth of the decline. Krugman recommended especially strong doses of government spending. "My advice to the Obama people is to figure out how much help they think the economy needs, then add 50 percent. It's much better, in a depressed economy, to err on the side of too much stimulus than on the side of too little."[67] Columnists did not only recommend abstract increases in spending, but also suggested where the money should go.

Although columnists did not connect the housing and financial crisis to the stagnant wages of working America, they did suggest that fiscal stimulus money should be spent shoring up wages that were likely to take a further hit in the recession. One particularly remarkable op-ed by Robert Rubin and Jared Bernstein noted that the problem of the early 2000s was that the benefits of "productivity growth have largely eluded working families." In this crisis, the state needed to address this by making it easier to unionize, maintaining tight labor markets, and "investing more of the benefits of trade in offsetting (workers') losses," through more effective safety nets, including universal health care and pension coverage.[68] Krugman's conversion to a more socially democratic economic platform was reflected in his admiration for Europe's welfare state. "Guaranteed health insurance and generous unemployment benefits ensure that, at least so far, there isn't as much sheer human suffering in Europe as there is in America. And these programs will also help sustain spending in the slump."[69]

On the issue of what should be done to restructure the economy, op-ed columnists had divergent views. In keeping with his belief that the financial crisis was caused more by naiveté than greed, Brooks argued for modest changes. "The greed narrative leads to the conclusion that government should aggressively restructure the financial sector. The stupidity narrative is suspicious of that sort of radicalism."[70] While Freidman was usually an advocate of letting poorly performing firms fail (GM, for example), he argued that the usual market mechanism of bankruptcy for the financial firms would have disastrous consequences. "You let the market clear them away, and we could all be wiped out with them." His solution was predictably favorable to business. The government should subsidize "private equity groups and hedge funds to get them to make the first bids for these toxic assets by guaranteeing they will not lose." Friedman recognized that this would appear to be a further subsidy for the very financial sector that caused the crisis, but that the only way to get the banking system back on its feet was by "rewarding some new investors." Over the longer term, Friedman recommended that a potential solution should be found through consultation with the business community in a Davos-style summit with "the country's 20 leading bankers, 20 leading industrialists, 20 top market economists and the Democratic and Republican leaders."[71] This supposed solution was typical of Friedman's association with, and trust in, the economy's elite. It was a faith that remained unshaken even after the economic crisis for which so many of those leaders were directly responsible. Someone more critical of the role of these very people in the crisis might be skeptical about the potential for genuine reform from this meeting.

The "tweaking" recommendations of Friedman and Brooks were not uncontested. Predictably, Krugman demanded a more drastic makeover, including, apparently, forced trips to the barber. "As I said, the important thing is to bail out the system, not the people who got us into this mess. That means cleaning out the shareholders in failed institutions, making bondholders take a haircut, and canceling the stock options of executives."[72] There was also an understandable desire to pursue charges for those who had actually crossed the line from the merely destructive to the legally criminal.[73] The columnists who favored a more dramatic reform of the industry were alarmed by the proposals that were coming out of Washington under both the Bush and Obama administrations. Krugman was worried that Bush's plan would spend billions of taxpayer dollars without solving the structural problems in the industry and warned, "if this plan goes through we'll all be very sorry in the not-too-distant future."[74] He didn't think Obama was doing much better. "The underlying vision remains that of a financial system more or less the same as it was two years ago, albeit somewhat tamed by new rules."[75]

What was missing in these packages was meaningful regulatory reform. "The lesson from the financial crises of the 20th century is that responsible politicians are not socialist demons trying to destroy capitalism. Carter Glass saved American capitalism through prudent regulation that prevented past excesses without stifling new innovation. The next administration will need to accomplish that feat again."[76] Even conservative William Kristol admitted that the deregulated financial system created "something close to Karl Marx's vision of an atomizing, irresponsible and self-devouring capitalism" and recommended legislating "monetary, fiscal and legal guardrails" that are needed for the market to work.[77]

The debate about the merits of nationalizing the failing banks mirrored that about the need for regulatory reform. University of Chicago economist Casey Mulligan claimed that the argument in favor of nationalization was based on faulty assumptions. "First, saving America's banks won't save the economy. And second, the economy doesn't really need saving."[78] Brooks argued that the banks may need saving, but the government was very poorly qualified to fill this role. "Governments are terrible managers of bad assets. There's no good history of governments doing that well." Geithner's caution about large-scale government involvement fit this role nicely. "If we're going to have a finance czar, he should at least dislike the role."[79]

Krugman was the most vocal advocate of nationalization. When Geithner declared his lack of transformative vision for his restructuring plan with the quote: "We have a financial system that is run by private shareholders, managed by private institutions, and we'd like to do our best to preserve that system," Krugman derided the move as "'lemon socialism': taxpayers bear the cost if things go wrong, but stockholders and executives get the benefits if things go right. If taxpayers are footing the bill for rescuing the banks, why shouldn't they get ownership, at least until private buyers can be found?"[80]

For the columnists, like Krugman, who were unsatisfied with the ambition of the restructuring, much of the blame for this lack of vision was due to the intimate connection between the finance industry and those charged with reforming it. When AIG paid out large bonuses to its executives even after it received bailout money to survive, Summers defended the practice by saying that the bonuses had been written into contracts that could not be broken. Dowd was skeptical, sarcastically pointing out that a contract that has a bonus structure of "if you ruin the world economy, we'll pay you an extra million" should probably not be that hard to get out from under. A more likely explanation for both the continued bonus payments and the lack of real industry reform was that Geithner "comes from the cozy Wall Street club" and the mistaken administration belief that the solution to the crisis could be found by "the same people who invented the risky financial tactics so they can unwind their own rotten spool."[81]

The op-ed section had a great deal in common with the news. Both were very critical of the finance and banking industry's role in both deregulations and advocated sweeping use of fiscal stimulus money. Both also largely steered clear of broader causes of the crisis that stemmed from American attempts to restore profitability, starting in the 1980s—from weak wages of the American worker to liberalization of trade and finance. The main difference between the sections was that the op-ed pages contained an explicit debate about the causes of the industry crisis and the extent of the government intervention needed to solve the problem. While all of the contributors agreed that the industry made some very costly mistakes, more conservative writers like Brooks and Friedman argued against a systemic explanation of the causes of the crisis and, therefore, advocated a cautious, limited regulatory response. Krugman's more systemic (less apologetic and more accurate) diagnosis of the problems in the financial industry led to much more sweeping and radical proposals, from a much stronger regulatory presence to state ownership in the financial system.

The *Times* and the Financial Crisis: Editorials

Much as it did with energy deregulation, the *Times'* editorial page started out with a cautiously optimistic take on banking deregulation. While one editorial criticized a draft of the deregulatory legislation in the runup to the repeal of Glass-Steagall, arguing that it would "seriously compromise the ability of the most important Federal regulators to supervise major financial institutions,"[82] the *Times* was more optimistic about the final draft. "The proposed deregulation is designed to help American companies expand abroad and become more efficient at home. But the breakthrough agreement was made possible by the lawmakers' willingness to try to protect consumers and poor communities from being trampled in the process." "The principle of freer competition is the economic engine of this era. But the other imperative is to demand openness, financial prudence and safeguards so that the vast new concentrations of wealth and power do not create new abuses."[83]

After it became clear that deregulation had "created new abuses," the editorial page had excellent hindsight. "Mortgage lenders blithely lent enormous sums to those who could not afford to pay them back, dicing the loans and selling them off to the next financial institution along the chain, which took advantage of the same high-tech securitization to load on more risky mortgage-based assets."[84] Editorials even provided some nice detail on specific abuses. "A.I.G. was a key player in a type of unregulated derivative called a credit default swap. Such swaps are often defined as a form of insurance because the seller guarantees payment to investors in case their investments go bust. They are not safe insurance in any familiar sense, however, because A.I.G. was not required to set aside reserves in the event of a claim. That is why, when the bubble burst and defaults rose, A.I.G. was unable to make good, provoking the bailouts."[85] Of course, this type of financial sleight of hand was "the result of antiregulatory bias and deregulatory zeal . . . that eclipsed not only rules and regulations, but the very will to regulate."[86]

The editorial page mirrored Krugman's prescriptions of fiscal policy targeted at social welfare programs. "The Bush administration . . . must now throw more money at the economic downturn. . . . Unemployment benefits, food stamps and federal aid to states and cities yield the biggest return for every dollar spent."[87] It also advocated tilting the labor market in favor of workers by strengthening unions. "Without a united front, workers will have even less bargaining power in the recession than they had during the growth years of this decade. . . . If pay continues to lag, it will only prolong the downturn by inhibiting spending."[88]

Editorials advocated dramatic intervention in the financial system in order to limit the extent of the crisis. They were very critical of the Republican hesitation to pass Bush's bailout package, describing it as a "display of pique and disarray . . . rooted less in analysis or principle than in political posturing and ideological rigidity. The House minority leader, John Boehner, conceded as much: 'While we were able to move the bill drastically to the right, it wasn't good enough for our members.'"[89] While editorials also had reservations about the financial bailout, these objections were the opposite of the Republican misgivings. The Republicans wanted less government intervention while the *Times* wanted more oversight from both the Bush and Obama packages. One editorial claimed that the Bush bailout was asking taxpayers to "write a check for $700 billion and trust the government and Wall Street to do the right thing—with inadequate regulation and virtually no oversight."[90] Obama's plan was described as so lacking in oversight that, "throwing money at the problem is becoming an end in itself."[91]

Bailout money must be accompanied by a restructuring of the industry that would prevent this type of crisis in the future. For a start, executive compensation needed to change. At the very least, the government "should tighten limits on executive compensation for bankers who have taken taxpayer money."[92] More generally, a new regulatory framework for the financial industry needed to be developed with the difficult task of "resolving future financial failures before they occur."[93] However, these types of measures did not feature prominently in the bailout discussion under either Bush or Obama, much to the dismay of the *Times*. Bush's restructuring was criticized for continuing with the fallacy that "market discipline is the most effective tool to limit risks to the financial system. . . . In the absence of rules—and regulators who are willing and empowered to enforce them—market discipline is a fantasy."[94] Obama offered little improvement. "Any new regime must be founded on a declared desire and willingness to regulate. Will

Mr. Obama deliver? Without a clear signal from the president-to-be, the early signs are not terribly encouraging."[95]

Editorials also proposed that financial assistance should be extended to house-holds struggling to pay their mortgages as well as to giant corporations. One edi-torial lamented that families were "left out of the administration's plan entirely," and suggested that people having trouble making their payments should have their "mortgages modified under bankruptcy court protection. That step should have been taken long ago to avert the foreclosures and house price declines that are at the root of the crisis."[96]

In keeping with its news and op-ed sections, editorials argued that the lack of regulatory restructuring or conditions accompanying the massive taxpayer bailout was due to the incestuous relationship between the industry and those in charge of its bailout. During the Bush administration, Treasury Secretary Paulson "hails from Wall Street and could, if he wanted to, return to Wall Street."[97] Obama's choice as Paulson's successor, Geithner, "was a key decisionmaker (as the president of the Federal Reserve Bank of New York) last September when the government let Lehman Brothers fail and then, two days later, bailed out the insurer American International Group for $85 billion. Those decisions proved cataclysmic."[98]

Conclusion

The *Times'* coverage of macroeconomics showed a desire for broad-based income gains, but failed to connect the wage stagnation of the last thirty years to policies that transformed the labor market to the benefit of firms and the detriment of work-ers. Its perspective on American foreign policy was similar. It was very critical of democratic countries that compromised the profitability of U.S. corporations and did not adequately investigate U.S. claims of non-intervention. Although it expressed frequent dismay at the consequences, the *Times* made no systematic effort to analyze and oppose conservative macroeconomics and predatory foreign policy. On the subjects of energy regulation and corporate crime the *Times* suffered from amnesia. With the exception of Krugman's insight into the energy scandal, each successive violation was treated as an unforeseen and surprising development. However, once the evidence of the malfeasance became obvious, the paper demanded both swift punishment for the offending parties and strengthened regulations to ensure that the offenses were not repeated.

The *Times* showed a more systemic, analytic approach to the financial crisis. Although it did not connect the income stagnation of U.S. workers to the rise in debt and collapse of the housing bubble, the proposed solutions to the economic crisis involved a return to a strong social welfare state. These were the very policies that had been destroyed by successive presidents and Fed chairs under the guise of fighting inflation in the 1980s and 1990s—a fight that the *Times* championed, lauding Greenspan's macroeconomic savvy. Perhaps this represents a belated recognition that these inflation-fighting policies, which were so successful in restoring corporate profitability, but so harmful for the bottom 80 percent of income earners, were detrimental to the long-term economic viability of U.S. business.

In contrast to energy deregulation, the *Times* was much more critical, far earlier, of the government's reduced role in finance. Although the op-ed page contained perspectives from people like Brooks and Friedman, who proposed a more business-friendly version of industry reform, the bulk of the content in the paper denounced deregulation from the very outset. It identified the systemic problems with the incentives in the industry as soon as the crisis started to unfold and called for drastic, immediate restructuring. In its search for a solution for the banking sector, the *Times* reached back in history for a return to Roosevelt's Glass-Steagall regulation and across the ocean for Sweden's bank nationalization. Interestingly, using Sweden as a template for turning private firms over to government control was in sharp contrast with most of its reporting on the Swedish economy, which consistently criticizes its hostility to profits.

The *Times* certainly had no qualms about attacking its corporate colleagues and potential advertisers. The largest financial firms were criticized both for their role in mismanaging their own corporate portfolios and lobbying the government for shortsighted, self-interested changes to the regulatory environment that made the mismanagement possible. Its sharpest words, however, were reserved for the government officials that presided over the deregulation. It used the opportunity of the crisis to reevaluate the legacies of previously deified public figures, most obviously Greenspan, but also people like Rubin and Summers.

The hypothesis of this book is that the *Times*' economic policy is wedded to neither conservative nor liberal positions, but rather favors the longer-term interests of U.S. business. On the issue of bank deregulation, the *Times* was liberal from the outset, criticizing the removal of Glass-Steagall. Once the crisis hit, the *Times*' debate was not between the merits of liberal and conservative policy but between a liberal return to regulation and options that could be considered far more radical, including nationalization and a dramatic overhaul of social welfare policies that would improve the bargaining power of the U.S. workforce. Advocacy of regulation on the now obviously self-destructive world of finance could easily be interpreted as protecting the broader interests of business at the expense of the short-term profits of a particular industry. However, the push for reregulation and changes to the rules of the labor market are not so easily dealt with.

The financial crisis finally revealed the extent of the sickness of the U.S. economy that had been constructed over the last thirty years. Given the current context of mounting bankruptcies and falling profits, it is difficult to imagine a policy environment that would be more harmful to business interests. The free-market, conservative policy prescriptions, not just in energy and finance, but also in the labor market and elsewhere, revived profitability temporarily, but lack of regulatory protection and income gains meant that it was unsustainable. Given the depth of the economic crisis, and its roots in unfettered free enterprise, it is possible that the *Times'* newfound social democratic perspective reflects the strength of the medicine needed to cure the ills of U.S. business and restore the conditions for long-term profitability, which at the moment include supporting worker incomes and constraining the freedom of profit-maximizing business.

Conclusion

Corporate Nationalism?

What have we discovered after reading sixty years of the *Times*? Is the Coulter/ O'Reilly perspective correct in arguing that the *Times* spreads liberal propaganda oddly in conflict with its own corporate interests? Or perhaps McChesney and Chomsky are right in arguing that the *Times* will be pro-business due to its need to curry favor with its corporate advertisers.

On big picture issues, what economists would generally call macro issues, the *Times* has been neither conservative nor liberal. On the issues of inflation, unemployment, and growth the *Times* advocated conservative, tight monetary policy under the guise of fighting inflation when it appeared as though profits were being squeezed by a tight labor market and strong unions. It opted for a more liberal, expansionary regime of lower interest rates when it felt that limited demand was constraining profits. The *Times* was conservative in its criticism of more progressive but equally successful economic entities like Sweden. So the *Times*' macro policy perspective was neither consistently liberal nor conservative, but was consistent in supporting the profitability of U.S. business.

With respect to foreign policy we chose cases in which the economic policies of democratically elected governments threatened the profitability of U.S. corporations. Here, the Chomsky theory appears to fit well. Although the *Times* emphasized its commitment to democracy, its overarching perspective was very critical of governments that nationalize U.S. firms or impose regulations that would limit their profits. This included not only constant criticism of these types of economic policies but also the need to ascribe dictatorial tendencies to the democratic leaders who implemented them. Conversely, the *Times*' default assumption was that the United States did not interfere with the sovereign affairs of nations, even those whose economic policies are badly misguided. In the area of foreign politics, the *Times* played the very conservative role of the fourth estate. The *Times* was in favor of democracy, but only when it did not interfere with U.S. corporate interests.

On matters of regulation, the *Times* was much more liberal. Although it toyed with the possibility that deregulation could create a more efficient energy industry, once the Enron scandal broke it demanded a return to strict regulation and stern punishments for the corporate criminals. This is not particularly difficult to interpret. The *Times* was willing to consider the conservative deregulatory policy only as long as it would benefit business as a whole by providing lower cost, more reliable energy supplies. When this proved to be a false assumption, the *Times* switched to praising a more stable, liberal regulatory regime. Its coverage of corporate crime and, in particular, OSHA may have been unsystematic, but the *Times* was morally on the side of workers, citizens, and consumers. Conservatives like Coulter and O'Reilly would find plenty of liberal ammunition for their attack on the *Times* in these areas. Here, the *Times*' willingness to "out" corporate offenders might well anger some potential advertisers. Instead it opted for the principled stand that American corporations have a responsibility not to kill or steal from their own.

The columns written by two of its star commentators, Krugman and Friedman, further reflect the conservative-liberal dichotomy. Friedman was relentlessly pro business, but argued in favor of certain liberal policies, like a gasoline price floor, in order to direct entrepreneurial activity. Krugman started out as a conservative on free trade and labor market policy and a liberal on regulation and health insurance. However, over time he has become much more socially democratic in his outlook.

In some ways the *Times*' perspective on the financial crisis mirrored Krugman's evolution. As the causes of the crisis became increasingly obvious and the negative impacts of the recession on the U.S. workforce became more troubling, the *Times* advocated a much more liberal, social democratic reform for both the banking system and broader macroeconomic policy.

The *Times* is first among the media gatekeepers in support of corporate ideology. It distills an acceptable line for capital to take on a particular issue, produces corporate ideology, and disseminates it to the public. In order to effectively play this role, it defines acceptable corporate and government behavior. It is critical of actions that threaten the accumulation of profits for the system or undermine the political legitimization on which it depends. It imposes discipline for the business class as a whole. The *Times* almost behaves like a responsible parent when U.S. business acts in a childish manner by punishing any self-destructive behavior that will jeopardize long-term growth. The *Times*' long-term profitability depends on its willingness to be critical of corporate and conservative state activity in prescribed historically specific ways. This makes the *Times* both a bulwark against reaction and a fetter on further progress against exploitation, imperialism, environmental destruction, injustice, and inequality.

The left accuses the *Times* of manufacturing consent in its economic coverage because of its economic dependence on advertising revenue and the corporate requirement of profitability. However, we have seen that the *Times* was not hesitant about criticizing corporate activity that harmed broader business interests or resulted in great societal harm. Indeed, the *Times'* prestige and long-run profitability depends on providing the appropriate forum for, and limits to, such criticism. This is why a for-profit media corporation like the *Times* would hire liberal journalists and let them indulge their views. The *Times* is not a lapdog of corporate America. Nor is it a raving apostle of liberal social engineers. Rather, it is both.

What the *Times* has consistently opposed are real threats to U.S. business interests. For example, it has criticized political movements and policies that, no matter how democratic, efficient, or equitable, shift power away from corporations. Further, its economic analysis only rarely systematically linked major social problems to the U.S. business class, preferring instead to rely on the "bad apple" explanation of individual wrongdoing.

The *Times* acted as an important gatekeeper for a perspective that promoted the long-term profitability of the U.S. business class by being both liberal and conservative. While the future of the *Times*, and the newspaper industry, currently looks bleak, there is no question that for the last sixty years the *Times* has been the leading voice of responsible corporate America. Whether it can continue to play this role given the pressures detailed in Chapter 1, however, remains to be seen.

Appendix

Methods for Collecting Articles

General Methods

Searches were in the ProQuest "Historical *New York Times* Database." Unless otherwise specified, all searches were in citations and document text. The search results were scanned for relevance to come up with a population of articles. Writing was separated into news articles, op-eds, and editorials. Editorials were easy to separate since they have no listed author and are categorized by the database. Op-eds were more difficult to separate out because they were not always correctly categorized in the database. Op-eds were identified by their location in the paper, often (but not always—for example, economic scene) on the page opposite the editorial page. We have also identified them when the writing is by a *Times* columnist or when the author's affiliation is identified (for example, Robert Chernomas is a professor of economics at the University of Manitoba).

Chapter 3: The *New York Times* and Macroeconomics: A Tale of Two Countries

U.S. Monetary Policy

To examine how the *Times* reported on monetary policy, inflation, and profitability we searched for writing containing the words "Federal Reserve" and "unemployment and inflation." We searched three time periods, 1950–1955, 1975–1985, and

1995–2000. All of the articles in the first time period were read. For the last two time periods there were a total of 530 news articles; we examined 50 percent of these for a total sample of 265. The entire population of editorials (66) and op-eds (67) was read.

Sweden

We searched the *Times* for its view of Sweden and its economy over a fifty-year period from 1950 to 2000. The writing in our sample responded to a search for the terms "Sweden" with "economy" (excluding the word Nobel to eliminate articles about the prize), "Meidner," and "Sweden" with "worker and ownership." A brief relevance scan of these search results yielded 182 news articles, only 6 op-eds, and 15 editorials.

Chapter 4: U.S. Foreign Economic Policy

Iran

This section draws from writing appearing in the *Times* between 1951 and 1960 that responded to searches on "Iran" with "economy," "Anglo-Iranian," and "Iran" with "CIA." Due to the large population of news articles for the search Iran and economy between 1950 and 1955 we used a sample of 150 out of the total of 307 relevant stories. The whole population of news stories between 1955 and 1960 was read. The total number of news stories in the sample was 289. The entire population of op-eds (5) and editorials (109) was read.

Venezuela

Our period of study spans the period of economic and political unrest at the beginning of the Chavez administration between 1998 and 2005. It also includes recent coverage between 2008 and February 2009 for its reporting on the constitutional referendums to extend term limits. We searched the *Times* for news articles, op-eds, and editorials that answered to the terms "Venezuela" with "economy" or "Chavez." The entire population of 141 relevant stories was used. This resulted in 86 news articles, 6 op-eds, and 49 editorials.

Chapter 5: Regulation

Enron

Writing was drawn from a search of the *Times* under the terms "California" with "energy crisis" between 1999 and 2005. In order to verify that this cast a sufficiently wide net, a search on "Enron" with "California" was also conducted, which turned up no additional writing. A quick scan for relevance resulted in 152 news stories in this time period, unsurprisingly clustered around the dates of the power failures and the Enron revelations.

There were 35 op-eds and 19 editorials using the same search techniques. All of the articles were read.

OSHA

Two searches of the *Times*' database were performed. The first was on "OSHA" and the second on "occupational safety and health administration." The writing was scanned for relevance to focus on the actual running of OSHA and the economic debates surrounding regulatory protection of worker safety and health. This meant weeding out stories about specific workplace incidents of the "individual died in shipyard, OSHA is investigating" variety. This scan left us with a total of 170 stories between 1950 and 2001. Of course, writing on OSHA only started appearing in 1971, after the founding of the agency. Of this total, there were 92 news articles, 35 op-eds, and 43 editorials. All of the articles were read.

Corporate Crime

The *Times* database was searched for the terms "corporate crime" and "white collar crime" between 1950 and 2000. Only those stories with some analysis of corporate crime were included. Much of the writing that responded to the white-collar crime search was very brief descriptions of a particular criminal investigation along the lines of "Conrad Black was arrested at his home today." A quick scan of the search results to weed out these types of stories left a population of 116 news articles, 33 op-eds, and 17 editorials. The entire population was used.

Chapter 6: Star Writers

Since all of the writing in this section is by columnists, there is no division between news stories, op-eds, and editorials.

Thomas Friedman

The search on the *Times*' database on Thomas Friedman's commentary yielded a sizeable 1280 articles after 2000. Once the columns were scanned to exclude all but the economic issues covered so far in this book (with the exception of articles on the 2008 financial crisis that is addressed in Chapter 7), 128 relevant op-eds remained, all of which were used.

Paul Krugman

A search of the *Times'* archive on Paul Krugman produced 872 stories. After a scan for relevance was conducted to eliminate all writing that was not on economics (he wrote a fair amount of political commentary, especially during elections) and that dealt with the current crisis (which appear in Chapter 7), 302 op-eds remained, all of which were used.

Chapter 7: The Financial Crisis

The *Times'* database was searched for the terms "economic crisis" or "financial crisis." The search started from August 2007, when Northern Rock in the UK received emergency funds from the bank of England, which was one of the earlier signs of serious trouble in the world banking system. A scan of the 1530 stories was conducted to weed out the consequences of the crisis on one particular industry, like automobiles or a report stating that "IBM slashed 5,000 jobs" in order to focus on the causes of, and solutions to, the broader crisis. This scan left 321 news articles that were relevant, from which a random sample of 33 percent was chosen, leaving 107 articles. There was also a second group of 95 articles that were classified as commentary and appeared in the business section. But they were written by staff reporters and were not classified as op-eds. These articles contained more analysis of the crisis than the regular news articles, which were often blow-by-blow accounts of declines in GDP or employment numbers, so they were sampled at a higher rate of 50 percent. The total sample, then, was 154 articles out of a population of 418. Given the importance of banking regulation in the financial crisis, we were also interested in the *Times'* reporting on the Glass-Steagall Act over a longer time period. The database after 1995 was searched separately for the terms "banking deregulation," "Glass-Steagall," or "Gramm Leach Bliley," which produced 88 articles, all of which were used. These same searches produced a total of 95 op-eds and 46 editorials, all of which were used.

NOTES

Notes to Chapter 1

1. Cohen, B. *The Press and Foreign Policy* (Princeton, NJ: Princeton University Press, 1963), pp 164–165.

2. Bowden, M. "The Inheritance," *Vanity Fair*, May, 2009, pp 128–135.

3. Lule, J. *Daily News, Eternal Stories: The Mythological Role of Journalism* (New York and London: The Guilford Press, 2001), p 6.

4. Bianco, A. "The Future of the *New York Times*," *Business Week*, January 17, 2005.

5. Gurley, G. "Coultergeist," *New York Observer*, August 21, 2002.

6. O'Reilly, B. "The Worst of Times," *New York Daily News*, June 21, 2004, Available at http://www.nydailynews.com/news/ideas_opinions/story/204738p-176737c.html, Accessed March 28, 2008.

7. Reynolds, A. "Classless Warfare Escalates," 2004, Available at http://www.cato.org/pub_display.php?pub_id=2486, Accessed January 5, 2008.

8. Boehlert, E. *Lapdogs: How the Press Rolled Over for Bush* (New York: Free Press, 2006).

9. Chomsky, N. *Understanding Power: The Indispensable Chomsky* (New York: The New Press, 2002), pp 21, 23.

10. Chomsky, N. "The Big Idea with Andrew Marr—Interview with Noam Chomsky," 1996, BBC, Available at http://www.zmag.org/Chomsky/interviews/9602-big-idea.html, Accessed March 20, 2008.

11. Chomsky, *Understanding Power*, p 23.

12. Bowles, S., David, G., and Thomas, W. "Power and Profits: The Social Structure of Accumulation and the Profitability of the Postwar U.S. Economy," *Review of Radical Political Economics*, 18, 1986.

13. McChesney, R. *The Problem of the Media* (New York: Monthly Review Press, 2004).

14. Sutter, D. "Advertising and Political Bias in the Media: The Market for Criti-

cism of the Market Economy," *American Journal of Economics and Sociology*, July 2002, pp 725–745.

15. Hamilton, J. *All the News That's Fit to Sell* (Princeton: Princeton University Press, 2004), p 25.

16. Bianco, "The Future of the *New York Times*."

17. Diamond, E. *Behind the Times* (New York: Villard Books, 1994), p 52.

18. Ibid, p 55.

19. Bianco, "The Future of the *New York Times*."

20. Bowden, "The Inheritance," pp 128–135.

21. Campaign Money. "New York Times Co.—Political Campaign Contributions," Available at http://www.campaignmoney.com/new_york_times.asp, Accessed July 9, 2009.

22. Chomsky, D. "The Mechanisms of Management Control at the *New York Times*," *Media, Culture & Society*, 21(5), 1999, p 582.

23. Diamond, *Behind the Times*, p 388.

24. New York Times Company. *The New York Times Circulation Data*, 2008a, Available at http://www.nytco.com/investors/financials/nyt-circulation.html, Accessed May 5, 2009.

25. New York Times. *Annual Report 2008*, p 3.

26. Ibid, p 2.

27. Diamond, *Behind the Times*, p 383.

28. Bianco, "The Future of the *New York Times*."

29. New York Times Company. *Advertising Research Department*, 2005, Available at http://nytmarketing.com/mediakit/n_readership.html, Accessed March 30, 2007.

30. Diamond, *Behind the Times*, p 119.

31. New York Times Company. *Annual Report 2005*, 2006, F9.

32. Bianco, "The Future of the *New York Times*."

33. New York Times, *Annual Report 2008*, p 27.

34. Bowden, "The Inheritance," pp 128–135.

35. New York Times, *Annual Report 2008*, p 27.

36. Ibid, p 27.

Notes to Chapter 2

1. Lott, J. Jr. and Hassett, K. "Is Newspaper Coverage of Economic Events Politically Biased?" American Enterprise Institute, 2004, Available at www.aei.org/docLib/20040915_LottHassett.pdf, Accessed March 17, 2008.

2. Ibid, p 22.

3. Groseclose, T. and Milyo, J. "A Measure of Media Bias," *Quarterly Journal of Economics*, CXX(4), 2005, pp 1191–1237.

4. Ibid, p 1212.

5. Lott and Hassett, "Is Newspaper Coverage of Economic Events Politically Biased?" p 8.

6. Berman, R. "Differences in American and European Worldviews," *Reason*, March 2004, Available at http://findarticles.com/p/articles/mi_m1568/is_10_35/ai_n6047486/, Accessed August 4, 2010.

7. Puglisi, R. "Being the *New York Times*: The Political Behavior of a Newspaper," London School of Economics, Political Economic and Public Policy, Working Paper no. 20, 2006, p 3.

8. D'Alessio, D. and Allen, M. "Media Bias in Presidential Elections: A Meta-Analysis," *Journal of Communication*, 50(4), 2000, pp 133–156.

9. Center for Responsive Politics. "Hedge Funds: Long Term Contribution Trends," Available at http://www.opensecrets.org/industries/totals.php?cycle=2010&ind=f2700, Accessed June 30, 2010.

10. Hamilton, J. *All the News That's Fit to Sell* (Princeton: Princeton University Press, 2004), p 1.

11. Sutter, D. "Advertising and Political Bias in the Media: The Market for Criticism of the Market Economy," *American Journal of Economics and Sociology*, July 2002, pp 725–745.

12. Herman, E. and Chomsky, N. *Manufacturing Consent: The Political Economy of the Mass Media* (New York: Pantheon, 2002).

13. McChesney, R. *The Problem of the Media* (New York: Monthly Review Press, 2004).

14. Ibid, p 73.

15. Ibid, p 50.

16. Ibid, p 186.

17. Ibid, p 73.

18. Sutter, "Advertising and Political Bias in the Media: The Market for Criticism of the Market Economy," p 732.

19. Strupp, J. "BP Runs Two Dozen Full Page *New York Times* Ads," *Media Matters*, June 28, 2010, Available at http://mediamatters.org/strupp/201006280009, Accessed July 7, 2010.

20. Sutter, "Advertising and Political Bias in the Media: The Market for Criticism of the Market Economy," p 731.

21. Ibid, p 732.

22. For example, see Weaver, D. and Wilhoit, G. *The American Journalist in the 1990s* (Mahwah, NJ: LEA, 1996).

23. Sutter, D. "Can the Media Be so Liberal? The Economics of Liberal Bias," *Cato Journal*, 20(3), p 442.

24. Boehlert, E. *Lapdogs: How the Press Rolled Over for Bush* (New York: Free Press, 2006), p 268.

25. Baron, D. "Persistent Media Bias," *Journal of Public Economics*, 90, 2006, pp 1–36.

26. Hamilton, *All the News That's Fit to Sell*, p 42.

27. Ibid, p 72.

28. Ibid, p 151.

29. Gentzkow, M. and Shapiro, J. "Media Bias and Reputation," *Journal of Political Economy*, 114(2), 2006, pp 280–316.

30. Cook, T. *Governing the News* (Chicago: University of Chicago Press, 1998), p 15.

31. Ibid, pp 165–168.

32. McChesney, *The Problem of the Media*, p 60.

33. Ibid, p 67.

34. Cited in Boehlert, *Lapdogs*, p 17.

35. Hallin, D. *The Uncensored War: The Media and Vietnam* (New York: Oxford University Press, 1986).

36. Ibid, p 8.

37. Ibid, p 70–71.

38. Ibid, p 9.

39. Ibid, p 28.

40. Ibid, p 208.

41. Ibid, p 208.

42. Kendall, D. *Framing Class: Media Representations of Wealth and Poverty in America* (Lanham, MD: Rowman & Littlefield, 2005), p 231.

43. Ibid, p 232.

44. Ibid, p 11–12.

Notes to Chapter 3

All of the references to the *New York Times* in the following chapters follow this format: month, date, year, page number. Page numbers cited are from ProQuest Historical Newspapers, the *New York Times* (1851–2007). For articles later than 2007, the page numbers were taken from ProQuest Newsstand, the *New York Times* (late edition, East Coast).

1. Macroeconomic policy involves the government's ability to influence employment, inflation, and economic growth. The most commonly discussed macro tools are fiscal (the use of taxation and government spending) and monetary policy (manipulation of interest rates by the central bank), but the broad macro structure of an economy is much more than these two isolated policy levers, involving, among other things, policies that affect the rate of innovation, capital accumulation, and the labor market. Predictably, these policies not only have an impact on employment, inflation, or growth, but also on corporate profits. As an obvious example, the fiscal policy of lower corporate tax rates should increase after-tax profits. Less obviously, increasing government spending can increase profits by raising the level of demand and productivity in the economy. Tight monetary policy, which is used to maintain low inflation rates by raising interest rates, increases the cost of borrowing funds, lowering the profits of firms that borrow money. It also reduces interest-sensitive consumption and investment spending, reducing demand in the economy, which makes it more difficult for firms to sell their products. However, the very same policy of increasing interest rates will also increase unemployment and lower workers' wage demands, which is beneficial (within limits) for the profitability of the business class as a whole, while protecting the assets of the financial sector from inflation. The opposite monetary policy, lowering interest rates, may be consistent with low inflation, high capacity utilization, growth, and profits, but only if wage expectations are sufficiently depressed.

Broadly speaking, liberal macroeconomic policy is more committed to an active macroeconomic role for the government than is conservative. Since liberals are more likely to believe that the economy needs some government assistance to achieve full employment of its productive resources, they tend to be more eager to prescribe increases in government spending and lower interest rate policies than are conservatives. Conservatives believe that other than an occasional random shock from nature (sunspots or floods, for example) the problems with capitalist economies can be usually traced to government spending, taxing, or regulating. The conservative policy prescription is that a smaller government means a larger economy.

A similar division can be seen when comparing liberal and conservative positions on the longer-term issue of economic growth. Liberals tend to advocate a crucial role for government funding of research and development (R&D) to foster the technological change on which economic growth greatly depends. Conservatives would prefer to leave R&D decisions in the hands of profit-making private firms.

2. Bowles, S., Gordon, D., and Weisskopf, T. *After the Wasteland* (Armont, NY: M.E. Sharpe, 1990), p 96.

3. Ibid, pp 53–56.

4. Thurow, L.C. *The Future of Capitalism* (New York: Penguin Books USA Inc, 1996), p 1.

5. Sepehri, A. and Moshiri, S. "Inflation-Growth Profiles across Countries: Evidence from Developing and Developed Countries," *International Review of Applied Economics*, 18 (2), April 2004, pp 191–207.

6. Sarel, M. Nonlinear Effects of Inflation on Economic Growth. IMF Staff Papers, 43, 1996, pp 199–215.

7. Galbraith, J.K. *American Capitalism* (Cambridge: Houghton Mifflin Co., 1952).

8. Pollin, R. "The Natural Rate of Unemployment: It's All About Class Conflict," *Dollars and Sense Magazine*, 219, September/October, 1998, pp 12–15.

9. Ibid, pp 12–15.

10. Cohen, N. "Gambling with Our Future," *New Statesman*, January 13, 2003, Available at http://www.newstatesman.com/200301130012, Accessed March 15, 2007.

11. Greenspan, A. Testimony Before the Committee on the Budget, United States Senate, January 21. Washington: Federal Reserve Board, 1997. Available at www.federal reserve.gov/BOARDDOCS/Testimony/1997/19970121.htm, Accessed March 12, 2007.

12. Greider, W. "Father Greenspan Loves Us All," *The Nation*, January 1, 2001.

13. Mishel, L., Bernstein, J., and Schmitt, J. *The State of Working America 1998–1999* (New York: Cornell University Press, 1999), pp 153–155.

14. Thurow, *The Future of Capitalism*, p 2.

15. Cited in Tasini, J. "The DLC Won't Talk About Corporate Power," *Huffington Post*, July 25, 2006.

16. Piketty, T. and Saez, E. "Income Inequality in the United States, 1913–1998," *Quarterly Journal of Economics*, 118 (1), 2003, pp 1–39.

17. Mishel, Bernstein, and Schmitt, *The State of Working America 1998–1999*, pp 153–154.

18. Foster, J. and Magdoff, F. "Financial Implosion and Stagnation," *Monthly Review*, December, 2008. Available at http://www.monthlyreview.org/081201foster-magdoff.php, Accessed June 10, 2009.

19. McNally, D. "Global Finance, the Current Crisis and Challenges to the Dollar," *Relay*, 22, April/June, 2008.

20. Mishel, L., Bernstein, J., and Shierholz, H. *The State of Working America, 2008–2009* (New York: Cornell University Press, 2009), pp. 286–287.

21. Swedish Institute. November 10, 2004.

22. Olsen, G. *The Politics of the Welfare State: Canada, Sweden and the United States* (Oxford: Oxford University Press, 2002), 13–17.

23. Bowles, Gordon, and Weisskopf, *After the Wasteland*, p 40.

24. Lopez-Carlos, A. *The Global Competitiveness Report 2005–2006: Video Interviews*, September, 2005.

25. Blyth, M. *Great Transformations: Economic Ideas and Institutional Change in the Twentieth Century* (Cambridge, UK: Cambridge University Press, 2002), pp 117–123.

26. Apr 26, 1953, E8.

27. Jun 3, 1950, 52.

28. Aug 3, 1952, E7; see also Jul 9, 1950, E10.

29. Feb 24, 1952, F7.

30. Dec 15, 1975, 61; see also Dec 26, 1976, F1; Feb 27, 1977, 110.

31. Jun 16, 1977, 85.

32. Aug 15, 1979, D2; for other articles that present it as a dilemma see Apr 29, 1975, 47; Mar 24, 1975, 49; Apr 11, 1976, 105; Jun 9, 1977, 75; Jul 11, 1977, 47; Jul 4, 1978, 24; Sep 9, 1979, F18.

33. Oct 27, 1977, 78.

34. Oct 30, 1977, 131.

35. Dec 26, 1977, D1.

36. Dec 18, 1977, 148.

37. Jan 21, 1975, 47.

38. Jul 30, 1975, 43; for other articles advocating easier monetary policy see also Jul 29, 1976, 41; Dec 24, 1976, 56; Aug 15, 1979, D2.

39. Apr 30, 1975, 69.

40. Oct 15, 1975, 61.

41. May 7, 1975, 59.

42. Jun 8, 1975, 163.

43. Dec 24, 1976, 57.

44. Aug 12, 1979, E1; see also Aug 8, 1975, 48; Oct 1, 1975, 65; May 28, 1976, 71; Dec 11, 1976, 46; May 4, 1977, 76; May 8, 1977, 103; Apr 6, 1978, D1; Apr 27, 1978, D1; Nov 21, 1978, D13.

45. Jul 18, 1976, 88.

46. Feb 3, 1980, F1.

47. Feb 27, 1977, 110; see also May 7, 1975, 59; Jun 8, 1975, 163; Feb 28, 1977, 49; Mar 8, 1977, 55; Nov 14, 1977, 69.

48. Jul 21, 1977, 71; Feb 2, 1978, D3.

49. Mar 28, 1976, 125; see also Jun 16, 1977, 85; Jun 2, 1977, 71; Jun 9, 1977, 75.

50. Aug 8, 1975, 48.

51. Dec 30, 1975, 31.

52. Mar 10, 1977, 53.

53. Jun 8, 1978, D11.

54. Jun 27, 1978, D2.

55. Dec 7, 1981, D1; see also Nov 20, 1981, D2; Nov 24, 1981, D1; Apr 1, 1982, D1.

56. Mar 10, 1982, D2.

57. Jan 29, 1984, F1.

58. Jul 15, 1983, D2.

59. Jun 20, 1983, D1.

60. Sep 18, 1981, D2.

61. Apr 29, 1984, F1.

62. Dec 2, 1984, F1.

63. Nov 14, 1977, 69.

64. Jul 1, 1976, 49.

65. Dec 24, 1976, 57; see also Sep 7, 1979, D2.

66. Jun 3, 1995, 31; see also Dec 9, 1995, 37; Jun 7, 1996, D1.

67. Oct 12, 1997, WK1; see also Apr 10, 1997, D2.

68. Aug 8, 1996, D4.

69. Jul 4, 1999, 64.

70. Feb 27, 1997, D6.

71. Jan 5, 1998, D1.

72. Apr 5, 1997, 37; see also May 8, 1997, D4; May 9, 1997, D1; May 7, 1999, C1; Jun 15, 1999, C2; Jun 17, 1999, C1; Nov 12, 1999, C1.

73. Nov 6, 1997, D1.

74. Jun 30, 1975, 29.

75. Oct 23, 1977, F14; see also Jun 18, 1978, SM4; Jun 4, 1979, A17.

76. Jan 16, 1980, F18; see also Aug 17, 1980, F16.

77. Oct 18, 1982, A17; see also Dec 28, 1980, F2; Jul 26, 1981, F2; Mar 12, 1982, A29; Jul 23, 1982, A23; Feb 8, 1983, A21; Jun 5, 1983, F3.

78. Jul 27, 1980, F16.

79. Oct 24, 1982, E21.

80. Apr 21, 1975, 29.

81. Feb 22, 1982, A17.

82. Oct 2, 1980, A23; see also Jun 26, 1981, A27.

83. Jun 18, 1978, SM4.

84. Nov 18, 1982, A27.

85. Nov 15, 1984, A30.

86. Feb 26, 1995, F25.

87. Feb 4, 1996, SM36.

88. May 3, 1998, WK1.

89. Oct 11, 1997, A11; see also Feb 2, 1997, F14; Sep 29, 1998, A25; Jan 26, 1999, A23; Apr 11, 1999, WK18; Apr 18, 1999, WK18; Jun 20, 1999, WK3.

90. Nov 20, 1997, A31.

91. Sep 20, 1998, WK15; see also Jan 18, 1999, A17; Nov 24, 1999, A23.

92. Mar 27, 1997, A29.

93. Oct 14, 1997, A27; see also Feb 2, 1998, A23; Aug 28, 1998, A25; May 29, 1999, A15; Aug 3, 1999, A15.

94. Aug 1, 1999, WK15.

95. Jul 31, 1997, A23; see also Apr 4, 1997, A35.

96. Aug 24, 1997, E13.

97. Jan 17, 1995, A19.

98. Jan 7, 1950, 11.

99. Jul 5, 1975, 12.

100. Mar 16, 1976, 34.

101. Feb 7, 1976, 20.

102. Feb 15, 1975, 28; Mar 16, 1975, E18; Jul 12, 1975, 12; Jul 17, 1975, 28; Aug 10, 1975, E14; Feb 1, 1976, E16; Nov 13, 1976, 17; Oct 24, 1977, 28; Sep 24, 1977, 15; May 13, 1978, A18; May 23, 1978, A18; Dec 13, 1981, E28; Jan. 16, 1982, A18; Sep 30, 1982, A30; Oct. 13, 1982, A30; Oct. 27, 1982, A26.

103. Mar 19, 1976, 31; Feb 21, 1978, 30.

104. Sep 26, 1975, 36.

105. Aug 22, 1975, 30; Sep 21, 1975, E16.

106. Aug 17, 1975, E14; Mar 19, 1980, A26.

107. Jul 8, 1984, E20.

108. Sep 22, 1996, E12; Feb 2, 1997, F14.

109. Feb 25, 1996, E14.

110. Sep 17, 1997, A30.

111. Jun 8, 1996, 18.

112. Jan 21, 1966, 86.

113. Sep 22, 1968, 183.

114. Jan 4, 1950, 69.

115. Sep 5, 1950, 12.

116. Jan 4, 1950, 69.

117. Sep 11, 1954, 20.

118. Jan 4, 1955, 75; Jun 12, 1955, BR13.

119. Jan 5, 1954, 62.

120. Jan 7, 1958, 66.

121. Sep 5, 1950, 12.

122. Sep 5, 1950, 12.

123. Jan 3, 1952, 72.

124. Sep 11, 1954, 20; Mar 15, 1955, 10.

125. Jan 5, 1954, 62.

126. Sep 9, 1954, 12.

127. Sep 9, 1954, 12.

128. Sep 17, 1956, 5.

129. Oct 23, 1965, 35.
130. Jan 9, 1962, 70.
131. Sep 14, 1969, 95.
132. May 25, 1964, 51.
133. Apr 4, 1965, F26.
134. Nov 6, 1968, 53.
135. Nov 6, 1968, 53.
136. May 24, 1974, 33.
137. Feb 13, 1975, 58; Sep 20, 1976, 65.
138. Oct 22, 1975, 10.
139. Jun 13, 1976, 115.
140. Apr 15, 1964, 58.
141. Oct 23, 1965, 35.
142. Mar 1, 1965, 37.
143. May 12, 1965, 72.
144. Feb 26, 1971, 3.
145. Apr 7, 1976, 61.
146. Apr 7, 1976, 61.
147. Apr 7, 1976, 61.
148. Jun 13, 1976, 115.
149. Sep 20, 1976, 65.
150. May 5, 1980, A2.
151. May 28, 1978, F1.
152. May 25, 1984, A20; Aug 17, 1988, B9.
153. Aug 20, 1980, A2.
154. Sep 19, 1982, 18.
155. May 5, 1980, A2.
156. May 19, 1985, E4.
157. Feb 20, 1990, A2.
158. Nov 16, 1980, E3.
159. Aug 5, 1977, 3.
160. Mar 24, 1978, 11; see also May 5, 1980, A2.
161. Oct 27, 1989, A3.
162. For example, May 14, 1980, A2; Jul 24, 1981, A3; Feb 20, 1990, A2.
163. Oct 27, 1989, A3.
164. May 11, 1985, 17; May 18, 1985, 35.
165. Jul 7, 1991, F5.
166. Mar 24, 1978, 11.
167. Feb 11, 1990, F15; Feb 16, 1990, A3.
168. Sep 21, 1998, A3; Sep 17, 1994, 4.
169. Sep 16, 1991, A1.
170. Apr 25, 1983, D6; see also May 19, 1985, E4.
171. Nov 14, 1983, D1; see also May 19, 1985, E4.
172. Sep 6, 1987, E4.
173. Oct 8, 1999, A1.

174. Jun 25, 1990, D13.
175. Oct 14, 1973, 168.
176. Aug 30, 1987, F3.
177. Feb 23, 1992, E3.
178. Sep 19, 1950, 30.
179. Sep 23, 1952, 32; for a virtually identical article see Sep 21, 1954, 24.
180. Nov 13, 1954, 14.
181. Sep 23, 1962, 196; see also Sep 19, 1968, 46.
182. Sep 23, 1962, 196.
183. Sep 24, 1964, 40.
184. Sep 23, 1970, 46.
185. Sep 23, 1976, 36.

Notes to Chapter 4

1. Blum, W. *Killing Hope: US Military and CIA Interventions Since World War II* (Monroe, Maine: Common Courage Press, 2004).

2. Sutton, 1955, cited in Paine, C. and Shoenberger, E. "Iranian Nationalism and the Great Powers: 1872–1954," *MERIP Reports* no. 37, May, 1975, p 24.

3. Ibid, pp 23–24.

4. Kinzer, S. *All the Shah's Men: An American Coup and the Roots of Middle East Terror* (Hoboken, NJ: John Wiley & Sons, 2003), p 6.

5. Gareau, F. *State Terrorism and the United States* (London: Zed Books, 2004) and Blum, *Killing Hope*.

6. Hooglund, E. "Iran," in Schraeder, P.J. (ed.) *Intervention in the 1980s: U.S. Foreign Policy in the Third World* (Boulder, Colorado: Lynne Rienner Publishers Inc, 1989), p 212.

7. Rodriguez, F. *Inequality Growth and Poverty in an Era of Liberalization and Globalization* (Oxford Scholarship Online Monographs, 2004), p 29.

8. Shifter, M. "In Search of Hugo Chavez," *Foreign Affairs*, 85(3), 2006, p 46.

9. Ibid, p 46.

10. BBC. "Venezuela Strike Falters," BBC News, January 28, 2003. Available at http://news.bbc.co.uk/2/hi/business/2701873.stm, Accessed March 3, 2009.

11. Central Intelligence Agency. 2009. *The World Factbook*. Available at https://www.cia.gov/library/publications/the-world-factbook/geos/ve.html#Econ, Accessed March 3, 2009.

12. World Bank. *Venezuela at a Glance*, 2008. Available at http://devdata.world bank.org/AAG/ven_aag.pdf, Accessed March 10, 2009.

13. Rodriguez, F. "Revolutionary Road: Debating Venezuela's Progress," *Foreign Affairs*, 87(4), 2008, p 161.

14. Weisbrot, M. and Sandoval, L. *Update: The Venezuelan Economy in the Chavez Years* (Washington, D.C.: Center for Economic and Policy Research, 2008), pp 10–11.

15. Economic Commission for Latin America and the Carribean. *Social Indicators*

and Statistics, 2008. Available at http://www.eclac.org/estadisticas/publicaciones/default.asp?idioma=IN, Accessed March 9, 2009.

16. Weisbrot and Sandoval, *Update*, p 14.

17. Central Intelligence Agency, *The World Factbook*.

18. PBS. "The Troubled Media," December 28, 2006. Available at http://www.pbs.org/newshour/indepth_coverage/latin_america/venezuela/media.html, Accessed July 14, 2009.

19. Mander, B. "Venezuelan Media Fear Fresh Assault," *Financial Times*, June 19, 2009. Available at http://www.ft.com/cms/s/0/4915a606-5cea-11de-9d42-00144fe-abdc0.html, Accessed July 14, 2009.

20. Oct 17, 1952, 5; see also Aug 31, 1951, 1; Jan 4, 1952, 3; Jan 27, 1952, E1; Aug 18, 1952, 4; Oct 17, 1952, 1; Jul 11, 1953, 6.

21. Sep 7, 1952, E5.

22. Mar 6, 1953, 3; see also May 21, 1951, 13.

23. Apr 10, 1951, 13; see also Mar 17, 1951, 4; Jun 24, 1951, 127; Jul 1, 1951, 13; Sep 29, 1951, 5.

24. Jun 10, 1951, 26.

25. Oct 23, 1952, 4; see also Oct 5, 1951, 5; Oct 7, 1951, 26.

26. Aug 17, 1952, E1.

27. Jan 6, 1953, 75.

28. Aug 17, 1952, E1.

29. Jan 8, 1951, 9.

30. Aug 23, 1953, E5.

31. Sep 28, 1952, 22.

32. May 25, 1954, 43.

33. Apr 20, 1952, E5.

34. Mar 10, 1952, 3; see also May 19, 1951, 4; Jun 26, 1951, 11; Jul 6, 1951, 6; Sep 5, 1951, 19; Oct 14, 1951, E5; Mar 10, 1952, 3; Mar 24, 1952, 4; Apr 20, 1952, E5; Jan 6, 1953, 75; Jan 31, 1953, 6; Feb 1, 1953, 22.

35. Dec 20, 1952, 28.

36. Sep 20, 1952, 5.

37. Mar 16, 1953, 12.

38. May 10, 1953, 4.

39. Aug 17, 1952, E5.

40. Oct 17, 1952, 1.

41. Aug 9, 1953, E4; see also Aug 24, 1953, 1.

42. Aug 30, 1953, E3.

43. Aug 21, 1953, 3.

44. Jun 26, 1956, 2.

45. Aug 23, 1953, E1.

46. Aug 21, 1953, 3; see also May 7, 1951, 11; Aug 22, 1953, 1.

47. Jul 27, 1958, E4; see also Sep 22, 1954, 5.

48. Sep 3, 1953, 6; see also Aug 30, 1953, E3; Sep 20, 1953, E6; Oct 2, 1953, 3; Oct 27, 1953, 6; Nov 22, 1953, 24; Jan 5, 1954, 66; Feb 6, 1954, 5.

49. Jul 25, 1954, E4.

50. Oct 29, 1958, 4; see also May 9, 1954, 54; Jul 28, 1954, 1; Oct 19, 1958, 26; Nov 5, 1958, 14.

51. Jan 13, 1959, 70.

52. Aug 23, 1953, E1.

53. Aug 21, 1953, 1; see also Aug 12, 1952, 1.

54. Jul 25, 1954, E4.

55. Jan 2, 1958, 5.

56. Feb 22, 1959, 65.

57. Aug 20, 1953, 2.

58. Dec. 15, 1952, 8.

59. Aug 20, 1953, 3.

60. Jul 30, 1952, 1.

61. Sep 18, 1952, 23.

62. Aug 25, 1953, 1; see also May 17, 1951, 58; May 25, 1951, 13; May 29, 1951, 10; Nov 21, 1951, 4; Dec 30, 1951, E5; Jun 23, 1952, 18; Jul 30, 1952, 1; Aug 17, 1952, E5; Sep 18, 1952, 23. ·

63. Aug 30, 1953, E3.

64. Aug 20, 1953, 1.

65. Dec 26, 1956, 31; see also Aug 21, 1953, 3; Jul 8, 1954, 6; Aug 8, 1954, 3; Nov 7, 1954, F1; Oct 14, 1955, 1.

66. Sep 9, 1951, SM19.

67. Feb 24, 1952, SM14.

68. Aug 30, 1953, SM13.

69. Sep 28, 1952, SM16.

70. Feb 22, 1959, SM15.

71. Mar 18, 1951, SM6.

72. Feb 22, 1959, SM15; see also Jun 7, 1953, SM9.

73. Sep 28, 1951, 28.

74. May 23, 1951, 34.

75. Mar 16, 1951, 30.

76. Jul 6, 1951, 17.

77. Jun 21, 1951, 26.

78. Sep 30, 1951, 122; see also Apr 30, 1951, 19; May 21, 1951, 26; May 25, 1951, 26; May 29, 1951, 22; Jun 4, 1951, 25; Jul 6, 1951, 17; Jul 11, 1951, 19; Aug 17, 1951, 16; Aug 23, 1951, 21; Oct 16, 1951, 30; Aug 9, 1952, 12; Aug 27, 1952, 26; Sep 1, 1952, 16; Sep 4, 1952, 26; Sep 9, 1952, 26; Sep 17, 1952, 30; Sep 26, 1952, 20; Oct 17, 1952, 26; Mar 2, 1953, 22.

79. Apr 30, 1951, 19.

80. May 21, 1951, 26.

81. Jul 19, 1951, 22; Sep 4, 1952, 26.

82. Jun 21, 1951, 26.

83. Mar 16, 1951, 30; see also Mar 18, 1951, E2; Apr 30, 1951, 19; Oct 8, 1951, 17; Oct 14, 1951, 160; Oct 15, 1951, 24; Oct 20, 1951, 12; Nov 16, 1951, 24; Apr 14, 1952, 18; Jul 25, 1952, 16; Nov 2, 1954, 26.

84. Oct 7, 1952, 28; Dec 9, 1952, 32.

85.   Jan 21, 1952, 14.

86.   Sep 3, 1953, 20.

87.   Aug 26, 1953, 26; see also Dec 15, 1954, 30.

88.   Oct 14, 1953, 28; see also Feb 2, 1954, 26; Mar 2, 1954, 24; Apr 12, 1954, 28.

89.   Jul 15, 1952, 20.

90.   Jul 18, 1952, 18; see also Jul 23, 1952, 22; Jul 29, 1952, 20; Nov 18, 1952, 30; Aug 4, 1953, 20; Aug 17, 1953, 14; Aug 20, 1953, 26.

91.   Aug 21, 1953, 16; Dec 15, 1954, 30; Oct 13, 1955, 30; Jul 13, 1956, 18; Feb 14, 1959, 20; Feb 18, 1959, 32; Feb 24, 1959, 28.

92.   Aug 26, 1953, 26; Nov 10, 1953, 30.

93.   Mar 16, 1951, 30; Jul 23, 1952, 22; Jan 1, 1953, 22; Dec 9, 1953, 10.

94.   May 21, 1951, 26; Jun 28, 1951, 21; Aug 4, 1951, 14; Oct 3, 1951, 32; Aug 9, 1952, 12.

95.   Oct 20, 1951, 12; Feb 29, 1952, 22; Mar 2, 1953, 22.

96.   Nov 29, 1955, 28.

97.   Feb 18, 1959, 32; see also Jul 20, 1954, 18; Jul 13, 1956, 18; Feb 14, 1959, 20; Feb 24, 1959, 28.

98.   Aug. 6, 1954, 16.

99.   Dec 6, 1998, A3.

100.   May 17, 2007, A8.

101.   Apr 10, 1999, A3.

102.   Feb 18, 1999, A3.

103.   Apr 17, 1999, C1.

104.   Sep 1, 1999, A3.

105.   Mar 11, 2004, W1; see also Feb 17, 2007, A3; Apr 10, 2007, A1.

106.   Dec 4, 2001, A10; see also Dec 19, 2003, W1.

107.   Jan. 9, 2007, A6.

108.   Nov 30, 2002, C3; see also Dec 4, 2002, A6; Dec 5, 2002, A6; Dec 6, 2002, A14; Dec 14, 2002, A3; Dec 16, 2002, A1; Dec 20, 2002, A14.

109.   Feb 26, 2003, C1.

110.   Apr 13, 2002, C1.

111.   Mar 21, 2003, A4.

112.   See, for example, Mar 21, 2003, A4; Dec 12, 2002, A16.

113.   Apr 30, 2003, A3.

114.   Mar 18, 2004, A17.

115.   Jul 28, 2000, A1.

116.   Oct 17, 2001, A3.

117.   Dec 16, 2003, W1; see also Jun 12, 2003, A8.

118.   Jan 15, 2009, A12; see also May 7, 2007, A6; Jul 23, 2007, A8; Dec 3, 2007, A1; May 18, 2008, A14; Aug 2, 2008, A7.

119.   Dec 8, 2002, A16; see also Dec 12, 2002, A16; Feb 9, 2008, A1.

120.   Dec 6, 1998, A3; see also May 7, 2001, A4.

121.   Apr 10, 1999, A3; see also May 25, 2003, A15; Oct 15, 2007, A9; Jun 10, 2008, A6; Nov 11, 2008, A8; Dec. 14, 2008, A8.

122. Feb 17, 2009, A6.
123. Nov 17, 2007, A1; see also Aug 16, 2007, A10; Aug 15, 2007, A6.
124. Jul 26, 1999, A8; see also Sep 5, 1999, A13.
125. Apr 26, 1999, A9.
126. Sep 11, 1999, A2.
127. Aug 1, 2000, A6.
128. Aug 2, 2000, A11.
129. Nov 25, 2008, A6.
130. Sep 10, 2000, A17.
131. Dec 5, 2000, A14.
132. May 7, 2001, A4.
133. Oct. 19, 2001, A8.
134. Dec 22, 2002, A10.
135. Feb. 14, 2009 A9; see also Jan 3, 2008, A1; Feb 9, 2008, A1; Jun 10, 2008, A6; Aug 6, 2008, A14; Jan 21, 2009, A12.
136. Apr 14, 2002, A1; see also Apr 14, 2002, A10.
137. Apr 15, 2002, A1.
138. Aug 17, 2002, A1; see also Oct 10, 2002, A8; Oct 14, 2002, A7; Oct 22, 2002, A16; Oct 26, 2002, A7.
139. Apr 12, 2003, A3.
140. Aug 21, 2003, A10.
141. Dec 1, 2003, A3.
142. Dec 20, 2003, A6; Mar 3, 2004, A9; May 31, 2004, A4; Jun 5, 2004, A2; Jun 9, 2004, A10.
143. Aug 14, 2004, A3.
144. Jun 5, 2004, A2; see also May 31, 2004, A4; Aug 14, 2004, A3.
145. Aug 17, 2004, A1.
146. Apr 14, 2002, D4.
147. Apr 16, 2002, A1.
148. Apr 20, 2002, A1.
149. Aug 20, 2004, A8.
150. Sep 30, 2004, C100.
151. Dec 3, 2007, A1.
152. Feb 27, 2000, D16.
153. May 11, 2007, A4.
154. Jan 7, 2003, A19.
155. Apr 4, 2007, A4.
156. Apr 16, 2002, A27.
157. Nov 29, 2007, A31.
158. Dec 1, 2007, A15.
159. Jun 2, 2002, 48.
160. Jan 26, 2003, D13.
161. Mar 5, 2003, A23; see also Aug 14, 2004, A15.
162. Mar 17, 2007, A15.
163. Apr 1, 2007, D5.

164. Dec 30, 2007, D8; see also Aug 26, 2007, WK3; Feb 3, 2008, WK17; Dec 1, 2007, A15.

165. Dec 6, 2007, A41.

166. Jun 6, 2007, A23.

167. Dec 3, 2007, A25.

168. Apr 4, 2000, A23.

169. Aug 23, 2007, A21.

170. Apr 4, 2007, A4.

171. Jan 7, 2003, A19; see also Apr 16, 2002, A27; Apr 18, 2002, A27.

172. Apr 21, 2007, A15.

173. Jun 23, 2003, A21.

174. Dec 8, 1998, A26.

175. Aug 28, 2003, A30; see also Dec 18, 2002, A34; Mar 23, 2007, A20.

176. Aug 18, 2004, A22.

177. Aug 2, 2000, A24; Apr 13, 2002, A16; Dec 4, 2007, A34; Dec 1, 2007, A14; Aug 22, 2007, A18; Jul 6, 2003, D8.

178. Aug 28, 2003, A30; see also Dec 18, 2002, A34.

179. Aug 2, 2000, A24.

180. Nov 25, 2008, A30.

181. Aug 18, 2004, A26; Apr 24, 2008, A24; also Aug 22, 2007, A18; Jan 10, 2007, A22.

182. Jun 15, 2008, WK11; see also Mar 23, 2007, A20.

183. Aug 2, 2000, A24.

184. Mar 7, 2007, A20.

185. Apr 13, 2002, A16; see also Apr 16, 2002, A26.

186. Feb 14, 2009, A22; for other editorials declaring Chavez an autocrat, authoritarian, or a strongman see Nov 6, 2000, A38; Feb 21, 2003, A26; Jun 10, 2004, A28; Jan 10, 2007, A22; Dec 4, 2007, A34; Dec 8, 2007, A16; Mar 25, 2008, A26; Aug 22, 2008, A18; Nov 18, 2008, A26.

187. Dec 1, 2007, A14.

188. Aug 22, 2007, A18.

189. Apr 4, 2002, A22.

190. Aug 2, 2000, A24.

191. Aug 18, 2004, A22.

192. Nov 25, 2008, A30; Jun 15, 2008, WK11; May 25, 2008, WK9.

193. Nov 28, 2008, A42.

194. Feb 14, 2009, A22.

195. Apr 16, 2002, A26.

Notes to Chapter 5

1. Polanyi, K. *The Great Transformation* (Boston: Beacon Press, 1963).

2. Blyth, M. *Great Transformations: Economic Ideas and Institutional Change in the Twentieth Century* (Cambridge, UK: Cambridge University Press, 2002), pp 181–185.

3. Consumer Reports. "Deregulated," *Consumer Reports*, July 2002, pp 30–35.

4. Frontline. "Interview: Jeff Skilling," *PBS Frontline*, March 28, 2001. Available at http://www.pbs.org/wgbh/pages/frontline/ shows/blackout/interviews/skilling .html, Accessed August 30, 2007.

5. CBS News. "Enron 'Mastermind' Pleads Guilty," October 17, 2002. Available at http://www.cbsnews.com/stories/2002/10/17/national/main526018.shtml, Accessed August 30, 2007.

6. Ibid.

7. Stiglitz, J. *Globalization and Its Discontents* (New York: Norton, 2002), p 261.

8. Guardian. "Enron: Web of Intrigue," 2007. Available at http://www.guardian .co.uk/flash/0,5860,634489,00.html, Accessed March 13, 2007.

9. National Energy Policy Development Group. *Overview: Reliable, Affordable, and Environmentally Sound Energy for America's Future*, 2001. Available at http://www .whitehouse.gov/energy/overview.pdf, Accessed March 12, 2007.

10. Stiglitz, *Globalization and its Discontents*, p 266.

11. ILO. *Occupational Injuries: United States*, 2009. Available at http://laborsta .ilo.org/STP/do, Accessed April 9, 2009.

12. Leigh, J. P., Steven, M., Marianne, F., Chonggak, S., and Philip, L. "Occupational Injury and Illness in the United States: Estimates of Costs, Morbidity, and Mortality," *Journal of the American Medical Association Archives of Internal Medicine*, 157(14), 1997, p 1557.

13. Morrall, J. "A Review of the Record," *Regulation*, 10(2), 1986, pp 25–34.

14. Weil, D. "If OSHA Is So Bad, Why Is Compliance So Good?" *The RAND Journal of Economics*, 27(3), 1996, p 618.

15. McQuiston, T., Ronda, Z., and Loomis, D. "The Case for Stronger OSHA Enforcement—Evidence from Evaluation Research," *American Journal of Public Health*, 88(7), 1998, p 1022.

16. Markowitz, G. and Rosner, D. *Deceit and Denial: The Deadly Politics of Industrial Pollution* (Berkeley: University of California Press, 2002).

17. US Department of Justice. *Homicide Trends in the US*, 2009. Available at http:// www.ojp.usdoj.gov/bjs/homicide/tables/totalstab.htm, Accessed April 9, 2009.

18. Graham, D. "FDA, Merck and Vioxx: Putting Patient Safety First?" Testimony before the US Senate Committee on Finance, November 18 , 2004. Available at http:// finance.senate.gov/hearings/testimony/2004test/111804dgtest.pdf, Accessed September 7, 2009.

19. Muller, N. Z. and Mendelsohn, R. "Measuring the Damages of Air Pollution in the United States," *Journal of Environmental Economics and Management*, 54(1), 2007, pp 1–14.

20. Clinard, M. and Yeager, P. *Corporate Crime* (New Brunswick, NJ: Transaction Publishers, 2005) p 12.

21. US Department of Justice. "F. Hoffmann-La Roche and BASF Agree to Pay Record Criminal Fines for Participating in International Vitamin Cartel," 1999. Available at http://www.usdoj.gov/atr/public/press_releases/1999/2450.htm, Accessed April 10, 2009.

22. Nightingale, A. and Hopfinger, T. "Valdez Ghosts Haunt Exxon with Spill

Prone Ships," *Bloomberg.com*, 2009. Available at http://www.bloomberg.com/apps/news?pid=20601109&refer=news&sid=a5vsMTT0Ywuk, Accessed April 10, 2009.

23.   Clinard and Yeager, *Corporate Crime*, pp 111–116.

24.   Oct 28, 1999, C1.

25.   Jul 29, 2000, A7; see also Jan 27, 2001, C1.

26.   Dec 9, 2000, A9; see also Dec 30, 2000, A8.

27.   Jan 12, 2001, C1; see also Jan 30, 2001, A20; Mar 24, 2001, C1; Mar 25, 2001, 24; May 11, 2001, C1; Jul 3, 2001, A10; Jul 10, 2001, A14.

28.   Dec 18, 2000, C6.

29.   Apr 1, 2001, BU13.

30.   Mar 1, 2001, C17; see also Mar 20, 2001, A16.

31.   Jan 10, 2001, A12; May 2, 2001, A14; Jan 3, 2002, A18.

32.   Dec 8, 2000, A28; see also Dec 30, 2000, A8.

33.   Dec 9, 2000, A9.

34.   May 11, 2001, A30.

35.   Jul 17, 2001, A14.

36.   May 29, 2001, A12; for other articles that present the issue as Democrat versus Republican see Feb 1, 2001, A16; Mar 23, 2001, A16; May 4, 2001, A16; May 18, 2001, A16; Jun 8, 2001, A23; Jun 20, 2001, A14; Aug 14, 2002, C1; Aug 16, 2003, B1.

37.   Mar 20, 2001, A16.

38.   Mar 23, 2001, A16.

39.   May 5, 2001, A21.

40.   Oct 9, 2001, A16.

41.   Nov 4, 2001, A29; see also Nov 19, 2002, C4.

42.   Nov 10, 2001, C1; see also Nov 30, 2001, C6; Apr 11, 2002, C1.

43.   Apr 12, 2002, C1.

44.   May 9, 2002, C8.

45.   Feb 5, 2003, C2.

46.   Jun 13, 2004, WK7; see also May 8, 2002, C1; May 8, 2002, C7; May 10, 2002, C1; Jul 9, 2002, C1; Oct 18, 2002, C1; Oct 21, 2002, C1; Jun 4, 2003, C6; Jun 3, 2004, A24.

47.   Feb 18, 2002, C1.

48.   Mar 4, 2003, A19; see also Jun 1, 2002, C2; Jun 2, 2002, B1; Jun 5, 2002, C1; Jun 8, 2002, C1; Aug 14, 2002, C1; Sep 18, 2002, A22; Nov 12, 2002, C1; Nov 19, 2002, C4; Dec 22, 2002, 28; Mar 27, 2003, A14; Jun 26, 2003, A20; Aug 29, 2003, C4; Apr 9, 2004, C5; Sep 10, 2004, A14.

49.   Jun 15, 2002, C3; Dec 3, 2002, C18.

50.   May 15, 2002, C1; see also May 22, 2002, C10.

51.   Jun 18, 2002, C1.

52.   Jun 8, 2002, C1; see also Dec 13, 2002, A30.

53.   Jun 8, 2001, A23.

54.   Nov 10, 2001, C1; see also Dec 4, 2001, C1; Jan 9, 2002, C4; Feb 1, 2002, C5; May 8, 2002, C7.

55.   Feb 9, 2002, C1.

56.   Dec 4, 2001, C1.

57. Feb 10, 2002, 33; Aug 1, 2002, C12; Aug 3, 2002, C2.

58. May 8, 2002, C1; see also Dec 22, 2002, 28; May 12, 2002, D4.

59. May 12, 2002, C1.

60. Jul 28, 2002, B1.

61. Jul 28, 2002, B12.

62. Jan 21, 2001, 20.

63. Feb 8, 2001, G1.

64. Mar 31, 2001, A8.

65. Aug 6, 2000, WK16.

66. Jan 11, 2000, A31.

67. Jan 11, 2001, C2; see also Apr 5, 2001, C2.

68. Jan 13, 2001, A13; see also Jan 14, 2001, WK4; Dec 15, 2001, A31.

69. Dec 31, 2000, WK9.

70. Mar 24, 2001, WK15; see also Apr 29, 2001, WK17; Jun 3, 2001, WK17; Feb 26, 2002, A25.

71. May 10, 2002, A35.

72. Jun 27, 2001, A21; Nov 11, 2001, WK13; Aug 16, 2003, A25; Aug 19, 2003, A21.

73. Sep 17, 2002, A29.

74. Mar 28, 2003, A17; see also May 10, 2002, A35; Jun 7, 2002, A27; Sep 27, 2002, A31; Apr 27, 2004, A25; Jul 11, 2004, A19.

75. Jun 3, 2001, WK18; see also Feb 2, 2001, A19; Mar 4, 2001, BU4; Feb 2, 2001, A19.

76. May 11, 2002, A17.

77. Jan 27, 2001, A14; see also Jan 16, 2001, A22.

78. Apr 21, 2001, A14; see also May 16, 2001, A26.

79. Jan 31, 2001, A20; see also May 16, 2001, A26.

80. May 8, 2002, A30.

81. May 18, 2001, A18; see also Sep 10, 2001, A28; Apr 10, 2002, A26; Sep 26, 2002, A28; Oct 5, 2002, A18; Mar 23, 2003, E12.

82. Jun 1, 2002, A14; see also Jun 6, 2004, WK12.

83. Apr 1, 2003, A18; see also Jul 1, 2003, A22.

84. May 27, 2002, A12.

85. Jul 12, 2004, A18.

86. Oct 31, 2003, A22.

87. Dec 27, 1971, 15.

88. Sep 21, 1975, F1.

89. Oct 6, 1977, 101.

90. Dec 22, 1996, F1.

91. Feb 9, 1975, 60; Dec 16, 1980, D21; Jul 28, 1991, E3.

92. Jun 14, 1987, F1.

93. Jun 22, 1978, A1.

94. Jan 2, 1975, 71; May 29, 1975, 24; Nov 9, 1979, A16.

95. Nov 18, 2000, C1.

96. Feb 19, 1978, F5.

97. Nov 22, 1978, D18; see also Dec 16, 1980, D21.

98. Dec 27, 1971, 15; see also Aug 5, 1975, 5; Sep 21, 1975, F1; Dec 15, 1976, 41; Jan 10, 1988, E5; Jul 28, 1992, A9.

99. Jan 14, 1983, A15; see also Apr 20, 1988, A21.

100. Apr 16, 1972, 44; for more examples of business opposition being blamed for OSHA failures see Jan 17, 1973, 137; July 16, 1974, 14; Feb 2, 1975, F5.

101. Sep 17, 1974, 33; see also Oct 28, 1976, 77.

102. Jan 16, 1976, 61; see also Nov 30, 1980, 37.

103. Feb 12, 1981, A19; see also Feb 13, 1981, 15.

104. Jul 14, 1977, 5.

105. May 8, 1977, 18.

106. May 1, 1979, D9.

107. Jul 15, 1977, 23.

108. Jun 29, 1980, 12; see also Sep 20, 1974, 51; Mar 4, 1976, 15; Dec 20, 1976, 39; Aug 25, 1977, 68; Dec 19, 1978, D3; Apr 1, 1979, E5; Aug 27, 1979, A14; Dec 20, 1979, D13; Dec 26, 1979, D2; Apr 1, 1980, 14; May 25, 1982, D22; May 27, 1981, B9; May 30, 1981, 8; Jul 13, 1981, A11; Oct 31, 1982, 39.

109. Mar 1, 1981, F1.

110. Jan 4, 1981, F1.

111. Feb 14, 1981, 29; see also Mar 20, 1978, D1; Apr 13, 1978, D1; Feb 18, 1981, D13; Nov 7, 1981, 28; Jan 10, 1982, NES32.

112. Nov 27, 1982, 7.

113. Nov 28, 1982, E8.

114. May 11, 1983, B6; see also Mar 13, 1983, N_J_1; Apr 17, 1983, 636; Nov 22, 1983, A18.

115. Sep 5, 1983, 9.

116. Nov 10, 1983, B12.

117. Jul 17, 1988, 18.

118. Feb 8, 1986, 7.

119. Aug 2, 1987, F1.

120. Apr 18, 1985, A18.

121. Aug 29, 1983, A16.

122. Apr 18, 1983, A15.

123. May 10, 1985, D22.

124. Sep 3, 1988, 24.

125. May 7, 1985, B8; see also Sep 21, 1983, A18; Dec 1, 1983, B12; Jan 1, 1984, 26; Feb 28, 1984, A14; Apr 9, 1984, B16; Jun 4, 1984, B11; Jun 17, 1984, N12; Oct 23, 1984, A20; Jun 27, 1985, A16; Nov 5, 1985, A17; Mar 6, 1986, B10; Nov 28, 1986, B16; Jun 26, 1987, A10; Apr 19, 1988, A21; Apr 20, 1988, A21; Apr 21, 1988, A25.

126. Jan 23, 1994, F25.

127. Feb 28, 1995, A20.

128. Jun 12, 1995, D1.

129. Sep 6, 1999, A14.

130. Dec 28, 1975, 109.

131. Oct 10, 1979, A24.

132. Mar 30, 1992, A8; see also Feb 14, 1982, E2; Aug 12, 1983, A8; Nov 20, 1983, F4.

133. Mar 17, 1976, 23.

134. Dec 20, 2000, G1.

135. Apr 29, 1979, F16.

136. Nov 23, 1980, F2; see also Mar 12, 1980, A27; Jan 4, 1981, F2.

137. Feb 3, 1993, A23.

138. Jun 10, 1979, SM26.

139. Sep 12, 1982, F8; see also Jul 28, 1977, 19; Jan 22, 1978, E7; Jun 18, 1978, E4; Sep 14, 2000, C2.

140. Dec 5, 1982, F2.

141. Oct 27, 1974, 272.

142. May 4, 1981, A23.

143. Dec 13, 1981, E29.

144. Aug 7, 1997, A31.

145. May 7, 1979, A21.

146. Sep 20, 1980, 19.

147. Sep 5, 1983, 19.

148. Aug 21, 1983, SM34.

149. Aug 22, 1983, A21; see also Dec 28, 1983, A23.

150. Aug 7, 1995, D2; see also Feb 2, 1992, F13.

151. Jun 6, 1977, 28; see also Aug 8, 1977, 22.

152. Jan 18, 1980, A22.

153. May 28, 1978, F13.

154. Jul 9, 1980, A18.

155. Nov 29, 1980, 22.

156. Jun 16, 1978, A26.

157. Mar 5, 1976, 25.

158. Mar 9, 1984, A28.

159. Nov 20, 1985, A30.

160. Apr 29, 1985, A16.

161. May 30, 1985, A22.

162. Jul 27, 1978, A18.

163. Jan 7, 1979, E18.

164. Jun 29, 1985, 24.

165. Mar 3, 1980, A18.

166. Apr 3, 1986, A26; for other examples of workplace-specific hazards see Jan 26, 1980, 20; Jun 9, 1984, 22; Nov 2, 1984, A26; Nov 1, 1987, E24.

167. Apr 16, 1985, A26; see also Sep 16, 1985, A16; Oct 10, 1988, A18.

168. Jul 14, 1987, A26; see also Aug 25, 1987, A20.

169. Mar 24, 1988, A34.

170. Jul 25, 1987, 30.

171. Dec 21, 1971, 55.

172. May 29, 1975, 39.

173. Feb 3, 1976, 65.

174. Jan 31, 1978, 57; Sep 9, 1987, B3.

175. Mar 31, 1978, D1.

176. Jun 14, 1980, 25; Oct 19, 1988, D1; Jan 1, 1989, E6; Jan 10, 1989, D1; Mar 7, 1992, 39; Dec 30, 1993, D1.

177. Nov 23, 1982, B1; Oct 19, 1996, 39.

178. Jun 8, 1984, F14; May 7, 1985, D1; May 12, 1985, F14; May 14, 1986, D24; Jun 6, 1986, D1; Mar 10, 1990, 33; Mar 31, 1990, 31; Mar 2, 1994, D2.

179. Sep 28, 1984, D1.

180. Nov 2, 1986, 45.

181. Feb 10, 1990, 33.

182. Dec 18, 1996, D1; Jan 8, 1997, D1.

183. Jul 20, 1974, 39.

184. Dec 2, 1978, 26.

185. Apr 10, 1980, D1.

186. Aug 11, 1991, 131.

187. Jun 9, 1995, D1.

188. Feb 12, 1978, F3.

189. Aug 1, 1976, 25.

190. Nov 21, 1976, 27.

191. Feb 9, 1978, D1; see also Aug 13, 1976, 26; Feb 16, 1977, 73; Mar 16, 1978, D1.

192. Dec 18, 1987, D1.

193. Jan 15, 1989, E28; for more stories on corporate penalties being too light see, for example, Dec 13, 1979, D4; May 7, 1985, D1; Jul 29, 1991, A10; Oct 4, 1998, WE1.

194. Oct 10, 1988, D1; see also Oct 12, 1988, D6; Jan 15, 1989, E28.

195. Apr 29, 1990, 23; see also Oct 16, 1990, A24.

196. Sep 14, 1985, 29; see also Sep 17, 1985, A22; Sep 20, 1985, A16.

197. Feb 20, 1992, D7.

198. Nov 20, 1992, D9.

199. Dec 10, 1990, D2; see also Feb 28, 1992, D1.

200. Dec 2, 1978, 26.

201. May 9, 1985, D4.

202. Sep 29, 1987, A24.

203. May 19, 1985, E2.

204. Mar 9, 1997, E7; see also Feb 2, 1986, 30.

205. May 29, 1988, E4.

206. May 6, 1990, E4.

207. May 11, 1975, E5.

208. Jun 9, 1985, F1.

209. Jun 9, 1985, F1.

210. Jan 3, 1993, F13.

211. May 4, 1975, 192.

212. Apr 16, 1980, A27.

213. Oct 14, 1984, F2; see also Nov 30, 1986, 163; May 5, 1991, F13.

214. Jul 24, 1988, SM18.

215. Mar 29, 1992, SM26.
216. Dec 12, 1976, F16; see also Nov 9, 1975, F16.
217. May 19, 1985, F3; see also Sep 14, 1985, 23; Dec 27, 1987, E13.
218. Mar 12, 1989, F2.
219. Oct 15, 1995, F11.
220. Dec 27, 1987, E13.
221. Oct 14, 1984, F2; see also Sep 14, 1985, 23; Apr 23, 1989, SM30.
222. Jun 19, 1975, 35.
223. Sep 9, 1975, 38.
224. Jun 18, 1976, 17.
225. Sep 7, 1976, 30; see also Jul 30, 1983, 20; May 10, 1985, A30; Oct 11, 1985, A34.
226. Feb 17, 1988, A22.
227. Nov 22, 1990, A26.
228. Sep 24, 1990, A18.
229. Apr 14, 1984, 24.
230. Jan 1, 1976, 16.
231. May 16, 1985, A30.
232. Jun 25, 1987, A26.

Notes to Chapter 6

1. Bivens, J. *Everybody Wins, Except for Most of Us: What Economics Teaches About Globalization* (Washington: Economic Policy Institute, 2008).

2. Pieper, U. and Taylor, L. "The Revival of the Liberal Creed: The IMF, the World Bank, and Inequality in a Globalized Economy," in Baker, D., Epstein, G., and Pollin, R. (eds.), *Globalization and Progressive Economic Policy* (Cambridge: Cambridge University Press, 1998), Ch. 2.

3. Rodriguez, F. and Rodrik, D. "Trade Policy and Economic Growth: A Skeptic's Guide to the Cross-National Evidence," *NBER Macroeconomics Annual 2000.*

4. Chang, H. *Kicking Away the Ladder—Development Strategy in Historical Perspective* (London: Anthem Press, 2002).

5. Anand, S. and Segal, P. "What Do We Know About Global Income Inequality?" *Journal of Economic Literature*, XLVI(1), 2008, pp 90–91.

6. Wade, R. "Globalization, Growth, Poverty, Inequality, Resentment and Imperialism," in Ravenhill, J. (ed.), *Global Political Economy* (Oxford: Oxford University Press, 2008).

7. ILO. *World of Work Report 2008: Income Inequalities in the Age of Financial Globalization, International Institute for Labour Studies* (Geneva: ILO, 2008).

8. Chen, S. and Ravallion, M. "How Have the World's Poorest Fared Since the Early 1980s?" *The World Bank Research Observer*, 2004.

9. Business Week. "How Rising Wages Are Changing the Game in China," *Business Week*, March 27, 2006. Available at http://www.businessweek.com/magazine/content/06_13/b3977049.htm, Accessed April 19, 2009.

10. Bureau of Labor Statistics. "Usual weekly earnings summary," 2009. Available at http://www.bls.gov/news.release/wkyeng.nr0.htm, Accessed April 19, 2009.

11. ILO. *Competitiveness Productivity and Jobs* (Bangkok: ILO Regional Office of Asian and the Pacific, 2008), p 1.

12. ILO. *Labour and Social Trend in Asia and the Pacific 2006* (Bangkok: ILO, 2006), pp 100, 111.

13. World Bank. *The Cost of Pollution in China* (Washington, DC: World Bank, 2007), p xi.

14. Ibid, p xvii.

15. Kahn, J. and Yardley, J. "As China Roars, Pollution Reaches Deadly Extremes," *The New York Times*, August 26, 2007.

16. Economist. "Up to Their Necks in It," *The Economist*, 388(8589), 2008, pp 49–50.

17. Seger, M. *Globalization: A Very Short Introduction* (Oxford: Oxford University Press, 2003), p 111.

18. Stiglitz, J. and Charlton, A. *Fair Trade for All* (Oxford: Oxford University Press, 2005).

19. May 25, 2005, A25.

20. Dec 24, 2008, A25.

21. Oct 20, 2006, A23; Jun 1, 2001, A19.

22. Jun 14, 2006, A 23.

23. Nov 12, 2008, A31.

24. Dec 17, 2008, A39.

25. Jul 28, 2002, 4.13.

26. Jun 9, 2000, A31.

27. Aug 3, 2005, A19.

28. Sep 22, 2000, A27.

29. Dec. 24, 2008, A25.

30. Oct 14, 2005, A25; see also May 4, 2005, A23.

31. Jun 24, 2004, A23; see also Jun 6, 2004, 4.13; May 20, 2004, A27; Apr 1, 2004, A23; Mar 21, 2004, 4.11; Mar 7, 2004, 4.13; Mar 4, 2004, A29; Feb 29, 2004, 4.13.

32. Jan 11, 2009, WK10.

33. Mar 1, 2006, A19.

34. Dec 7, 2008, WK10; see also Aug 10, 2008, WK11; Dec 16, 2007, 4.10; Oct 17, 2007, A27; May 13, 2007, 4.12; Feb 3, 2006, A23.

35. Jun 24, 2007, WK14; see also Jun. 3, 2007, 4.15; May 13, 2007, 4.12; Apr 28, 2006, A23; Mar 1, 2006, A19; Mar 2, 2001, A23.

36. Jun 22, 2008, WK11.

37. Sep 21, 2008, WK11; see also Jul 30, 2008, A17; Jan 17, 2007, A23; Jan 10, 2007, A23; Dec 6, 2006, A29; Feb 3, 2006, A23.

38. May, 24, 2006, A27; see also Mar 29, 2006, A23; Aug 10, 2008, WK11; Sep 7, 2008, WK9.

39. Mar 22, 2006, A25.

40. Jun 22, 2008, WK11.

41. Sep 14, 2008, WK11.

42. Aug 13, 2008, A21.

43. Apr 30, 2008, A19.

44. Sep 21, 2008, WK11; see also July 30, 2008, A17.

45. July 1, 2005, A17; see also Jun 29, 2005, A23.

46. Jun 24, 2005, A23.

47. Jun 3, 2005, A23.

48. Boltho, A. "What's Wrong with Europe?" *New Left Review*, 22, July–Aug, 2003, pp 5–26.

49. Feb 2, 2003, 4.15.

50. Thorpe, K., Howard, D., and Galactionova, K. "Differences in Disease Prevalence as a Source of the U.S.-European Health Care Spending Gap," *Health Affairs*, 26(6), 2007, pp 678–686.

51. Sep 22, 2002, C13.

52. Apr 14, 2000, A31.

53. Kearney, A.T. "A Quick Look," 2009. Available at http://www.atkearney.com/index.php/About-us/quick-look.html, Accessed July 15, 2009.

54. Oct 5, 2008, WK9.

55. Aug 11, 2002, 4.13.

56. Sep 22, 2002, 4.13.

57. Mar 17, 2002, 4.15.

58. Dec 24, 2008, A25.

59. Dec 1, 1999, A23.

60. Jul 20, 2001, A21.

61. Apr 14, 2000, A31.

62. May 23, 1999, 24.

63. Dec 30, 2003, A21; see also Jul 14, 2006, A17; Sep 1, 2006, A15.

64. Nov 22, 2002, A27.

65. Jan 21, 2003, A23.

66. Dec 5, 2005, A23.

67. Jun 16, 2006, A31.

68. Feb 27, 2006, A19.

69. Aug 18, 2006, A17.

70. Jun 10, 2005, A21.

71. Dec 3, 2002, A31.

72. Jul 13, 2007, A19; see also Oct 28, 2001, 4.13; Oct 31, 2001, A15; Jan 8, 2002, A19; Jan 7, 2003, A19; May 9, 2003, A31.

73. Feb 23, 2000, A21.

74. May 28, 2003, A43.

75. Jan 23, 2000, 4.15; see also Feb 23, 2000, A21; May 10, 2000, A31.

76. Jan 23, 2000, 4.15; see also Feb 13, 1997, 33.

77. Feb 27, 2004, A27; see also May 21, 2000, 4.17.

78. Feb 13, 1997, 33.

79. May 10, 2000, A31.

80. Jul 5, 2000, A17.

81. Apr 22, 2001, 4.17.

82. Jan 23, 2000, 4.15.

83. Feb 23, 2000, A21.

84. Apr 23, 2000, 4.11.

85. Apr 22, 2001, 4.17.

86. May 14, 2007, A19.

87. Dec 28, 2007, A23.

88. Mar 29, 2000, A25.

89. Jul 29, 2005, A23.

90. Jun 21, 2002, 21.

91. Aug 21, 2001, A17.

92. Dec 17, 2004, A35; see also Jul 22, 2001, 4.13; Aug 8, 2001, A17; Dec 5, 2003, A30; Dec 16, 2003, A35.

93. Aug 27, 2004, A21.

94. Apr 15, 2005, A19; see also Apr 22, 2005, A23.

95. Jun 13, 2005, A17.

96. Aug 27, 2004, A21.

97. Nov 25, 2005, A39; for more on universal health care see Oct. 3, 2005, A21; Jan 5, 2007, A17; Feb 16, 2007, A23; Aug 11, 2008, A17; Oct. 6, 2008, A29; Nov 7, 2008, A35.

98. Jul 23, 2000, 4.15.

99. European Medicines Agency. "European Medicines Agency Recommends Restricted Use for Piroxicam," European Medicines Agency Press Release, June 25, 2007, Doc. Ref. EMEA/265144/2007.

100. Dec 16, 2005, A41.

101. Apr 5, 2000, A23.

102. Oct 22, 2002, A31.

103. Jan 29, 2002, A21; see also Mar 19, 2007, A15.

104. May 21, 2007, A19.

105. Jun 13, 2008, A29.

106. Jun 13, 2008, A29.

107. May 17, 2002, A25.

108. Jan 27, 2004, A23; see also Feb 3, 2004, A23.

109. May 27, 2003, A25.

110. Apr 4, 2001, 4.17.

Notes to Chapter 7

1. This introduction is drawn from chapters by the authors in Guard, J. and Anthony, W. (eds). *Bailouts & Bankruptcies* (Winnipeg: Fernwood Press, 2008).

2. Warren, E. "The Middle Class on the Precipice: Rising Financial Risks for American Families," *Harvard Magazine*, January/February, 2006. Available at harvard-

magazine.com/2006/01/the-middle-class-on-the.html, Accessed January 10, 2009, p 28.

    3. Ibid, p 31.

    4. Foster, J.B. and Magdoff, F. "Financial Implosion and Stagnation: Back to the Real Economy," *Monthly Review*, December, 2008. Available at http://www.monthlyreview.org/081201foster-magdoff.php, Accessed April 22, 2009.

    5. Mishel, L., Bernstein, J., and Allegreto, S. *The State of Working America 2006/07* (Ithaca, NY: Cornell University Press, 2007), figures 5LA and 5LB.

    6. Duca, J. "Making Sense of the U.S. Housing Slowdown," *Economic Letter—Insights from the Federal Reserve Bank of Dallas*, 1, 2006,11. Available at http://www.dallasfed.org/research/eclett/2006/el0611.html, Accessed April 20, 2009.

    7. Getter, D., Jickling, M., Labonte, M. and Murphy, E. "Financial Crisis? The Liquidity Crunch of August 2007," *Congressional Research Service Report for Congress, 2007*, September 21, 2007, Washington, DC: Congressional Research Service, p 1.

    8. Barth, J., Brumbaugh, R., and Wilcox, J. "Policy Watch: The Repeal of Glass-Steagall and the Advent of Broad Banking," *Journal of Economic Perspectives*, 14, Spring, 2000, 2.

    9. Kroszner, R. and Rajan, J. "Is the Glass-Steagall Act Justified?" *American Economic Review* 84(4), 1994.

    10. Public Broadcasting Service. "The Long Decline of Glass-Steagall," 2008. Available at http://www.pbs.org/wgbh/pages/frontline/shows/wallstreet/weill/demise.html, Accessed on December 12, 2008.

    11. General Accounting Office. *Financial Derivatives: Actions Needed to Protect the Financial System* (Washington, D.C.: General Accounting Office, 1994).

    12. Getter, et al. Financial Crisis, 2007.

    13. Mortgage Bankers Association. *National Delinquency Survey, 4th quarter 2007* (Washington, DC: Mortgage Bankers Association, December 31, 2007).

    14. Getter, et al. Financial Crisis, 2007.

    15. Oct 23, 1999, 1.

    16. Apr 7, 1998, D8.

    17. Nov 13, 1999, C3.

    18. Nov 5, 1999, A1; see also Nov 13, 1999, C3.

    19. Nov 7, 1999, 4.2.

    20. Apr 12, 1998, 4.1.

    21. Oct 26, 2003, 3.4; for other articles criticizing Rubin's role in the merger see Oct 27, 1999, A1; Nov 18, 1999, C17.

    22. Jul 28, 2002, 3.1.

    23. Jun 5, 2005, 3.1; see also Feb 10, 2002, 3.1; Jul 28, 2002, 3.1; Sep 8, 2002, 3.1.

    24. Mar 3, 2009, A1.

    25. Jan 1, 2009, A1.

    26. Oct 26, 2008, A1.

    27. Oct 15, 2008, B1.

    28. Oct 18, 2008, A1.

29. Apr 4, 2009, B3.
30. Dec 18, 2008, A1.
31. Feb 5, 2009, B1.
32. Jan 25, 2009, A1.
33. Oct 26, 2008, BU1.
34. Mar 11, 2009, B1.
35. Oct 9, 2008, A1; see also Oct 26, 2008, BU1.
36. Oct 24, 2008, B1.
37. Nov 17, 2008, A1.
38. Oct 26, 2008, BU1.
39. Apr 27, 2008, BU1.
40. Dec 21, 2008, A1.
41. Dec 21, 2008, A1.
42. Dec 21, 2008, A1.
43. Dec 21, 2008, A1.
44. Jan 27, 2009, B1.
45. Nov 14, 2008, B1.
46. Mar 20, 2009, B4.
47. Oct 26, 2008, BU1; see also Apr 7, 2009, B1.
48. Nov 14, 2008, B1.
49. Mar 26, 2009, F8.
50. Nov 25, 2008, B1.
51. Apr 6, 2009, A1; for a similar story on the head of the SEC, Mary Schapiro, see Jan 12, 2009, B1.
52. Feb 16, 2009, B1.
53. Mar 21, 2009, B1; see also Oct 18, 2008, A1; Mar 23, 2009, A10.
54. Jan 25, 2009, A1.
55. Jan 23, 2009, B1.
56. Mar 11, 2009, B1.
57. Oct 22, 2008, B1.
58. Apr 16, 1998, A.23.
59. Aug 5, 2002, 4.9.
60. Mar 27, 2009, A29.
61. Sep 23, 2008, A29.
62. Mar 20, 2009, A27.
63. Mar 30, 2009, A29.
64. Apr 3, 2009, A29.
65. Mar 17, 2008, A19.
66. Sep 30, 2008, A27.
67. Nov 10, 2008, A29; see also Feb 2, 2009, A21; Mar 16, 2009, A23.
68. Nov 3, 2008, A31.
69. Mar 16, 2009, A23.
70. Apr 3, 2009, A29.
71. Mar 11, 2009, A31.
72. Mar 17, 2008, A19.

73. Dec 28, 2008, WK9.

74. Sep 22, 2008, A23.

75. Mar 27, 2009, A29.

76. Sep 13, 2008, A19.

77. Nov 17, 2008, A27.

78. Oct 10, 2008, A33.

79. Feb 10, 2009, A27; see also Mar 8, 2009, BU5.

80. Feb 2, 2009, A21.

81. Mar, 18, 2009, A27; see also Sep 23, 2008, A29.

82. May 14, 1999, A26.

83. Oct 24, 1999, 4.14.

84. Sep 19, 2008, A18.

85. Mar 15, 2009, WK11.

86. Mar 19, 2009, A30; see also Apr 3, 2008, A26; Sep 23, 2008, A28.

87. Nov 9, 2008, WK8; see also Jan 27, 2008, WK15; Sep 20, 2008, A18; Jan 20, 2009, A32.

88. Dec 29, 2008, A24.

89. Sep 30, 2008, A26.

90. Sep 23, 2008, A28.

91. Nov 30, 2008, WK7; see also Dec 15, 2008, A34.

92. Nov 8, 2008, A20.

93. Aug 20, 2008, A22.

94. Apr 3, 2008, A26.

95. Jan 8, 2009, A30.

96. Sep 23, 2008, A28; see also Nov 19, 2008, A34.

97. Sep 23, 2008, A28.

98. Dec 15, 2008, A34; see also Nov 25, 2008, A30; Jan 8, 2009, A30; Feb 9, 2009, A22.

INDEX

Note: NYT indicates *New York Times*; t. indicates table.

About the Authors

Robert Chernomas is a professor of economics at the University of Manitoba. He has published extensively on the topics of macroeconomics, globalization, the social determinants of health, and the history of economic thought, specializing in the work of Marx and Keynes.

Ian Hudson is an associate professor of economics at the University of Manitoba. He has published several articles in the area of political economy, focusing on the role of the state and economic development.

Robert Chernomas and Ian Hudson have previously collaborated on the book *Social Murder and Other Problems with Conservative Economic Policy* (2007).